Policing Methamphetamine

Policing Methamphetamine

Narcopolitics in Rural America

William Garriott

NEW YORK UNIVERSITY PRESS
New York and London

NEW YORK UNIVERSITY PRESS
New York and London
www.nyupress.org

References to Internet websites (URLs) were accurate at the time of writing.
Neither the author nor New York University Press is responsible for URLs
that may have expired or changed since the manuscript was prepared.

Library of Congress Cataloging-in-Publication Data

Garriott, William Campbell, 1977–
Policing methamphetamine : narcopolitics in rural America / William Garriott.
p. cm.
Includes bibliographical references and index.
ISBN 978–0–8147–3239–7 (cl : alk. paper) — ISBN 978–0–8147–3240–3
(pb : alk. paper) — ISBN 978–0–8147–3241–0 (e-book)
1. Methamphetamine—West Virginia—Baker County. 2. Methamphetamine
abuse—West Virginia—Baker County—Prevention. 3. Drug traffic—
Investigation—West Virginia—Baker County. 4. Methamphetamine abuse—
United States—Political aspects. 5. Police—United States. I. Title.
HV5831.W4G37   2011
362.29'9—dc22   2010039828

New York University Press books are printed on acid-free paper,
and their binding materials are chosen for strength and durability.
We strive to use environmentally responsible suppliers and materials
to the greatest extent possible in publishing our books.

Manufactured in the United States of America
c   10 9 8 7 6 5 4 3 2 1
p   10 9 8 7 6 5 4 3 2 1

For Sarah

Contents

Acknowledgments

First and foremost, I want to thank the residents of that area of West Virginia that I call Baker County for their kindness, hospitality, and willingness to share their lives. It was their generosity that made this research possible. I regret that the need for anonymity makes me unable to thank them by name. Particular thanks goes to "Christie" who went above and beyond in sharing her life experience with me.

Financial support was provided by the Graduate School at Princeton University, the Center for the Study of Religion at Princeton University, the National Science Foundation, and the Fellowship of Woodrow Wilson Scholars. I thank them for their generosity.

I am very thankful to those who commented on the manuscript and offered their support over the course of this project. There are too many to name here, but I would like especially to acknowledge John Borneman, Nancy Campbell, Summerson Carr, Jessica Cattalino, Isabelle Clark-Deces, Leo Coleman, Susanna Drake, Cassie Fennell, Angela Garcia, Abdellah Hammoudi, Stephanie Kane, Mindie Lazarus-Black, Rena Lederman, Peter Locke, Moira Lynch, Anne-Maria Makhulu, Joseph Masco, Dawn Moore, Kevin O'Neill, Philip Parnell, Jason Pine, Eugene Raikhel, Carolyn Rouse, Jane Schneider, Michelle Stewart, Mariana Valverde, Matthew Wolf-Meyer, Carol Zanca, and Jessica Zuchowski. My sincerest thanks goes to James Boon and Lawrence Rosen who provided invaluable feedback on an early draft of the manuscript. I owe an enormous debt of gratitude to Carol Greenhouse and João Biehl, who offered support beyond measure over the course of this project. Without their encouragement and insight this project would not have been possible.

A heartfelt thanks goes to my colleagues in the Department of Justice Studies at James Madison University: Linda Barbosa, Terry Beitzel, Tammy Castle, Glenn Hastedt, Suraj Jacob, Roberta Mitchell, Peter Pham, Peggy Plass, Christine Robinson, Suey Spivey, Scott Vollum, and Jacki Buffington-Vollum. I would also like to thank Lara Knowles who provided invaluable assistance during the preparation of the final manuscript.

Jennifer Hammer and her colleagues at New York University Press have helped in innumerable ways with the preparation of this book. I would like to thank them as well as the three anonymous reviewers for their insights.

Portions of the manuscript were presented to audiences at Indiana University, the University of Chicago, Princeton University, McGill University, and the University of Toronto, as well as at the annual meetings of the American Anthropological Association, the Law and Society Association, and the Midwest Political Science Association. My sincerest thanks to all who attended those presentations and critically engaged with my work.

Parts of this book were first published in other venues. An earlier version of chapter 2 was published in the *Canadian Journal of Law and Society* as "Targeting the Local: Policing Methamphetamine in a Rural U.S. Community."

Words cannot express the debt of gratitude I owe my family. For their support and encouragement I thank my parents, William and Mary Beth Garriott, both of whom assisted me directly in researching and thinking about my project. I also thank my brothers Pat Garriott and Miles Garriott for their encouragement and support. Thanks also to the Swanson family, Nina, Michael, Pete, and Erik, as well as Thor and Brianne Trone, Chris Trone, and David and Siri Trone.

Finally, I could not have completed this project without the support of my wife, Sarah. She has been with me every step of the way, from grant writing to fieldwork to the final draft. For the innumerable ways in which you continue to support and inspire me, Sarah, thank you.

Introduction

On March 9, 2006, George W. Bush signed into law the USA PATRIOT Improvement and Reauthorization Act. True to its name, the 2006 version of the PATRIOT Act was largely a reauthorization of the initial legislation, with the same general emphasis on combating "terror" in the name of homeland security. There was, however, one major exception. The new act included legislation focused on *methamphetamine*, the synthetic substance *Newsweek* had recently dubbed "America's most dangerous drug" (Jefferson 2005).

In his comments during the signing, President Bush spoke directly about the "growing threat" of methamphetamine and the measures taken by the legislation to address it. "Meth is easy to make. It is highly addictive. It is ruining too many lives across our country," President Bush stated. "The bill introduces commonsense safeguards that would make many of the ingredients used in manufacturing meth harder to obtain in bulk, and easier for law enforcement to track. . . . The bill also increases penalties for smuggling and selling of meth. Our nation is committed to protecting our citizens and our young people from the scourge of methamphetamine."[1]

Methamphetamine is the first drug to generate national concern in the United States in the twenty-first century. Its spread from the West Coast to the Midwest and now into the Southeast has prompted many to speak of the meth problem as an epidemic. And as with previous drug epidemics in the United States, the problem has been framed overwhelmingly as a law enforcement issue. The legislation contained in the PATRIOT Act, for instance, authorized *double* the amount of funding for law enforcement initiatives in "meth hot spots" as what it allocated for stopping the importation of meth from Mexico, improving the health of children affected by meth, assisting incarcerated female meth offenders with their children, and funding meth lab cleanup initiatives—combined.[2] Thus the response to methamphetamine has involved repetition of the same punitive paradigm that has come to characterize efforts to address illicit drugs in the United States (Bertram et al. 1996).

This book examines contemporary concerns over methamphetamine in order to understand the abiding role played by illicit narcotics in American political life. Specifically, it examines the response to methamphetamine in one rural American community to show how the focus on narcotics has transformed the workings of law, the exercise of police power, and the practice of politics in the contemporary United States. Over the past century, the concern with narcotics has left its imprint on practically every corner of U.S. politics. Narcotics, a vernacular term used to refer generally to illicit drugs, have been and continue to be of significance to the election of officials, the administration of justice, the practice of law enforcement, the shaping of legal consciousness, the process of lawmaking and the formation of public policy (both foreign and domestic), the allocation of social services, the use of military force, the interpretation of law, and the behavior of the judiciary, to name but a few relevant areas of concern. Perennial political conflicts over race, class, gender, immigration, criminal justice, and social welfare, among others, have all been refracted through the lens of narcotics.

Nowhere, however, have the effects of the focus on narcotics been more acutely felt than in the legal system. Efforts taken to address narcotics through the law have brought about fundamental shifts in the legal culture of the United States itself. The criminal justice system has been at the forefront of these changes. Whether one looks at police, courts, or corrections, the criminalization of narcotics over the past century has left no component of this system untouched. Police forces have been reorganized and reoriented around drug enforcement; courts spend vast amounts of time and resources adjudicating drug offenders; and the corrections system, which has gone through an exponential period of growth in the last decades, now faces a range of bureaucratic, programmatic, and ethical challenges as its role in society has expanded and changed (Wacquant 2009a, 2009b).

These changes in the criminal justice system are only a part of a more fundamental shift that has taken place with regard to the state's efforts to control, monitor, and shape the actions of its citizens by means of the concern with narcotics. That is, the focus on narcotics has transformed the exercise of what is known in legal terms as "the police power" of the state in the United States. When one hears the word "police," the image that comes to mind is of the uniformed police force. But the exercise of the police power is a much broader enterprise. Generally speaking, the police power of the state refers to that modality of governance concerned with achieving and sustaining the "well-regulated society" (Novak 1996). To this end it is concerned with the broad objectives of maintaining order and avoiding future ills (Pasquino

1991, 109). As Markus Dubber writes, "The police power of the state is the power to order its constituents so as to maximize the 'public welfare' according to rules of expediency" (Dubber 2001, 833n.7). He goes on to quote William Blackstone's definition of police from the influential *Commentaries on the Laws of England* as "the due regulation and domestic order of the kingdom: whereby the individuals of the state, like members of a well-governed family, are bound to conform their general behavior to the rules of propriety, good neighbourhood, and good manners: and to be decent, industrious, and inoffensive in their respective situations" (ibid.).

This definition highlights the fact that, in practice, the state is not alone in the exercise of police power. The analogy Blackwell draws between the kingdom and the "well-governed family," as well as his reference to the "good neighbourhood," "good manners," and "rules of propriety," illustrates that institutions such as the family, the community, even "society" itself are all likewise sites of police and sources of police power—even if only in potential. Thus, just as the uniformed police force is but one modality of the police power of the state, so, too, is the police power of the state but one modality of police power itself.

Similarly, while the police power is typically associated with law—the use of the term "law enforcement" in the United States to refer to the uniformed police force is perhaps the most overt instance of this association—this relationship is an ambiguous one. The two often function as separate modalities of governance (Dubber 2005, 3). And while the legitimation, exercise, and control of police power is in many ways rooted in law, law is not the source of police power in any straightforward way. Indeed, in some instances, law may function as a tool of police power, rather than the reverse. This reflects one of the defining features of the police power in Western political history: its tendency to defy definition or limitation.

Calibrating the relationship between law and police, at least insofar as these function in the service of governance, becomes the task of politics in this context. Governance is here "understood in the broad sense of techniques and procedures for directing human behavior" (Foucault 1997, 82). The introduction of illicit narcotics into this equation has resulted in a particular mode of political practice that I term *narcopolitics*, which works to rationalize the practices of governance in terms of the problems associated with narcotics.[3]

From this perspective, the various approaches taken within the United States to address narcotics, including enforcement, treatment, and education, are not competing alternatives (as they are often treated in policy debates) but components of a broad "illicit drug regulatory apparatus" (Stalcup 2006, 3). An apparatus, according to Michel Foucault, is composed of "discourses, institutions, architectural arrangements, policy decisions, laws, administrative measures, scientific statements, philosophic, moral, and philanthropic propositions" (quoted in Stalcup 2006, 3). As will be seen throughout this book, the illicit drug regulatory apparatus has been woven into the very fabric of American political life.

Treating the various approaches to narcotics regulation as components of the same apparatus should not be taken as a sign that each component functions equally. On the contrary, the illicit drug regulatory apparatus in the United States has long been organized around enforcement. The effect of this emphasis is that other components of the apparatus, such as treatment and education, are often incorporated into enforcement efforts. This particular approach to narcotics should not be accepted uncritically. The focus here, however, will not be on evaluating the effectiveness of this approach, but on situating its effects on the workings of law and the exercise of police power within the context of political life in the United States.

Methamphetamine is the most recent in a long line of substances to be framed as a national threat and treated as the horizon against which a broad array of interventions may be staged. To highlight this political role of methamphetamine is not to suggest that there is no reason for concern. On the contrary, journalists and scholars have documented how methamphetamine has caused significant harm to families and communities, particularly in rural areas (Weisheit and White 2009; Reding 2009; Owen 2007; Pine 2007). This work lends support to the findings of a report issued by the Mayo Clinic, which noted methamphetamine's potential to unleash a "perfect storm" of medical and social complications (Lineberry and Bostwick 2006). Moreover, the idea that methamphetamine use has reached epidemic proportions is not without evidence. According to the Drug Enforcement Administration (DEA), meth lab seizures in middle America increased 126 percent between 1999 and 2003. Meth-related treatment admissions increased 87 percent over the same period. And by 2004, the National Survey on Drug Use and Health was reporting that approximately 11.7 million Americans aged twelve and older had tried methamphetamine at least once during their lifetimes.[4]

At the same time, there is evidence that the proliferation of methamphetamine is neither as new nor as extensive as has been suggested. Although *Newsweek* dubbed methamphetamine "America's most dangerous drug" in 2005, this was not the first major article the magazine had published on the subject. In 1989 *Newsweek* published an article titled, "The Newest Drug

War," in which it similarly stated that crank—a type of methamphetamine—
was a growing problem in rural America (Baker et al. 1989; see also Weisheit
and Fuller 2004, 52). There has also been something of a journalistic backlash
to the initial coverage of methamphetamine, with articles that question the
representation of the methamphetamine problem in earlier accounts (Shafer
2005, 2006; Valdez 2006; Egan 2009).

These debates resemble those that followed in the wake of other substances positioned as the "most dangerous" drug in the United States. In this
regard, there is something familiar in both the initial frenzy over methamphetamine and the backlash. What is significant, however, is not the debates
themselves but the wider political process of which they are a part. They are
one small dynamic in the ongoing use of narcotics for the purposes of governance; they are part and parcel of narcopolitics.

Narcopolitics

Narcopolitics refers to any practice of governance whose rationalization
lies in the concern with narcotics. My focus is the United States, the world's
largest consumer of illicit drugs (a.k.a. "narcotics"), but one could certainly
find variations of the same phenomenon elsewhere (e.g., Campbell 2009;
Penglase 2009; Moore 2007; Arias 2006; Taussig 2004; Zhou 1999). Indeed,
because of the inherently global nature of the illicit trade in narcotics, narcopolitical practices are inevitably interconnected and can only ever be loosely
contained in the discrete frame of the nation-state. Despite this inherent
interconnectedness, however, the specific form that the narcotics trade and
anti-narcotics practices take in a particular place can vary considerably,
resulting in important differences, which an anthropology of narcopolitics
such as this must be careful to articulate.

Contemporary narcopolitics began taking shape in the sixteenth century
with the rise of the global trade in psychoactive substances (Courtwright
2001). The transformation of products such as sugar, opium, and tobacco
into global commodities redefined the geopolitical map of the age and created new forms of sociality, labor, trade, governance, and experience (Mintz
1986; Ortiz 1995). Indeed, the commodity form is one of the defining features
of contemporary narcotics, creating particularly modern anxieties about
technology and personal enjoyment—pleasure in the age of mechanical
reproduction (Derrida 2003).[5] These global commodities, in turn, paved the
way for new generations of psychoactive substances, including the heroin,
cocaine, marijuana, and methamphetamine of today.

The practice of narcopolitics was a defining feature of American statecraft in the twentieth century (Musto 1999; Musto and Korsmeyer 2002; Bertram et al. 1996; Tracy and Acker 2004; Campbell 2000; Reinarman and Levine 1997; Agar and Reisinger 2002a, 2002b; Schneider 2008). Even before the formal declaration of the War on Drugs, the concern with narcotics provided an avenue through which the U.S. government could carry out a vast array of projects—everything from the regulation of schools and neighborhoods to the reshaping of military intervention and foreign policy to the reinterpretation of the constitution and other fundamental sources of legal rights. Citizens, too, participated in this process, using the issue of narcotics to make demands related to education, public safety, and the shaping of civic space. Today, narcotics continue to provide a robust medium through which broader anxieties over immigration, poverty, and intergenerational conflicts, to name just a few, are articulated and managed by both citizens and the state (Wacquant 2009a, 2009b; Andreas 2009; Bourgois and Schonberg 2009; Acker 2004; Moore and Haggerty 2001; Musto 1999).

If the topic of narcotics does not hold the prominent place it once did in American political discourse, such as during the Reagan administration's escalation of the War on Drugs in the 1980s, this is not because the issue is no longer viable. On the contrary, the concern with narcotics is now such a taken-for-granted component of American political life that it provokes little debate or comment. Thus students in public schools accept the drug education they receive through the DARE (Drug Abuse Resistance Education) program, as well as the regular drug searches performed by police, as routine components of their educational experience. Similarly, the rampant use of drug testing to manage groups as diverse as athletes, inmate populations, and factory workers strikes no one as odd or unreasonable. Rather, it seems like a commonsense strategy for a society that appears to be perennially plagued by drugs.

This book counteracts the "hidden-in-plain-sight" quality of narcopolitics by providing an ethnographic analysis of the practices at the heart of the contemporary American narcopolitical state. This ethnographic approach underscores both the forms these practices take and the ways in which they are lived. The focus is on methamphetamine because of its current position as America's most dangerous drug. Like previous drug threats, it is methamphetamine's addictiveness, availability, association with crime and violence, and capacity to cause harm to users and communities, regardless of social standing, that has been emphasized (Jefferson 2005).

Despite these similarities, however, there is much that distinguishes methamphetamine. Unlike comparable drugs such as cocaine and heroin, meth does not need to be imported. It can be manufactured locally using everyday household items such as cold tablets, iodine, and drain cleaner, which are then "cooked" using "recipes" readily available on the Internet. "Meth labs"—the name given to places where methamphetamine is manufactured—have been found everywhere: in hotel rooms, cars, and even suitcases, though ordinary homes located inconspicuously in rural areas remain the most common location. Furthermore, methamphetamine is having a disproportionate effect on rural areas, in precisely those places assumed to be least susceptible to such social problems as drugs, addiction, and crime. Finally, concern over methamphetamine has emerged at a time when the public feels acutely ambivalent about the War on Drugs. While the majority of Americans feel that fighting the drug war is still necessary, they no longer feel it can be won (Pew Research Center for the People and the Press [hereafter PEW] 2001). Even so, though methamphetamine has a unique profile, the prevailing response has emphasized the same narcopolitical strategies used against previous drug threats.

The location of the study is Baker County, a small, rural community in West Virginia.[6] Between 2006 and 2007 I conducted ethnographic research looking at the methamphetamine problem there. For more than a year I combed through archives, spoke with local residents, and observed the impact meth was having on the local community. During this time I was particularly attuned to the way community members responded to methamphetamine. I watched as prosecuting priorities of the courts shifted toward meth offenders, increasing workloads, and bringing new people into the criminal justice system; as community groups advocated for expanded drug testing in schools, causing tension between teachers and students, parents and children; as rumors circulated over who had been seen going to receive treatment for addiction at the local mental health facility; and as addicts, driven into a life of crime by their use of methamphetamine, were sent to overcrowded regional jails and state prisons where they received little medical treatment. Upon their release they struggled to find a place for themselves in the community where they lived with the double stigma of both their criminal record and their addiction. Attending to these developments, I documented how narcopolitical practices were deployed in Baker County in the wake of methamphetamine.

The prevailing response to methamphetamine in Baker County demonstrates how the practices and logics of narcopolitics have become embedded in everyday expressions of political life in the United States—even in those places, like Baker County, assumed to stand at some remove from the problem of illicit narcotics. This includes such basic components of political life as the legitimation of state authority, the exercise of police power, the upholding of rights, and the provision of order and security. Each chapter illustrates a different instance in which these basic political practices took place vis-à-vis the concern with methamphetamine.

This analysis reveals three key features of contemporary narcopolitics:

1. THE TARGETING OF SUBSTANCES AND THEIR EFFECTS, RATHER THAN PEOPLE AND THEIR ACTIONS, TO STRUCTURE THE FIELD OF INTERVENTION. The prevailing U.S. drug control strategy has been based on the assumption that the surest way of countering the negative impact of narcotics is to limit—and ultimately eliminate—their availability. As a result, the various elements of the narcopolitical order, from drug laws to police practices to judicial decisions, are united by the common focus on the substance and its effects as the object and means of regulation and intervention. This concern is ancillary to the narcopolitical practices that focus on people and their actions, such as the arrest of specific buyers, sellers, distributors, traffickers, and users of the drug. To be sure, the dramatic expansion of the U.S. prison population that occurred with the escalation of the War on Drugs in the 1980s involved the prosecution of people. Yet it is only through the targeting of the drugs themselves that these arrests have been possible.

Take, for example, the spike in the use of possession offenses—such as drug possession—to prosecute criminal offenders that occurred over the latter half of the twentieth century. According to Markus Dubber, this use of possession offenses marks "the end of criminal law as we know it." This is because the policing of possession is concerned neither with crime, understood as the "serious violation of another's rights," nor with law, understood as a "state run system of interpersonal conflict resolution," but with *threats*, understood here as the potential harm posed by an illicit object—and by extension, the possessor of that object—such as a drug (Dubber 2001, 834). The objective of the criminal justice system here is not to remedy a harm done but to neutralize a potential threat, in this case, by disrupting the circulation and use of an illicit object.

This approach toward the policing of possession offenses marks a shift away from the retributive concerns of traditional criminal law and toward a focus on prevention and incapacitation. This focus both drives and is driven by the focus on possession. Furthermore, it has turned U.S. criminal justice into a system of "penal police" concerned less with punishing crimes than policing threats. "Persons matter neither as the source, nor as the target, of threats," Dubber states. "Penal police is a matter between the state and threats" (ibid.).

Similarly, several landmark Supreme Court decisions regarding the use of drug detection technologies during police searches have redefined such basic aspects of political life as the right to privacy and protection from unreasonable search and seizure. These have taken the threat posed by drugs themselves for their justification. This has enabled police to carry out searches that would otherwise be unthinkable apart from the concern with narcotics (Marks 2007). Thus, though it is people, ultimately, who are sent to prison, have their belongings searched, or are forced to submit to a drug test, it is the specific materiality of the drug and its effects, whether real or imagined, that serves as the precondition for these interventions. And as we will see with methamphetamine, this has come to include the precursor chemicals out of which the drug is made.

2. THE SIMULTANEOUS USE OF MULTIPLE METHODS OF INTERVENTION TO DO THE WORK OF NARCOTICS CONTROL. The uniformed police officer is the most visible sign of both the state's police powers generally and of drug enforcement specifically. But this figure is the tip of the iceberg when it comes to the broad array of practices deployed to control the flow of drugs. For example, one of the most significant pieces of narcotics legislation is the Harrison Act of 1914. This act created a federal system of drug regulation that quickly shaped the drug markets of the era. The Harrison Act was not criminal law, however, but tax law. Nevertheless, its passage fundamentally altered the landscape in which narcotics were used, policed, and traded, setting the stage for the criminalization of narcotics that has characterized the U.S. approach ever since (Acker 2002).

More recent antinarcotics legislation has likewise attempted to engage the governmental capacities of the state on multiple registers. Legislation enacted during the Reagan administration, for instance, involved the allocation of almost $2 billion to address illicit narcotics. Specific initiatives included a drug-testing program for federal employees, stiffer federal sentences for drug offenders, including the death penalty for so-called drug kingpins, continued sponsorship of international drug eradication programs, and penalties against countries identified as drug producers who did not cooperate with U.S. eradication efforts (Goode and Ben-Yehuda 1994).

Increased use of the military has also been a hallmark of the campaign against illicit narcotics. In 1981 Congress revised a century-old law that prohibited the military from engaging in civilian law enforcement. As a result, the military was allowed to "loan equipment to the civilian police, train law enforcement personnel, and directly assist in some aspects of interdiction efforts" (Kraska 2003, 301). The law also authorized military officials to arrest traffickers in other countries (these powers were later suspended following the controversial arrest of Manuel Noriega).

More recent efforts have tended to downplay the military approach. The two most recent administrations have emphasized treatment, education, community, and faith-based initiatives. In the summer of 2009, the Obama administration "drug czar" Gil Kerlikowski announced that they would no longer be using the phrase "War on Drugs," in large part to signify the administration's shift toward a more public-health–oriented approach. "It is a change," Kerlikowski stated. "The change in emphasis is to look at this as a public health problem. Law enforcement and prevention and treatment are all big parts of it. But clearly, the public health problem is the way we should be viewing this" (U.S. Outlines New Drug War Strategy 2009).

And yet the same year saw the Obama administration issue the *National Southwest Border Counternarcotics Strategy*, a transnational law enforcement effort strictly focused on fighting Mexican drug cartels and stopping the flow of drugs and guns along the U.S. border with Mexico. Similarly, such enforcement efforts increasingly overlap with other military conflicts, particularly in Afghanistan where the DEA is poised to assume an even greater role in the conflict (Associated Press 2009).

3. THE BRIDGING OF PUNITIVE AND ACTUARIAL MODES OF GOVERNANCE. When drugs are constituted in political discourse as threats, there is an inevitable blurring of morality-based and risk-based reasoning that takes place. The moral opposition to drug use in the United States is well known. Its puritan heritage continues to cast a long shadow over the way particular substances are valued. Those taken to increase productivity tend to be embraced unproblematically while those taken primarily for pleasure are largely disdained (Levine 1978; Valverde 1998). As a result, illicit drugs are typically cast in moral terms, and this moral evaluation extends to those involved with drugs. The "drug dealer" has become a particularly maligned "figure of criminality" (Rafael 1999) in the public imagination (Garland 2001). Drug dealers are cast as "wicked individuals who have lost all legal rights and all moral claims upon us" (ibid., 192). This fuels a particularly punitive and "expressive" approach to drugs and drug-related crime, one that is "overtly moralistic, uncompromising, and concerned to assert the force of sovereign power" (ibid., 191; cf. Bertram et al. 1996).

But while drugs continue to incite moral opposition, they have also enabled practices for managing drug offenders that are not morality-based but risk-based. Such practices are not punitive but actuarial. They view criminal involvement with illicit narcotics less as a moral failing to be reproached than as a risk factor to be managed. A person's involvement with drugs is understood to increase the likelihood of their involvement with crime (beyond the criminal act of the drug possession and use itself). Drug possession is thus constituted as both a crime in itself and a predictor of additional and/or future criminality.

This association has given rise to such techniques as drug testing, drug sweeps, and drug courier profiling, all of which target drugs as a way to manage criminality and other associated risks. These techniques are now a central component of the way the criminal justice system polices threats and also does the work of risk management. From the risk-based perspective, then, narcotics are targeted, not because they are inherently bad (at least not just) but because there is a statistical (as well as discursive) correlation between drugs and crime. Thus institutional incentives make narcotics the focus of criminal justice practice just as much as a sense of moral outrage (Feeley and Simon 1992, 1994).

The attractiveness of narcopolitics is its ability to bridge both the morality-based and risk-based framings of narcotics and their corresponding punitive and actuarial approaches. This creates a potent system in which moral objections fuel the continued politicization of narcotics and sustain a largely punitive model of intervention, while simultaneously enabling the development and implementation of ever-more sophisticated forms of surveillance and "offender management" focused on mitigating risk.

These key features of contemporary narcopolitics form the backdrop to the response to methamphetamine that occurred in Baker County. They provided a general foundation for the more specific interventions that took place.

Methamphetamine Comes to Baker County

West Virginia shares many of the same characteristics as other states that have been heavily impacted by methamphetamine.[7] It is one of the whitest and most rural states in the United States. Its population is also one of the poorest and least educated, with 18 percent of residents living below the poverty line.[8]

The DEA's profile of West Virginia notes that its proximity to major metropolitan areas, including Pittsburgh, Baltimore, and Washington, D.C., makes it a strategic location for drug trafficking. The state's location, near the Shenandoah Valley of Virginia, just miles from where I conducted my research, also positions it at the center of national and international drug trafficking operations. Moreover, even though the law enforcement officers I interviewed would not officially confirm it, I was told that the Shenandoah Valley was part of a larger meth trafficking pipeline that stretched down through Virginia, the Carolinas, Georgia, Texas, and into Mexico. In short, West Virginia's rural character, its poverty, and its proximity to major metropolitan areas and drug trafficking routes made it fertile ground for methamphetamine to take root as it had in other areas (Ove 2006).

I chose to focus on West Virginia, rather than on a state where meth had already had a significant impact such as Missouri, Oregon, or Hawaii, in order to see the methamphetamine problem as it emerged. Conducting research in West Virginia between 2006 and 2007 provided precisely this kind of opportunity. At this time, West Virginia's methamphetamine problem was just beginning to gain widespread recognition. Between 2003 and 2005 the number of meth lab incidents statewide tripled, causing great concern.[9] Federal organizations such as the Drug Enforcement Agency targeted West Virginia as the leading edge of the methamphetamine epidemic as it moved eastward. A growing appreciation of the Shenandoah Valley's significance in the regional and global meth trade added to the concern. Indeed, as I began my research, a Federal Drug Task Force was wrapping up a two-year operation in the area focused on disrupting local networks of meth production and distribution between local dealers in West Virginia and producers and suppliers in the Shenandoah Valley.

In response, West Virginia lawmakers, particularly the newly elected governor, Joe Manchin, targeted the methamphetamine problem for regulatory intervention. They followed the lead of lawmakers in other states and passed legislation increasing the criminal penalties for meth-related crimes and strengthening the regulations on precursor chemicals used in the methamphetamine production process. These regulatory interventions involved the mobilization of significant sectors of the population, who were given new responsibilities under the legislation, particularly with regard to the monitoring of those precursor chemicals used in the methamphetamine production process. Conducting my research in West Virginia at this time thus allowed me to observe an epidemic "in-the-making," as it were, enabling me to see how people responded in the midst of the methamphetamine problem rather than in its aftermath.[10]

I focused my research on a cluster of five rural counties in the eastern part of West Virginia. This area sits just north of the Shenandoah Valley of

Virginia. To better insure the anonymity of my subjects, however, I have chosen to write about the area as if it were one county that I call Baker County. Like other parts of rural America, this area continues to undergo significant economic, demographic, and social changes. Small-scale farming used to be the primary occupation of most residents. Such farming is no longer viable, so many now work in the local poultry industry either as growers, drivers, or workers in the processing plant. Many others commute to work at similar factory jobs an hour or more away. The area's proximity to Washington, D.C., roughly three hours away, has made it an increasingly popular location for retirees from the city, as well as for tourists looking for weekend getaways. Some of these people came to the area shortly after 9/11, seeing safety in the area's rural location.

There is likewise an increasing Latino/Latina presence in the area, as immigrants, largely from Mexico and Puerto Rico, move there to work, primarily in the poultry industry. Along with the influx of "Mexicans," there is also a rising population of "Baltimore people"—white, mostly poor individuals and families seeking a new life in the rural setting away from the drugs and violence of the city. While local residents who were native to the area were still proud to call it home, there was nevertheless an underlying sense that the best years of the community might be behind them. Social changes such as these were often spoken of in terms of moral decline. I was told numerous times about the dwindling of parenting skills, of ethics and morals, and of common sense. "This used to be a real nice place to live," my neighbor, Elmer Jones, told me as we chatted on his porch one summer evening, looking at the home of the "Baltimore people" across the street with its crumbling facade and unkempt lawn. "Nowadays, people just don't know how to take care of themselves."

Any discussion of methamphetamine usually took place during talks about these more widespread changes. For instance, residents said repeatedly there was no family that had not been affected by drugs in some way. Concern over methamphetamine was particularly acute. Police officers I spoke with estimated that anywhere from 50 to 90 percent of all the crime they dealt with, such as breaking and entering, burglary, and domestic violence, had something to do with methamphetamine.

Such perceptions were not just limited to law enforcement. Those in the mental health field—substance abuse counselors, psychologists, and psychiatrists—spoke of increasingly unmanageable caseloads, as did social workers, health department employees, and those in child protection services. Administrators at the poultry processing plant instituted random drug testing as a standard practice to control the use of meth by their workers. They expressed frustration at the high turnover rates that resulted from employees either testing positive for drugs and being fired, or quitting rather than submit to a drug test.

This concern among professionals was mirrored in the community. Anxieties over the rise in methamphetamine use were particularly high. These anxieties were consistently articulated as a concern over crime. Local residents indicated that they had not experienced a dramatic rise in crime per se, but that they had begun to suspect that much of the crime they read about in the newspaper, or heard about from friends and neighbors, was somehow related to methamphetamine. Articulating their concerns in this way prompted residents to turn to the law, rather than to religion, public health, or some other institutional context, to address the growing methamphetamine problem, albeit in different ways.

Some were working to make law enforcement more accountable for handling the drug problem. One group of citizens came together and formed the community watch group "Concerned Citizens United Against Crime." This group formed shortly after a drug-related shooting at the local VFW. Members demanded that police take a harder stand on drugs and drug-related crime, monitored courts to make sure that those convicted of drug crimes received appropriate sentences, and prompted discussion about the lack of treatment resources available in the community for addicts and their families.

In other areas, citizens turned to the law in less formal ways to express their concerns over meth-related crime. Individuals called police with anonymous tips about possible dealers, reported signs of meth production discovered on their property or in the woods, and paid close attention to the behavior of their neighbors, especially newcomers, for any signs that drug dealing or using was taking place.

And elsewhere, there was little more than a feeling that "something should be done" about the growing drug problem, and a sense that law enforcement was responsible for doing it. Though unwilling to assist personally for fear of reprisal from the family members and neighbors on whom they'd be reporting, these residents nevertheless become frustrated when police were slow to arrest someone that, as I often heard, "everybody knows is selling drugs."

Such frustration often led to speculation about who was really behind the rising drug problem in the community. Rumors circulated about the role the mayor, the sheriff, and other officials were playing in facilitating the local drug trade. Residents whispered stories about suspicious nighttime rendezvous at the area's tiny airport that were presumed to be drug related. A local journalist caused a major stir when she wrote a column about a group of attorneys who were rumored to be involved in the drug trade. No evidence ever arose to substantiate the rumors, and the officials in question were quick to dismiss them as nothing more than gossip. However, when someone who, in the eyes of the community, should have gone to jail did not, it just seemed to further substantiate the rumors, maintaining the suspicions of many that the local drug problem was as bad as it was because the officials in charge of addressing it were actually involved in it.

And in the midst of all this concern and speculation were those struggling with methamphetamine addiction. Options for these individuals were extremely limited. Although there was a regional treatment facility, its scope, like similar facilities in rural areas, was modest. It was a strictly outpatient facility, with only a handful of certified substance-abuse counselors and three licensed psychiatrists who were responsible for providing mental health services for the entire region.

Inpatient treatments and hospitalizations were available only in larger cities, the nearest being one hundred miles away. There were those in the community who made daily trips to these facilities to maintain their treatment, but many more went without, often ending up enmeshed in the criminal justice system after committing a crime to sustain their habits. Further complicating the issue was the sheer difficulty of treating methamphetamine addiction itself. Local addiction counselors estimated their success rate with methamphetamine users at 30 percent, a figure that program participants felt was grossly inflated. Thus the limited effectiveness of treatment, and the difficulty of its implementation in rural areas, increased the probability that the criminal justice system—rather than the family, the church, or some other institution—would assume responsibility for the meth addict and his or her rehabilitation.

Methods

I conducted my research using an ethnographic approach. Information was assembled in three ways: (1) through the collection and analysis of all known criminal cases involving methamphetamine, (2) through regular court attendance in each of the five counties and interviews with individuals involved in court cases, and (3) through interviews and conversations with more than one hundred individuals in the five counties who were most knowledgeable about the local meth situation, including those who worked in a profession that dealt with meth use and its associated crimes, participated in one of the citizen action organizations focused on addressing the meth problem, or had been personally affected by meth in some way, real or imagined.

In ethnography it is always hard to know where to begin. I began by exploring the experiences and responses to the problems associated with methamphetamine among those most involved with addressing it. I made connections with key administrators and professionals working in institutions that were addressing the methamphetamine problem directly. These included the local hospital, courthouse, police station, schools, and churches. The goal here was to understand the professional bureaucracy in place for dealing with methamphetamine in the area.

I conducted interviews with key officials and administrators within these institutions. I mapped the bureaucratic processes in which they were involved, such as the process governing a person's arrest, trial, and sentencing, the protocol teachers followed when they suspected a student of using drugs, and the use of drug testing by administrators within a range of institutions to manage the populations under their supervision. Building on this work, I moved from the professional context to the world of ordinary citizens. The goal here was to understand the effect methamphetamine was having on everyday life, first of all by participating in the activities of a number of community action groups that were focused on methamphetamine. These included the group Concerned Citizens United Against Crime previously mentioned, as well as another group called the Substance Abuse Prevention Coalition. I attended meetings and interviewed members of these groups, paying attention to the ways they talked about drugs, crime, and addiction, and the kinds of action they were involved with or wanted to see taken to address the meth problem.

I also participated as fully as possible in the life of the local community. I sang in the community choir, went to Bible studies, and served as a judge in the elementary school social studies fair. I volunteered at the nursing home on bingo night and attended community events, such as the annual summer festival and the weekly bluegrass jam session at the senior citizen community center. Participating in community events this way gave me a more robust sense of life in the area. It also demonstrated the pervasiveness of the concern about methamphetamine, as conversations with local residents often and quickly turned to the topic.

Over the course of the research period I conducted detailed "person-centered" (Levy and Hollan 1998) interviews with a small number of recovering methamphetamine addicts. I documented in detail the experiences of these individuals with methamphetamine. In addition to obtaining detailed personal histories, I recorded each person's version of his or her addiction experience as well as accounts of arrest, conviction, and/or rehabilitation as applicable.

Additionally, I examined the case files on individuals convicted of a meth-related crime. These files included the history and full legal proceedings of each individual's case, transcriptions of confessions, preliminary evaluations by a psychologist and probation officer, letters of support (or vilification) from friends and other community members, full transcription of court proceedings if the case had gone to trial, and, if the person was convicted, letters from the person to the judge asking him or her to reconsider. Examining these files provided a crucial supplement to my interview work, enabling me to see the way these individuals were figured as criminals in the criminal justice system and beyond.

Proceeding in this way, this book provides a detailed account of how one community responded to the methamphetamine problem. It shows how, in their response, the residents of Baker County drew from patterns of enforcement that are now deeply engrained in American political life. It is these patterns of enforcement, and the politics by which they are sustained, that I term "narcopolitics." Understanding the significant role played by narcopolitics in contemporary American political life, particularly with regard to the workings of law and police power, is the focus of what follows.

1

"The Most Dangerous Drug in America"

I did not initially focus on the policing of methamphetamine in Baker County. As originally conceived, my project was going to be an examination of the treatment experiences of addicts working to overcome their addiction to meth—what I thought of as the "therapeutic trajectory" of their recovery process. I was interested in this question because of my reading in the scientific literature on methamphetamine addiction. Clinical reports have emphasized the neurological impact of methamphetamine, noting that in addition to being highly addictive, methamphetamine results in acute and/or chronic psychosis.[1] This complicates the already dim prospects for successful treatment. I was interested in how meth addicts learned to live with their addiction under these conditions, particularly in the resource-poor settings of the rural United States.

Thus, I began my research by speaking to those who worked in therapeutic services related to addiction. I made arrangements to interview the head addiction counselor, Carl Ferguson, at the local mental health clinic. I met him at his office, in the small brick building that housed the clinic. He welcomed me into his office, shaking my hand. He was younger than I had expected, seeming at most to be around forty. Stills from *The Andy Griffith Show* hung on the walls, providing the only decoration.

"How in the world did you end up here?" he asked, smiling, as we sat down. I explained my interest in methamphetamine and the impact it was having on rural communities. Carl began to explain in detail all of the problems the clinic and the community were having with meth. Because meth was so addictive it was nearly impossible to treat. Carl estimated that, at best, the clinic had a 30 percent success rate treating meth addicts. In his experience, treatment worked only when people really wanted to stop using the drug. Users, however, seldom got to that point and so rarely sought treatment on their own. The clinic probably wouldn't see any meth users, Carl wagered, if the court system did not send them to the clinic as often as they did. Indeed, the court played a vital role in the work of the clinic. "The court is the hammer that keeps them in treatment," he said.

This movement from the clinic to the court (and back again, and vice versa) became a theme that recurred in my early conversations with others involved in addiction therapeutics. I contacted the pastor of the First Baptist Church where, according to the newspaper, there was a Narcotics Anonymous meeting on Thursdays. In a brief email he replied that he knew nothing about the group; he wasn't even sure if they were still meeting. In any case, if I was really interested in learning about addiction issues, the person to talk to was Janice Cochran, head of the anti-drug group Concerned Citizens United Against Crime. She had been working to put pressure on local law enforcement to be more aggressive in their pursuit of drug offenders. In the process, she had become something of a local expert on drug issues, at least with regard to the criminal dimension of the problem.

A group of professionals in the social service field—social workers, community organizers, the high school guidance counselor—met regularly at the local hospital. The focus of their meetings was to develop prevention and treatment programs that met the county's specific needs. I began attending their meetings. After conducting interviews with the two primary organizers of the group, however, they suggested I speak to the local deputy sheriff, Daryl Montgomery. Daryl was the real expert on methamphetamine.

Daryl's expertise came from two years of experience working as part of a Federal Drug Task Force focused on arresting methamphetamine traffickers in the area. I asked Daryl how law enforcement dealt with the medical issues related to meth use and addiction. He admitted that they did not do much to address them. "They all want treatment when they get caught," Daryl stated. But few stayed with it. "I see treatment as an easy getaway," he continued. "Some people call me hardcore, but I think jail's the best treatment for them." The prosecuting attorney for the county shared Daryl's view and was very aggressive in obtaining felony convictions for drug offenders. He rarely agreed to treatment as an alternative to incarceration. "We're very lucky," Daryl stated.

During these early interviews, a pattern developed in which I found myself being constantly directed to members of law enforcement whenever I began asking questions about methamphetamine. This underscored the degree to which drug problems generally, and the methamphetamine problem specifically, were framed locally as matters for the criminal justice system. Eventually I began simply contacting members of the criminal justice system myself. One of these was the prosecuting attorney for the county,

Daniel Gardner. I called his office one morning and after two rings a man with a decidedly un-West Virginian accent picked up the phone. I introduced myself and explained my interests. "Uh huh," he said, distractedly. I could hear papers rustling in the background.

"I was wondering if you could tell me about some cases in which drugs were involved," I asked.

"I don't really have time to do that," he said, papers still rustling. "Just go to the circuit clerk's office and start looking through files. If you have any questions about specific cases let me know."

This was the first of many brush-offs I received during my fieldwork, or so I thought. I followed his instructions and went to the circuit clerk's office where all of the criminal case files for the county were housed. I introduced myself to the clerk and posed the same question I'd asked of the prosecuting attorney, but this time with more specificity: "Could I see the files for any cases in which drugs were involved? I'd be particularly interested in seeing any related to methamphetamine."

The clerk looked back, silently, lips pursed as though she were about to say something. I could not tell whether her expression was one of annoyance, confusion, or both. I braced myself for another brush-off. Then she spoke. She was trying to figure out the best way to respond to my request. The problem, she explained, was that so much of the crime they saw was drug-related. There were the cases of possession and distribution, crimes in which drugs were explicitly involved, but it was also the crimes committed with more regularity—breaking and entering, theft, domestic abuse, etc.—that were often drug-related, even though this was not reflected in the charges. She concurred with the prosecuting attorney's suggestion: the best thing to do was simply go through the file drawers. It would not take long to find drug-related cases.

In this way I discovered that the criminal justice system in Baker County was taking the lead in the response to methamphetamine and that the local treatment options, such as they were, were inseparable from this wider system of drug enforcement. To understand this system would require going beyond the concern with treatment per se, to a consideration of deeper patterns of drug control, of which the local treatment options were but a part.

Taking this approach would also require locating the response to methamphetamine in Baker County within the more general history of U.S. drug control. Illicit narcotics have long been framed as a law enforcement matter, the centerpiece of a broader "enforcement apparatus" that also includes drug treatment, education, and research, as well as legal regulations outside of criminal law (Stalcup 2006; Bertram et al. 1996). This framing has become so well engrained into U.S. political culture, in fact, that law enforcement—and criminal justice more generally—are virtually unthinkable today apart from the concern with narcotics. Thus, though the use of the criminal justice system to address illicit drugs has had a direct impact on the manifestation of the "drug problem," the deeper impact has been on the practice of criminal justice itself, which has been reoriented around the demands of drug enforcement. Notably, the process by which methamphetamine became "the most dangerous drug in America," to quote the former attorney general Alberto Gonzales, is part and parcel of this history, providing new venues for U.S. drug control and the exercise of police power.

Methamphetamine at the Dawn of the Twenty-First Century

Methamphetamine is a synthetic stimulant. It is a white or brown crystalline powder that may be smoked, injected, or taken intranasally (i.e., "snorted"). Since the mid-1990s, there has been a shift from snorting to smoking as the preferred method of administration (Rawson 2007, 2). In its smoked form, meth goes by various names including "ice," "crystal," "crank," and "glass." Other names include "chalk," "speed," and "Tina" (NIDA 2006, 1). Meth is part of the wider family of amphetamine-type stimulants (ATS), use of which has spiked globally in recent decades (UNODC 2005).

Users report experiencing a "rush" that includes increased energy, enhanced feelings of well-being, heightened libido, and appetite suppression. The anthropologist Jason Pine has suggested that this reflects a desire on the part of the user to reduce the body to little more than a "vector" for speed (Pine 2007, 358). But this desire is not without its consequences. In addition to the initial rush, users may also experience or display a variety of psychological effects, including paranoia, agitation, violent behavior, psychosis, talkativeness, anxiety, or depression. Hallucinations are also common. Some users report seeing bugs underneath their skin, which they then try to remove, injuring themselves in the process. Additionally, the systemic effects of prolonged meth use on the body can be extensive, affecting dermatologic, dental, cardiac, pulmonary, metabolic, immune, renal, and/or neurologic systems (Lineberry and Bostwick 2006, 81).

The methamphetamine production process likewise carries numerous physical risks. Though the majority of methamphetamine is produced outside the United States, it is also possible to produce it domestically in so-called meth labs using widely available chemicals such as iodine, cold tablets, and drain cleaner. The chemicals used are toxic, as are the chemical by-products, which are typically dumped by "cooks" on the side of the highway or in the woods. The production process is also extremely volatile, so meth labs—which can be anywhere from a house to a suitcase—carry a high risk of explosion. Thus everything from a severe burn to psychosis to tooth loss to cardiac arrest can be a symptom of methamphetamine. Meth's prevalence and potency, the risk it poses to users, their friends, family, and communities, and the "collateral damage" inflicted on legal, medical, and social services, led a Mayo Clinic report to label meth a "perfect storm" of medical and social complications (Lineberry and Bostwick 2006).

Methamphetamine was first synthesized in Japan in 1893. The militaries of Japan, England, Germany, and the United States used the drug during World War II to increase energy and enhance the performance of soldiers and other personnel. It likewise continues to have a commercial use in nasal decongestants and bronchial inhalers. A Schedule II drug, it is available with a prescription in small, nonrefillable quantities, and has been used for the treatment of attention deficit hyperactivity disorder (ADHD) and narcolepsy.

Domestic use of amphetamine and methamphetamine in the United States can be traced back to the early 1930s when the medicinal uses of the drugs were discovered. Between 1932 and 1946, the pharmaceutical industry promoted a list of thirty-nine generally accepted medical applications for the drugs. These included everything from the treatment of schizophrenia and head injuries to low blood pressure, radiation sickness, and hiccups (Miller 1997). Amphetamines were even promoted as a treatment for addiction itself, following in the footsteps of both heroin and cocaine, which were likewise promoted as anti-addiction medications (Bourgois 2000).

Amphetamine tablets were available without a prescription in the United States until 1951 and amphetamine inhalers until 1959. During the 1950s and '60s, amphetamines and methamphetamine were marketed and prescribed for the treatment of depression, obesity, and narcolepsy. They also began to be used licitly for the purposes of self-enhancement: housewives used amphetamines for weight loss and to be more productive around the house; students, businessmen, and laborers (particularly truck drivers) used them for their anti-fatigue effects (Campbell 2000; Miller 1997).

Production of amphetamines soared during this period. From 1958 to 1970 the annual legal production of amphetamines grew from 3.5 billion to 10 billion tablets. Approximately 20 million prescriptions were written each year during the 1960s, peaking in 1967 when 31 million prescriptions for amphetamines were written. Even so, licit production consistently exceeded licit use. Of the 100,000 pounds of pharmaceutical amphetamine produced each year up until 1971, it is estimated that between one-half and two-thirds were diverted to the illicit market (Miller 1997).

Use of methamphetamine began to take off in the late 1950s when some doctors began to prescribe its intravenous administration for the treatment of heroin addiction. The introduction of injectable methamphetamine set the stage for increased illicit use of the drug. Demand grew as heroin users, who were already using illicit drugs, became familiar with it. Illegal prescriptions written by pharmacists and doctors became more common. Aware of the growing illicit market in amphetamines and methamphetamine, the Department of Justice tightened regulations. In 1971 they set quotas on the amount of amphetamine that pharmaceutical manufacturers could produce. They also successfully pressured pharmaceutical manufacturers to voluntarily remove injectable methamphetamine ampoules from the outpatient prescription marketplace. The shrinking of the licit market created opportunities and demand for more extensive illicit production and distribution (Miller 1997). Thus methamphetamine is the product of the process Anne Lovell has called "pharmaceutical leakage" (Lovell 2006). As Lovell demonstrates in the case of high-dose buprenorphine, the licit development and sale of pharmaceuticals is always shadowed by the creation of an illicit market in which the drug simultaneously circulates. The interdependence of the two markets makes it extremely difficult to regulate either in isolation.

Illicit use of methamphetamine had long been thought to be limited to West Coast states and Hawaii. Meth use has been common there since at least the 1960s, and the first meth labs emerged in San Francisco in 1962. Then, biker gangs were the primary producers and distributors of methamphetamine (Miller 1997). But beginning in the mid-1990s, meth began spreading east. The precise reasons for this are not entirely known, but a number of factors contributed. The first was that clandestine production and distribution changed. No longer limited just to biker gangs, smaller groups of friends and family began using low-tech labs to produce limited amounts of meth. The new production process required a less sophisticated level of chemical knowledge. What it did require, however, was a recipe. This was the second change. Throughout the 1980s, recipes were carefully guarded secrets. But in the 1990s, detailed instructions of the methamphetamine production process began to circulate and eventually found their way to the Internet. This made instructions for meth use easily accessible to anyone interested in manufacturing it (Owen 2007). It also meant that methamphetamine could be accurately described as the first drug epidemic of the digital age.

A third key factor in the eastward spread of methamphetamine was that truckers who ran routes from the East to the West and back again became involved with its delivery. Truckers were some of the earliest users of amphetamines going back to the 1950s when they were still widely available without a prescription. The drugs helped drivers maintain wakefulness while spending long hours on the road. As amphetamines became more difficult to obtain licitly, the illicit market grew, creating demand for crank and other types of methamphetamine. One of my informants, a trucker named Ken, told me about his father, also a trucker, who introduced him to the use of "bennies" (Benzadrine) and other amphetamine-type stimulants as a regular component of work. Once these drugs became illegal, Ken and other truckers like him began to look for replacements. When Ken started driving regular routes from West Virginia to California, he was introduced to methamphetamine. As a means of paying for their own supply of meth, Ken and other truckers like him began to transport it east.

The domestic production of methamphetamine in clandestine meth labs also increased significantly during the 1980s. By 1992, the Drug Enforcement Administration (DEA) was reporting that methamphetamine was the most prevalent clandestinely manufactured controlled substance in the United States (Miller 1997). Though levels of illicit drug use are always hard to measure, the general trend over the next decade pointed toward expansion. One measure of this was the spike in treatment admissions for methamphetamine addiction. According to an official report released by the National Institute on Drug Abuse (NIDA) in 2006, only five states reported high rates of treatment admissions for methamphetamine in 1992. By 2002 the number of states had increased to twenty-one. Not surprisingly, the total number of treatment admissions for methamphetamine increased significantly as well, from 21,000 to 150,000 between 1992 and 2004. Similarly, methamphetamine-related hospital emergency department visits increased more than 50 percent between 1995 and 2002 (NIDA 2006). And by 2005 *Newsweek* magazine had dubbed meth "America's Most Dangerous Drug" (Jefferson 2005).

No Place to Hide

Methamphetamine is used by diverse populations. However, it has increasingly come to be seen as a white, rural drug. One of the first studies to make this association was produced by the National Center on Addiction and Substance Abuse at Columbia University (CASA). This study, tellingly titled, "No Place to Hide: Substance Abuse in Mid-Size Cities and Rural America," found that contrary to popular belief, rates of drug, alcohol, and tobacco use in rural and small town areas were equivalent to those in urban locations. Among young teens, rates of use were actually higher. The study presented methamphetamine as a case in point, noting that children twelve to fourteen years old were 104 percent more likely to use methamphetamine than their urban peers. In his introduction to the study, the executive director of CASA, Joseph Califano Jr., located these findings in a broad cultural narrative of national decline, concluding that "As we begin the twenty-first century in America, there is *no place to hide* from the problems of substance abuse and addiction" (CASA 2000, ii).

This representation of methamphetamine as a white, rural drug is not unfounded. It is supported by certain measures of rural methamphetamine use, particularly among arrestees and the incarcerated. For instance, a DEA report published in 2002 found that 94 percent of arrestees for methamphetamine were white, compared with 61 percent of cocaine users and 18 percent of crack cocaine users. Similarly, a study of incarcerated offenders published in 2001 in the *American Journal of Drug and Alcohol Abuse* found that 23.1 percent of rural inmates and 30 percent of the most rural inmates reported having used amphetamines prior to incarceration compared with only 10.6 percent of urban inmates (Weisheit and Fuller 2004, 139). More recently, a 2006 study of "the criminal effect of methamphetamine on communities" conducted by the National Association of Counties (NACo)—the premier lobbying organization for rural governments—found that methamphetamine was by far the number-one drug problem facing rural governments; that robberies, burglaries, and domestic violence had all increased as a result of meth; and that meth had increased the workload of public safety staff (NACo 2006; but see Owen 2007).

Perhaps the biggest reason that methamphetamine has come to be seen as a rural, white drug is because clandestine manufacturers have tended to locate in rural areas. The CASA study notes that there was a sixfold increase in the number of meth labs seized by the DEA during the mid-nineties, the majority of which were located in less-populated areas. The number of states in which labs were found likewise increased during this period. Already by 1999, the Shenandoah Valley of Virginia was being identified as the methamphetamine distribution hub for the eastern United States (CASA 2000, iii). All of this may explain why a poll conducted by the PEW Research Center in 2001 found that "drugs" was the number one "problem facing the community," according to residents of rural areas, ahead of unemployment, education, taxes, and infrastructure (PEW 2001, 3–4).

Global Trends

These changes in the consumption patterns of methamphetamine in the United States are part of a global trend. Amphetamines are now the second most-used drugs in the world behind cannabis. The United Nations Office of Drugs and Crime (UNODC) estimates that for a twelve-month period between 2003 and 2004 approximately 26 million people worldwide used amphetamines. By contrast, approximately 14 million used cocaine and 11 million used heroin. Nor is the use of amphetamines a strictly American or even Western phenomenon: countries throughout Eastern Europe, the South Pacific, Southeast Asia, Australia, and, increasingly, Africa, report problematic levels of use (Rawson 2007).

Methamphetamine production and circulation are likewise global in scope, but in a unique way compared to other drugs. The key ingredients used in making methamphetamine, ephedrine, and pseudoephedrine are manufactured in just nine factories in the world, located in only four countries, India, China, Germany, and the Czech Republic. The production process is extremely technical (much more so than producing methamphetamine from precursor chemicals), requiring sophisticated chemical knowledge and instruments. Again the process of pharmaceutical leakage is visible here, as the illicit trade in methamphetamine is uniquely dependent on the licit pharmaceutical market.

Ephedrine is used in asthma and diet pills, while pseudoephedrine is the key ingredient in a number of cold medications, the most prominent being Pfizer's Sudafed. The cold medication market alone is a $3 billion industry and is itself the product of an FDA decision in the 1970s that made a number of prescription medications, including those containing pseudoephedrine, available over the counter. Indeed, before 1976, any product containing pseudoephedrine could not be purchased in the United States without a prescription. Thus, just as the market in amphetamines was being more tightly regulated, the market in medications containing ephedrine and pseudoephedrine was being deregulated and expanded.

This is a crucial point to consider: the illicit market in amphetamines and methamphetamines has always been dependent on the licit market for these medications. This means that the methamphetamine problem is the product, not just of a quirk in the manufacture of a specific medication but of the more general rise of pharmaceuticals in the management of health that has occurred since the middle of the twentieth century and the explosion of over-the-counter medications that accompanied it (cf. Petryna et al. 2006;

Dumit 2002). Pharmaceuticals are now at the center of the way humans, at least those with access to medications, manage their health, well-being, and social relationships. Governments have taken note of and participated in this transformation, using the regulation of pharmaceuticals as a key domain in which to carry out the work of governance (Biehl 2005).

The journalist Steve Suo was one of the first to uncover the symbiotic relationship that exists between the licit and illicit markets in substances containing pseudoephedrine in a series of articles published in the *Oregonian* newspaper in 2004. In a series titled "Unnecessary Epidemic," Suo charted the various factors at work in creating the methamphetamine problem in the United States. His key finding was that regulatory decisions made by the U.S. federal government, enforcement agencies such as the DEA, and international organizations such as the International Narcotics Control Board in Vienna, Austria, had directly impacted the course of the meth problem in the United States. Specifically, the reluctance of U.S. legislators to restrict the sale of over-the-counter medications containing ephedrine in the 1980s and pseudoephedrine in the 1990s, or to better regulate the bulk sales of these chemicals, despite evidence that significant amounts of the medications were being diverted toward illicit use, enabled the proliferation of both home-made methamphetamine labs as well as meth produced in Mexican "super-labs" (Suo 2004; Pine 2007).

Suo's series was a damning critique of the collusion between government and industry, and brought swift response from legislators. Before his five-part series finished running, the governor of Oregon had already written a letter to the paper promising to make the meth problem a priority and to follow many of the recommendations made by Suo to better regulate the precursor chemicals used in the meth-making process. One of these was an executive order to the Oregon Pharmacy Board to immediately "enact emergency administrative rule" and put any products containing pseudo-ephedrine behind the pharmacy counter. Anyone wishing to purchase these products would have to show a valid identification, and the vendor would be required to keep a record of the purchase (including who it was and how much they purchased). This has now become law in Oregon and the majority of other states, as well as federal law since the passage of the Combat Meth-amphetamine Epidemic Act as part of the renewal of the PATRIOT Act in 2006 (Kulongoski 2004).

Similarly, powerful senators criticized by Suo for their inaction, such as Dianne Feinstein of California and Orrin Hatch of Utah, were prompted to publicly commit to doing more to address the meth problem. This took the form of putting anti-meth bills on the "fast track" in the Senate and pressuring international leaders to do more to control the flow of meth within their boarders.

In 2005, the House voted 423 to 2 to approve a bill that would cut U.S. aid to countries that imported too much pseudoephedrine, the key ingredient in meth (Suo 2005a). Heads of influential agencies such as the DEA, whom Suo had portrayed as not taking the meth problem as seriously as heroin or cocaine (he quoted one source at the DEA who said agents referred to meth derisively as "kiddie dope"), contested the characterization and took steps to illustrate publicly that meth was a priority. To this end, Attorney General Alberto Gonzales stated publicly and unequivocally that meth was indeed an "epidemic," and that "In terms of damage to children and to our society, meth is now the most dangerous drug in America" (Suo 2005b). Even though Suo's article was not distributed nationally, it did much to increase concern among legislators, who in turn began treating methamphetamine seriously as a national problem to the effect of calling it an epidemic.

The categorization of methamphetamine use as an epidemic had a number of consequences. On the one hand, it escalated the sense of threat and urgency, enabling anti-methamphetamine legislation to be enacted expeditiously. On the other hand, it "naturalized" the problem. That is, the clinical categorization of methamphetamine as an epidemic erased the political history that created the problem in the first place. State regulators and the pharmaceutical industry were thereby cleansed of responsibility, and efforts to confront the problem quickly became the focus of largely familiar law enforcement tactics used in the fight against other drug epidemics.

The most significant step in the federal legislative reaction to meth (at least symbolically) came on March 9, 2006, when President George W. Bush signed into law the USA PATRIOT Improvement and Reauthorization Act. The newly reauthorized act included the "Combat Methamphetamine Epidemic Act," a multimillion-dollar package aimed primarily at increasing the criminal penalties for making, possessing, and distributing methamphetamine. It was the most significant piece of legislation to be added to the PATRIOT Act, and the only piece that appeared to deviate from the legislation's wider focus on terrorism.

The actions taken (and not) by federal officials and the pharmaceutical industry combined with U.S. policy toward illicit drugs to create a regulatory field in which local responses to the problem took shape. In the process, those communities affected by methamphetamine were further incorporated into the ongoing efforts of the United States to eradicate the problem of illicit drugs.

Methamphetamine is hardly the first drug to generate such national concern in the United States. Cocaine, crack, heroin, opium, and marijuana—to say nothing of alcohol—have all taken their turn as the most dangerous drug in America. In each case, the general focus has been on finding legal solutions to the problem, with a particular emphasis on criminalization (Acker 2002; Musto 1999).

The response to methamphetamine has been largely a repetition of this pattern.[2] The funding of law enforcement initiatives in "meth hot spots" through the legislation contained in the PATRIOT Act is a prime example.[3] Similarly, within the federal government's drug control budget, which has totaled approximately $13 billion since 2006, the largest single expenditure was for domestic law enforcement ($3.6 billion) followed closely by interdiction ($3.3 billion). Together these expenditures constitute over half of the federal drug control budget, with $2.4 billion more going to law enforcement and interdiction than to treatment, prevention, and research (ONDCP 2007). Thus, even though methamphetamine has been figured as a new and unique problem, the response to methamphetamine has involved a repetition of the same punitive strategy of deterrence through criminalization that has long been the hallmark of the U.S. approach to the problems of drugs and addiction.

The search for legal remedies to the problem of illicit drugs in the United States goes back at least to the passage of the Harrison Act in 1914, but contemporary drug control efforts are largely the product of the War on Drugs, now well into its fourth decade. It was during the administration of Richard Nixon (1969–74) that the War on Drugs began in the United States in earnest. President Nixon used the phrase in a speech delivered in the summer of 1971 in which he likewise labeled drug abuse "public enemy No. 1."[4] In a speech delivered to Congress later that summer, Nixon continued the war motif, declaring that, "The [drug abuse] problem has assumed the dimensions of a national emergency. I intend to take every step necessary to deal with this emergency." ("Excerpts from President's Message on Drug Abuse Control" 1971).

From the beginning, the War on Drugs was envisioned as a national project. Like other such projects, it was imagined as a bold effort with broad implications through which a variety of policy goals could be pursued (Masco 2006; Lutz 2001). At the center of this effort was the relationship assumed to exist between drugs and crime. As David Musto and Pamela Korsmeyer have written:

Richard Nixon seized upon the issue of increasing use of illicit drugs in the United States as an opportunity to discredit "Great Society" liberalism . . . and to make good on a promise to lead an attack on crime. The people in charge of implementing his directives tended to accept at face value the proposition that a relationship existed between drug use and criminal behavior. . . . Even those White House planners who were skeptical about such links were aware of the political potential of the issue—the logic of the relationship between drugs and crime was easily communicated to the public, and the desirability of eliminating such a pernicious habit seemed self-evident. (Musto and Korsmeyer 2002, xviii)

The "self-evident" quality of both the relationship between drugs and crime and their need to be eliminated may explain why the War on Drugs has continued unabated since its declaration. It may also explain the "hidden-in-plain-sight" quality that surrounds its effects on American life. A series aired on National Public Radio in 2007 called the War on Drugs "The Forgotten War" (NPR n.d.). Mary Pat Brady has argued that the War on Drugs is not so much forgotten, as it is "disavowed" and "unremembered." This is true, despite (or even, perhaps, because) of the fact that major components of American law and public policy have been altered in the name of carrying out the drug war. These include everything from search and seizure laws, asset forfeiture laws, and terms of imprisonment, to money laundering laws, civil liberties, and foreign policy. Changes in government spending, the creation of new federal agencies, and unprecedented military operations have all resulted from the drug war as well. The justification for these changes, Brady argues, has been through the same narratives of emergency invoked by Nixon at the inauguration of the War on Drugs and implied by the war motif. This is why it is Brady's contention that the War on Drugs is indeed the "critical but disavowed" model for the War on Terror itself (Brady 2002, 446).

In addition to these more direct (albeit hidden) effects of the War on Drugs, the deeper impact has taken place at the level of everyday life. "Perhaps the War on Drugs' greatest achievement," Brady writes, "has been to make war familiar and largely banal—less terrifying" (ibid., 447). The War on Drugs is thus a component of the domestic militarization that Catherine Lutz has documented, even though it remains unremarked in her own account (Lutz 2002). It goes unremarked, perhaps, because it is now unremarkable. The drug war has become so familiar to the U.S. public, its continuation now goes without saying.

Statistics maintained by the U.S. Department of Justice's Bureau of Justice Statistics paint a vivid picture of just how extensive the effects of the War on Drugs have been, particularly on the criminal justice system.[5] "Drug-abuse violations" are now the single largest type of offense for which arrests are made in the United States.[6] This reflects the steady increase in the number and percentage of drug-abuse violation arrests over the past twenty-five years. For instance, of the roughly 14 million arrests made by state and local authorities in 2005, over 1.8 million were for drug-abuse violations. This reflects a tripling in the number of drug-abuse violation arrests since the 1980s, rising from 538,100 in 1982 to approximately 1.8 million in 2005. The percentage of total arrests for drug-abuse violations has nearly doubled over the same period, from 7.4 percent in 1987 to 13.1 percent in 2005. Finally, though these statistics are significant in themselves, they do not capture the more tacit forms of drug-focused policing—such as the stop and search of suspicious persons or vehicles—that are common, particularly in marginal communities, but often do not result in a formal arrest (Chambliss 2001).

This speaks to the impact that the focus on drugs has had on the organization and administration of law enforcement in everything from policing to prosecution. In 2003, more than 90 percent of police departments serving populations of 2,500 or more performed drug enforcement responsibilities. Similarly, 97 percent of all local police officers were employed by departments where drug enforcement was regularly performed. The same was true for sheriff's offices, with 90 percent reporting that they regularly performed drug enforcement functions.

The prosecution of drug offenders has likewise steadily increased. Over one third (35%) of all federal criminal prosecutions are for drug violations, up from less than a quarter in 1982 (21%). Similarly, U.S. attorneys initiated investigations involving 37,501 suspects for drug offenses in 2004 alone. The conviction rate for drug offenders is high and has grown. In 2004, 92 percent of drug defendants were convicted compared to 76 percent in 1981. Of those convicted, an increasing number—and more than any other type of criminal offender—are sentenced to prison. Indeed, as the proportion of all defendants sentenced to prison increased from 54 percent to 78 percent between 1988 and 2004, the proportion of drug offenders sentenced to prison increased from 79 percent to 93 percent. Very few of these convictions are the result of a trial. In 2002, for instance, 95 percent of drug trafficking convictions resulted from guilty pleas compared to 2 percent from jury trials and 3 percent from bench trials.

The prosecutorial emphasis on drug offenders has transformed the prison population as well. Drug convictions were responsible for more than 80 percent of the increase in the federal prison population between 1985 and 1995 (U.S. Dept. of Justice 1997). As of 2007, U.S. prisons and jails held approximately 2.3 million inmates, the highest number of any nation. The majority of these were there for drug-abuse violations. Although much has been made of the U.S. prison population, it is dwarfed by the number of individuals on probation. As of 2005 there were approximately 4.1 million adults on probation. Of these, 28 percent were drug offenders.

But perhaps the most significant impact of the War on Drugs, and the one that ties the whole complex together, is the deepening of the fundamental association between drugs and crime itself. Indeed, this association, though itself an artifact of U.S. drug-control policies, has become a focal point around which American government is organized and governance takes place (cf. Moore 2007).

No longer is the association between drugs and crime simply rhetorical or speculative. On the contrary, one of the fruits of the drug war is that this association is now statistically measurable. In 2004, for instance, 17 percent of state prisoners and 18 percent of federal inmates reported that they committed their current offense in order to obtain money for drugs. Similarly, 32 percent of state prisoners and 26 percent of federal prisoners reported that they had committed their current offense while under the influence of drugs.

Among all state prisoners, well over half (56 percent) were found to be dependent on or abused alcohol or drugs, regardless of their crimes. Among those diagnosed as mentally ill, the number was even more significant, with 74 percent of state prisoners dependent on or abusing alcohol or drugs.

As of 2002, 56 percent of jail inmates convicted of robbery reported using drugs at the time of their offense, along with 56 percent of those convicted of weapons violations, 55 percent of burglaries and 55 percent of motor vehicle theft. These percentages were even higher when alcohol was included, with 85 percent of burglaries, 79 percent of weapons violations and 75 percent of drug possession.

When incarcerated individuals were asked to report any previous drug use, the percentages become even more significant. In 2002, 82.2 percent of jail inmates reported having ever used drugs, 68.7 percent reported having ever used drugs regularly, 54.6 percent in the month before their offense and 28.8 percent at the time of the arrest. A more recent survey found that among state prisoners with a mental health problem, 62 percent had used drugs in the month prior to the offense.

Such numbers are significant, if for no other reason than they justify the state's continued prioritization of drugs in crafting public policy. For if, as these statistics would seem to indicate, drugs are implicated in most acts of criminality—whether it is a formal drug offense or not—then a continued focus on drugs and drug-related offenses seems like common sense. Moreover, as a result of this continued focus on drug offenders, the drug–crime connection increasingly becomes not just a statistical correlation but also an experiential fact. That is, as those individuals employed within the criminal justice system carry out their day-to-day duties, they experience the magnitude of the drug problem and the impact that drug offenders have on the criminal justice system firsthand. Again, while this is an artifact of U.S. drug-control policies that prioritize the arrest and prosecution of drug offenders, it makes the impact no less experientially real for those given the task of administering the policies. Thus, for these individuals—ranging from judges to social workers to police officers to ordinary citizens—the association between drugs and crime is not just a political assertion or statistical correlation but a matter of experience.

To put it simply, the association between drugs and crime has become a social fact in the United States. It would not be unfair to say that to live in the United States today is to participate, however modestly or vicariously, in the War on Drugs. It is noteworthy then how pessimistically the U.S. public views the state's efforts in the drug war. A poll conducted by the PEW Research Center in 2001, just as methamphetamine was gaining national attention, found that nearly three-fourths of the population (74%) believed that the United States was "losing the drug war." Moreover, the same percentage stated that the drug war could not succeed, agreeing with the statement, "Demand is so high we will never stop drug use" (PEW 2001, 1). My fieldwork gave me no reason to suggest that attitudes have changed.

And yet, despite this pessimism, there was little interest expressed in stopping the drug war or even considering alternative strategies (such as the establishment of more drug-treatment programs for drug users or the decriminalization of drugs). Indeed, even the de-escalation of certain components of the drug war (such as the rolling back of mandatory minimum sentences for nonviolent drug offenders) received only tepid endorsement from those surveyed (only 45% thought it was "a good idea"). Ultimately, the American public still views criminalization and interdiction as the best policy, despite the fact that it is viewed less favorably than it was even a decade ago. Thus, the majority of Americans appear committed to fighting a war they feel cannot be won, using a strategy they no longer believe in. This has created a paradoxical foundation for the political culture emerging from this context.

These historical developments in U.S. drug policy have shaped the practice of narcopolitics in the United States. In particular, they have sustained the framing of illicit drugs as an enforcement issue. This has put the criminal justice system at the forefront of efforts to address drug problems. It is no surprise, then, that this is the domain in which the political focus on narcotics has had its deepest impact.

The response to methamphetamine has involved the repetition of old patterns of enforcement but also the introduction of new trajectories. Chapter 2 explores one of those new trajectories, an assemblage of policing practices made possible by the fact that methamphetamine can be produced domestically using everyday household items. The focus of politicians, lawmakers, and criminal justice officials on stopping this form of domestic production has introduced new avenues for the exercise of police power, including its extension beyond the formal domains of law enforcement. It thus marks a new chapter in the history of narcopolitics.

2

"It Could Be Here . . .
It Could Be My Neighbor"

At one of the final meetings of the Substance Abuse Prevention Coalition, a regional coordinator presented the findings from a "Community Readiness Assessment" she had conducted for Baker County the previous month.[1] Jennifer Gaines was in her mid-twenties and worked for the West Virginia Prevention Resource Center (WVPRC) as a "community development specialist." The primary task of the WVPRC was to assist community groups in developing programs to promote health and well-being in the state, particularly those emphasizing prevention.

Jennifer explained that "readiness" was, like "social capital," one of those buzz words common in community development. It referred to a community's awareness of a problem, in this case substance abuse, and their willingness to address it. Jennifer had been able to establish the county's "readiness score" by asking various members of the community to complete a standardized questionnaire.

Before presenting the county's score, Jennifer referred to a chart showing the various levels of readiness. There were nine levels, ranging from level one, "No Awareness," to level nine, "Professionalization." Baker County was a level three, "Vague Awareness." This stage was just one step above "Denial" and indicated that "Most feel that there is a local problem, but no immediate motivation to do anything about it."

The members of SAPC were visibly disappointed with the assessment and began offering explanations as to why their score was so low. Some thought that using alcohol, tobacco, and drugs was something of a community norm, perhaps even a rite of passage, which parents tolerated because they themselves had done the same when they were younger. Others pointed to the fact that there were a large number of elderly residents who weren't particularly concerned about the drug problem. "A lot of it is our Appalachian culture," one woman insisted. One particularly frustrated woman, citing her own experiences trying to raise awareness about substance abuse in the county, felt that even though the score was low, it still overestimated the readiness of the county. Others nodded in agreement as she spoke about the strong "state of denial" that persisted in the community. Rather than acknowledge the drug problem and take steps to address it, the woman stated, most county residents simply denied that a problem even existed, insisting, "that's not here."

Jennifer stepped in at this point. She attempted to reassure the members of SAPC that there was still hope by suggesting a strategy for increasing readiness in the community. Jennifer explained that in doing the community readiness assessment, she had discovered that there was a strong reaction to significant drug-related events right after they happened, such as a drug-related death or a large drug bust, but that this sentiment faded the farther removed from the event people became. This suggested that county residents could potentially be mobilized but only if the group was able to find a way to harness this initial reactive spirit and transform it into a sense of readiness, replacing the idea that "that's not here" with the sense that "it could be here; it could be my neighbor."

A Vague Awareness?

This conversation surprised me. In my own interviews with community members, local awareness of drugs and drug abuse was anything but vague. Indeed, over the course of the time I lived in Baker County, I was amazed at just how frequently talk turned to the topic, referred to in the vernacular simply as "the drug problem." This form of talk seemed to have become even more prominent as concern with methamphetamine grew. And while community members might not have reached the level of readiness that would make them anxious to participate in the kind of prevention programs being developed by the Substance Abuse Prevention Coalition, they certainly displayed the awareness that, "it could be here; it could be my neighbor."

For example, I was at a Bible study one evening when conversation took an unexpected turn toward the topic of methamphetamine. It was a small group, gathered in the basement of the Methodist church. A friend, Joey Corbin, had invited me. I accepted Joey's invitation for the same reason I accepted Sandy Hinkle's invitation to be a judge in the elementary school social studies fair, and Chris Worthen's invitation to assist with bingo at the nursing home on Thursday nights: out of the ethnographic imperative to immerse oneself as thoroughly as possible in the field site, but also because, in such sites, talk frequently turned to the topic of methamphetamine.

The group was composed of older men and women in their fifties and sixties. Joey and I were two of the last to arrive. Those who had already gathered chatted with each other, some sitting in the metal folding chairs that had been arranged in a circle in the middle of the room, some still on their feet, grazing on the impressive spread of cookies, cake, coffee, and tea that was standard fare at such gatherings.

I followed Joey as he walked over and sat down in a folding chair next to a large man in jeans, a gray T-shirt, and a camouflage baseball cap; beside him sat a small, frail-looking woman in a blue dress. Both appeared to be in their early sixties. The older man gave a slight nod to Joey as we approached.

"How are you, Billy?" Joey asked in greeting.

"Not too bad," the man said, pausing briefly before adding, "My back is still killing me though. The doctor changed my medications around but it ain't doing no good."

Joey nodded in sympathy. He had had his own problems with pain. While working at the local poultry processing plant, Joey had been in a severe accident that left him with burns over a significant portion of his body and had been hospitalized for three months. He survived, but his body was covered with scars and he was missing most of the fingers on his left hand.

During the time Joey was in the hospital, he was given morphine for the pain. "I got hooked on it," he said. "I had to wean myself off it there at the end." This personal experience with drugs and addiction led Joey to the topic of methamphetamine. "But that [morphine] ain't nothing compared to what kids are putting into their bodies today," he said, moving up on the edge of his chair to make the point. "We got a boy selling meth right up the street from us over there. I believe he's making it, too. We had a house burn down over there from where they was making it."

This brief exchange between three friends in the basement of a church typified the kinds of contexts in which concerns about methamphetamine were expressed. I witnessed and/or participated in similar conversations while waiting to vote, while at the hardware store, and at Wal-Mart. In these exchanges, meth was a concern because of its prevalence and proximity. People were aware that meth seemed to be having its primary impact on rural areas, and if the arrest records in the local paper were any indicator, their community was hardly immune to its effects. Without being prompted, local residents expressed their deep concern about methamphetamine with stories about people they knew—or people that they knew, knew—had had some kind of personal encounter with methamphetamine. In this way, they embodied the level of awareness that the Substance Abuse Prevention Coalition was looking for. Indeed, Joey's story, focused as it was on the meth cook and meth dealer in his neighborhood, literally expressed the feeling that "It could be here; it could be my neighbor."

For most, knowledge of methamphetamine came from second- or third-hand sources. The court proceedings published by the local newspaper were a key source. So, too, were awareness-raising campaigns such as those carried out by police officers and community groups like the Substance Abuse Prevention Coalition. Many local residents had been made aware of meth at work, either through training programs or as a result of new responsibilities related to meth. Taken as a whole, these various forms of awareness-raising created a palpable sense of methamphetamine and the threat it posed to the community.

This sense of methamphetamine was amplified as knowledge gained from second- and third-hand sources such as training seminars and the local newspaper was coupled with firsthand experience. For those, such as Joey, it produced a sense of astonishment comparable to that expressed by Freud upon seeing the Acropolis for the first time: "So all this really *does* exist." (Freud 1936, 240). Such individuals served as crucial nodes in the wider networks of methamphetamine-related talk, enhancing its circulation and verisimilitude.

Everything about methamphetamine was a cause for concern for residents of Baker County. Its addictiveness, its prevalence in rural areas, the uncanny fact that "the people you'd never suspect" were the most likely users. But the aspect of meth that caused the most concern was the way in which it was produced. Unlike comparable drugs such as cocaine and heroin, meth could be manufactured locally using everyday household items. Meth labs had been found everywhere, in hotel rooms, cars, and even unassuming homes in rural areas. These "laboratories" often consisted only of a small ensemble of tools and ingredients, compact enough to fit inside a briefcase. Meth "cooks" largely opted to work in rural areas, where the potent chemical smell that accompanied the production process was less likely to be detected, and the toxic by-products that resulted could be easily dumped. The DEA reports that between 1999 and 2004 the number of meth lab incidents—situations involving an active meth lab or its remnants—nationally rose from 7,438 to 17,170 (DEA, n.d.c).

This image of the meth lab as rural, hidden, and impossible to detect aside from a few telltale signs has become a key symbol of methamphetamine. Indeed, what the crack house was for cocaine, the meth lab has become for methamphetamine. More importantly, the fact that methamphetamine can be produced from chemicals that were, until recently, widely available, has directly affected the way citizens have been called upon to aid in addressing the problem. Specifically, the association of methamphetamine with everyday items has led to the expansion of the number and kinds of individuals involved in policing their circulation. This broadening of scope has happened within the field of law enforcement, where officers from agencies such as the Department of Natural Resources are now much more involved in drug enforcement, but also among ordinary citizens, who have become increasingly involved in the policing of their communities through a growing awareness of the signs of possible meth production and use.

Legislation introduced to formally regulate the chemicals used in meth production, particularly products like certain over-the-counter medications containing pseudoephedrine, has encouraged this awareness among citizens and sought to build on it, creating new regulations that either formally or informally require citizens to participate in police work. As part of this effort, law enforcement officials, politicians, and community groups have all sought to increase public awareness of the signs of methamphetamine production and use, thereby incorporating local residents into the work of drug enforcement.

Making Methamphetamine

"I've seen what drugs can do to a lot of people." Justin Stokes sat across the table from me. I continued to sip my coffee while he (and the waitress) had long forgotten about his empty glass of iced tea. Three years earlier Justin had been convicted of multiple counts of possession of methamphetamine with intent to deliver. He served two years in the regional jail and was completing his sentence on probation. A high school friend of Justin's had introduced us when he heard I was doing research on methamphetamine.

Justin lived alone in a small farmhouse on top of the mountain that stood between Meadville, the county seat of Baker County, and the small town of Dove. For reasons he never made clear, Justin had no telephone. To reach him, I had to call his cousin, who would then walk next door to see if Justin was home. On my third attempt, I reached him, and he agreed to meet. Justin suggested we meet at Annie's, the restaurant attached to the bowling alley in downtown Meadville.

Justin was already sitting on a bench outside the restaurant when I arrived, his short, dark hair mostly covered by his baseball cap. Justin was stocky, though he explained as we entered the restaurant that he actually weighed fifty pounds less than he had a year ago, a fact that he attributed to the healthy lifestyle he'd adopted since his release from jail, but others, including his probation officer and ex-wife, saw as a clear sign he was again using methamphetamine. Justin dismissed these suspicions as the standard gossip that had always followed him in the town, the kind of talk that made it a difficult place for him to live, even before he became involved with meth.

I was somewhat surprised Justin had chosen Annie's to meet. Annie's was the most public place in town. According to locals, half of the town ate at least one meal a day there. My surprise at Justin's choice grew as the waitress slowly approached our table. I sensed a coldness in her demeanor, something I'd not sensed before when I'd been there alone. I assumed she knew who Justin was, and was probably wondering who I was, other than a stranger having public dealings with one of the most notorious drug dealers in town. I learned later that the waitress's son, David, had also been sent to jail for selling methamphetamine. Indeed, Justin and David were part of the same string of arrests that came after a Federal Drug Task Force began to focus on the area.

Justin spoke in hushed tones. He smiled his crooked smile on occasion but mostly remained serious. He had been convicted of selling meth but not of producing it. Justin claimed, nevertheless, to have been involved with both. Indeed, he started producing because he refused to steal (or worse, "sell his body," as he'd seen others do) to maintain his habit. "After I knew how to make it [meth], it was *on*," he said excitedly. "I'd just go up here to the hardware store, get my stuff, come back to the house and cook it."

"Were you able to get everything you needed just at the hardware store?"

"Hardware store, Rite Aid [a national pharmacy chain]. . . " Justin replied. "I don't know if you know what it's made out of."

"I know basically," I said, "but I don't know specifics."

Justin began listing the ingredients. "Boranic Acid, witch hazel, Nasenex, Sudafed; I've seen it made with ether, sulfur . . . " As he spoke he became progressively more excited, seeming to take pleasure in his own ingenuity.

Although he did not name it as such, Justin was describing the so-called Nazi method for producing methamphetamine. The folk etymology of this term holds that it was developed by Nazis during World War II to produce methamphetamine and other amphetamines consumed by the Nazi military and key officials including, supposedly, Hitler himself. Until the new regulations limiting sale of the precursor chemicals used to produce meth, it was the most common method of production, gaining prominence first among Hell's Angels and other biker gangs in the West, and then going national once such recipes, which had been secretly guarded, were made public knowledge via the Internet (Owen 2007).

Here is how Donnie Grate, another local methamphetamine cook, described the production process to the prosecuting attorney of Baker County:

> You take the Sudafed, pop them out of the pack, crush them and grind them, put them in a bucket. Take your batteries, peel them off and get the lithium strip out of them. Put the pills and the lithium in a bucket and pour the anhydrous on it. Then you throw Coleman to it, it will bubble . . . a white stream of liquid. Then you take the lid off, put it in a jar. Then you take a pop bottle with tubing, three inch tubing, and then you put salt liquefier in it and smoke it. Put it in a jar and smoke that liquid. Then you filter that into another jar and get the meth out.

Recent anti-meth legislation has targeted this kind of domestic production by heightening regulations on chemicals used in the cooking process. Though new, this legislation is part of a long history of attempts to regulate amphetamines and related precursor chemicals, which have moved in and out of formal legality for decades (Weisheit and Fuller 2004). Whereas previous efforts focused largely on the national and international flows of bulk supplies, the recent legislation foregrounds local intervention at point of sale. This has required the involvement of a wider range of individuals at the local level to enforce the regulations.

That the police power of the state has been channeled through the local is hardly surprising. In the United States, much of the "heavy lifting" involved in criminal justice takes place in local jurisdictions (Scheingold 1991). This reflects what Lawrence Friedman has called the "major structural contradiction" inherent to the U.S. criminal justice system: "The causes of crime, the reach of crime, the reality of crime—all these are national in scale and scope. Criminal justice, on the other hand, is as local as local gets" (Friedman 1993). Indeed, as Markus Dubber and Marianna Valverde have observed, there is a strong tendency in the United States to delegate the state's police power to municipalities. "In fact," they write, "'the police power' is sometimes imagined as essentially local" (Dubber and Valverde 2006).

But this arrangement affects the constitution of "the local" as much as the administration of police power. That is, just as there is a tendency in U.S. law to imagine police power in local terms, so there is also a tendency to imagine the local in terms of police power. This is evident in the approach taken toward clandestine methamphetamine production. To police this problem, residents of rural communities have been equipped with a new field of vision, a new way of perceiving the local landscape centered around meth-amphetamine. Immanent in this new field of vision is a set of responsibilities to police the local landscape for signs of meth. In this way, the anti-meth legislation has remapped what the sociologist Pierre Bourdieu would have called the "juridical field" of local communities, generating a distinct "legal habitus" centered on the policing of clandestine methamphetamine produc-tion (Hagan and Levi 2005).

This habitus is based, not on struggle, competition, and conflict (as per Bourdieu's account) but on suspicion, apprehension, and—in certain cases—a sense of loss (ibid., 1502–3). Indeed, though some participated in the policing of methamphetamine enthusiastically, others did so with reluctance, indiffer-ence, or at significant personal cost, including the loss of the local—under-stood here as a particular sense of community and perception of the social and physical landscape—as they imagined it. For these individuals, knowledge of clandestine methamphetamine production was a "poisonous knowledge" that revealed an illicit potential in the community about which they would have preferred to remain unaware (Das 2000). Thus the new legal habitus ushered in by anti-meth efforts was occupied differently by different actors, even as it expanded the range of individuals involved in the policing process.

Policing at Work, Work as Policing

Many of the new regulations on precursor chemicals regulate their circula-tion at point of sale. This means that policing these chemicals is now part of the daily work routine for employees of businesses where such chemicals are sold. Pharmacists are a key example. As mentioned above, pharmacists have been given significant responsibilities under the new anti-meth legislation. The legislation effectively created a new category of medications: over-the-counter medications that are kept behind the pharmacy counter. In addition to maintaining the state registry that records the names of those purchasing products containing ephedrine or pseudoephedrine, pharmacists must now limit the amount of medication individual customers buy and do triage work in distinguishing legitimate from illegitimate customers.

I often went to the pharmacy in town. It was a locally owned operation and, as a business, functioned more like a general store. In addition to filling the majority of prescriptions for local residents—outdoing the local chain stores, including Wal-Mart—they offered a small selection of books and magazines, groceries, tools, kitschy West Virginia souvenirs, home décor, and clothing.

The Mackies, the family who owned the store, were friendly but generally reserved. They would share anecdotes with me about experiences they had had with "druggies" but were reluctant to reveal much of the inner workings of their business. This was understandable. As the primary purveyor of medications in the town, they were entrusted with knowledge about the health of the community on both an aggregate and individual scale. If they were guarded, it was because they were aware of the sensitivity of the information they possessed. And they took their role as stewards of this information very seriously.

The Mackies enforced the new regulations as they were required to, though Jerry Mackie expressed doubts that the new laws would have much effect. They posted a sign informing customers that all medications containing ephedrine or pseudoephedrine were now held behind the pharmacy counter. Those who requested to purchase one of these products were asked to show an ID and sign the state registry. Most of these sales were benign, and so the Mackies were not particularly moved by the new requirements. Indeed, they were, in many ways, already involved in this kind of triage work, but in a different way.

I would often see Dustin Mackie, Jerry Mackie's son, out in town. He was quiet but would often comment when they had had someone trying to get access to drugs illegally. For instance, he told me about a woman who came in with a prescription that had obviously been forged. They knew it had been forged because there were only two doctors in town, and they were very familiar with both their signatures and their prescribing practices. "Even if I'd believed the signature," Dustin explained, "there's no way Dr. Jenkins would have prescribed as much Vicodin as that prescription said." Thus, for Dustin, this local knowledge acquired through long-term relationships was a superior method for monitoring the illicit acquisition of prescription drugs than the state's bureaucratic measures.

And yet, in other areas, the state was finding ways to put this local knowledge to work. A sheriff in one county told me about an old friend who ran one of the many "country stores" that dotted the rural landscape in his jurisdiction, providing groceries and convenience items that gas stations stock in more urban areas. The sheriff had gone to the owners of these stores to warn them that there were people making meth in the area, and to pay attention to anyone buying a lot of cold medicine, cooking fuel, or batteries, or asking for anything strange, like plastic tubing. His friend looked surprised, and told him about an "old boy" that had started showing up and buying all his cold pills just as quickly as he could stock them, saying he had bad allergies. The sheriff's friend thought it was strange but hadn't been aware of the methamphetamine problem, or the fact that it could be made with cold medicine and other such items.

But the state is not the only institutional actor restricting access to precursor chemicals. National chain stores that are common in rural communities, such as Wal-Mart, Tractor Supply, and Southern States, have developed their own policies that complement the new regulations contained in the legislation. I would regularly go to Tractor Supply to get dog food for my two dogs. One evening I noticed a Meth Watch sticker on the front door.[2]

"Have you been having a lot of problems with meth?" I asked the cashier as I checked out.

She was in her forties and, without even looking up at me, began explaining the program.

"They gave us a list of things we're supposed to watch out for," she said, wrestling the large bag of dog food over the scanner and back into my cart.

"What are you supposed to do if you see people buying those things?" I asked.

"Well, if they're buying a whole bunch of something, or if we think they might be using it to make meth, then we're supposed to sell it to them and then follow them to the parking lot and see what vehicle they get into and write down the license plate number."

"What do you do then?"

"Well, we give their license plate number to the manager, and I think they call the police."

I asked her if employees at other stores were having to do the same kind of monitoring of purchases. She told me about a friend who worked at Southern States, an agricultural supply store. She and her co-workers were asked to monitor the sale of certain chemicals that could be used in the meth production process. Employees there drew directly from the their relationships with local farmers to carry out this task. The employees knew these farmers well, including the amount of each chemical they would need in a typical year. If a stranger came and started buying a lot of one of these chemicals, or a regular customer seemed to be ordering more than they should need over the course of the year, the employees were to notify law enforcement.

Businesses were not the only sites at which people were being asked to monitor chemicals and other products associated with methamphetamine production. Nor was regulation at point of sale the only means through which rural residents were being mobilized. State road workers and civic volunteers, among others, were given instructions on how to recognize the signs that a meth lab had been in operation. These instructions included how to distinguish garbage carelessly strewn along the highway from meth lab remnants. Having such knowledge was important as a safety measure, but it was also a way to aid law enforcement in the detection of local methamphetamine producers. In this way, road workers and volunteers added a new temporality to the policing of clandestine methamphetamine production. While the retail workers' policing of precursor chemical sales was forward looking in its orientation, seeking to prevent clandestine methamphetamine production from taking place, the road workers' policing of meth lab remnants was backward looking, seeking to find meth producers after the fact. Thus the targeting of methamphetamine production enabled the expansion of police power locally in both space and time, "allowing the governance of the past to be articulated with the governance of the future" (Dubber and Valverde 2006).

Kent MacAfee, a retired army contractor who was involved with numerous volunteer organizations in the community, was enlisted in this way into the work of policing methamphetamine. He brought me a sheet from the West Virginia Division of Environmental Protection he had received while doing volunteer road cleanup as an "Adopt-A-Highway" volunteer. These were the instructions given to participants:

Do not pick up the following items, as they may be associated with methamphetamine preparation:

Containers and glassware with white residue or powder
Grinders
Coffee filters
Funnels
Glass or plastic tubing
pH papers
Coolers and condenser tubes

Volunteers were further warned that:

The items listed above are often found in plastic grocery store bags that have been tied shut and thrown on the side of the road. Opening the bags can result in burns, blindness, and serious health problems. They may even explode.

These instructions educated volunteers on the signs of clandestine methamphetamine production. They also told volunteers what to do should they encounter the remnants of a meth lab:

Leave the bags where they are and call 911. After calling 911 please report any meth lab items you find while picking up litter to the Adopt-A-Highway Program. (emphasis in original).

These instructions gave participants in the Adopt-A-Highway program a new orientation toward their work. What had previously been a benign form of volunteerism was now a potentially dangerous activity. Such objects posed a direct threat to those involved, and required them to call local law enforcement if they encountered anything suspicious. Knowledge of local meth production was transforming participation in the Adopt-A-Highway program by drawing attention to potential threats in the local landscape and issuing new responsibilities to citizens to police the problem.

The same kind of instruction was given to state road workers. Charlie Kent, a man I met through singing in the community choir, worked for the Department of Transportation. He showed me a publication he received informing road workers about the dangers of methamphetamine production. After presenting some general information about methamphetamine provided by the DEA, the article concluded with instructions on what road workers should look for and do with regard to meth labs. The section titled "Road Workers Need to Be Alert" stated:

> Like hunters and Adopt-a-Highway volunteers, road workers are among those likely to stumble upon a meth waste dump.
>
> Be alert. What may initially look like harmless trash in a ditch may be lethal meth waste material.
>
> Do not go near the material(s).
>
> Do not touch or move anything in the area. In addition to being dangerous to yourself, disturbing the area may hinder law enforcement agencies [sic] efforts to trace the lab location and/or the manufacturers.
>
> Contact your supervisor immediately. Your supervisor should contact law enforcement personnel with the exact location of the possible meth waste dump.

Thus state road workers have been given the same instructions and responsibilities with regard to methamphetamine as Adopt-A-Highway volunteers. However, the instructions were even more explicit in discussing state road workers' role in police work. Road workers were instructed not to touch anything that might be a meth lab remnant, not only because of the threat to their safety but also because it could interfere with law enforcement efforts to locate the cooks. For their part, then, road workers were instructed to participate in the policing of methamphetamine through vigilance in looking for signs of meth production and precision when reporting the location of meth lab remnants to law enforcement.

In each case, the protocols given to pharmacists, road workers, retail clerks, and volunteers provided a new way of seeing the local landscape in terms of methamphetamine. Previously benign objects, such as a plastic bag on the side of the road or an over-the-counter cold medicine, were resignified as potential threats through their association with clandestine meth production. Furthermore, this knowledge carried with it the responsibility to act, to engage in the work of policing on the spot, and/or provide information to local law enforcement. In this way, the range of individuals policing the methamphetamine problem was expanding as the local landscape was re-imagined in terms of meth.

Expanding the Field of Drug Control

This expansion of police power was also taking place within the field of law enforcement itself. A significant group in this regard was Department of Natural Resources (DNR) officers. These officers were in charge of monitoring state-owned land, particularly state parks and reserves. Their primary duties consisted of enforcing laws related to these areas, particularly those regulating hunting, fishing, camping, and the like. A typical day for a DNR officer would include traveling through a section of state park making sure no one was hunting out of season or fishing without a license. Methamphetamine, however, was changing this role. Meth cooks' preference for secluded, rural areas meant that these officers had to be on the lookout for meth production.

The first person I spoke to about these changes was a DNR officer named Matt Keezle. Matt had been an officer for nearly ten years. An avid outdoorsman himself, working for the Department of Natural Resources was the closest he would ever get to hunting and fishing for a living. I met Matt through a mutual friend, someone that Matt would go fly-fishing with on occasion.

The office of the DNR was on an empty stretch of the highway twenty miles in either direction from the nearest towns. When I arrived, Matt was sitting in a swivel chair in front of a small desk. His receding hairline and green uniform made him seem older than he actually was. A plug of chewing tobacco bulged slightly from his lower lip, and a small Styrofoam cup, which he raised to his mouth occasionally to spit, sat between his legs.

When I told Matt that I was doing research on methamphetamine, he began telling me about a course he had taken a year or two earlier that all of the DNR officers had been required to attend. "They gave me a big folder full of information," he said, and began to search through the office to find it. "I know it's here somewhere," he assured me, rummaging through bookshelves stacked somewhat haphazardly with training manuals, file folders, and other bits of bureaucratic miscellany. I asked Matt if he had had much direct involvement with methamphetamine. Matt explained that the most significant things he had encountered were remnants of meth labs no longer in use. By the time he found them, the cooks were usually long gone.

DNR officers had the jurisdiction and responsibility to deal with these former labs, Matt explained, but they tried to avoid it if possible because it was dangerous. Matt relayed a story of a local police officer who had inadvertently come upon an active meth lab, and it had caused either liver or lung damage (Matt couldn't remember which). There was also a "you touch it, its yours" policy that governed jurisdictional issues among the various branches of law enforcement in the area. Cleaning up after a meth lab was so time-consuming and expensive that those at DNR avoided doing it if at all possible, preferring to let the sheriff's department or state police handle it. This revealed an important yet overlooked dimension of national efforts to stop clandestine methamphetamine production. Beyond the standard bureaucratic squabbles, the cost associated with cleaning up a meth lab is significant. County governments and state agencies in rural areas like West Virginia have limited funds for such activities, creating a financial disincentive to seek out signs of meth production.

Matt finally abandoned his effort to find the folder he had received at the meth training course and sat back in the swivel chair. The class had taught him a lot, though, he assured me. For instance, he knew now to check "burn piles" (small amounts of waste that campers burn as a means of disposal) for evidence that they had been making methamphetamine. He also knew to look for packages of Sudafed and other products containing pseudoephedrine. He had heard that as these products had become harder to come by, cooks had turned to other products, including the rather aptly named "Deer Cocaine," which was a bright pink liquid available at almost any store that hunters used to bait deer. Indeed, during hunting season the local Wal-Mart devoted an entire wall near the check-out lanes to a display of Deer Cocaine.

But Matt was not just involved in policing meth production; he was also involved in policing its use. Even before methamphetamine became a concern, Matt encountered people doing drugs on the side of secluded state roads. He stood up and reached for a small shoebox on top of a nearby bookshelf. The box contained all of the drug paraphernalia he had confiscated over the years. Most of the items were homemade pipes fashioned out of everything from plastic cups to a bear-shaped honey container.

Matt reached into the box and pulled out the empty shaft of a ballpoint pen. He had found the pen after he stopped two boys in a state park he suspected of using drugs. Matt had not found any drugs on the boys when he looked into their car, but noticed that the pen piece was on the ground after they left. Matt knew from his training that these pen pieces were often used to smoke meth. The user would put the meth on a piece of tin foil, hold a lighter underneath, and use the ballpoint pen "pipe" to smoke the meth as it rose up. Matt said he could have pursued the two boys but didn't because he knew it would have been nearly impossible to bring charges against them. Since he did not find the pipe in their possession and had not found any actual methamphetamine, the prosecuting attorney for the county probably wouldn't have even pursued the case.

The phone rang. Matt answered it, still holding the shoebox full of drug paraphernalia. "Hey," he said casually. "I'm talking to that guy I told you about who wanted to know about meth." A small smile appeared on Matt's face as he listened to the officer on the other end. "No, I didn't tell him about *that*," he said with a laugh. Matt then told the officer he would talk to him later and hung up the phone.

"Tell me about what?" I asked.

Matt smiled sheepishly and began telling me about a recent encounter. He had been doing his normal patrol through the back roads of the national forest when he noticed a truck parked in a small clearing beneath a tree. Matt parked and approached the truck. When he got there, he found a man sitting in the truck by himself, smoking meth and masturbating. Matt chuckled again, somewhat awkwardly, and shook his head in amazement. "That isn't even the first person I've caught doing that, either," he said, telling me briefly about another man he had found likewise sitting in his truck smoking meth and using a "pocket pussy" to masturbate.

I returned Matt's sheepish smile, embarrassed both for him and the men he had discovered. We sat in awkward silence for a moment until a state trooper came into the office. The DNR shared the building with the state police. The officer had come by to pick something up from his desk on his way home from work. Matt flagged the officer down as he came in and introduced me. His name was Gil McDonald. Like Matt, he was increasingly encountering meth as part of his work, including the same kinds of remnants of meth lab production.

Gil was also seeing more of it in his patrol work. In fact, he had just been involved in an undercover drug bust with a person who was selling methamphetamine. He unlocked a drawer on his desk and pulled out a small envelope marked Evidence. To my surprise, he unsealed the envelope and pulled out four small baggies containing a brownish crystalline substance that resembled unrefined sugar. He also pulled out a small metal tube, roughly three inches long, with a screw-off top. The meth had been in the metal tube on the person's key chain when they arrested him. Gil, too, had undergone training about methamphetamine. "That's how I knew what to look for," he said proudly.

Matt and Gil's experiences demonstrate how methamphetamine has created a common denominator for all forms of police work. The training they received about methamphetamine, like that given to state road workers, retail clerks, and others, heightened their awareness of meth and created new responsibilities to police it. This expanded the work of drug enforcement into seemingly unrelated domains, such as the daily patrol work of DNR officers. While this was likely but a shift in focus for Gil, Matt was given a much more significant set of requirements regarding the policing of state lands for signs of possible meth production. By his own admission, he carried out these new duties with a mix of enthusiasm and reluctance, seeking to fulfill his obligations in detecting former meth labs without creating a financial and administrative burden for the DNR. Furthermore, his range of encounters with meth users seemed a befuddling part of the job for Matt. The fact that he had arrested none of the users he encountered suggested reluctance on Matt's part to fully assume the role of drug enforcer. Nevertheless, by simply being aware of what to look for, Matt was involved with policing methamphetamine, even when this resulted only in informal intervention.

Locating the Meth Lab

As these various cases show, efforts by federal, state, and local governments to curtail the spread of methamphetamine have expanded the range of individuals involved in police work by increasing awareness of the signs of meth production and use. Though local knowledge and conflicting professional obligations could limit these efforts, they could also provide new avenues for their implementation. This was certainly evident in the most significant meth lab bust that occurred in Baker County. The discovery of this meth lab took place through the inadvertent deployment of local knowledge in response to the observation of suspicious activity, combined with a more professionally nuanced awareness of the (admittedly subtle) signs of meth production. This action, in turn, revealed a much deeper and more complex web of participants in the local meth trade.

In the fall of 2004, a Department of Natural Resources officer received an anonymous tip that someone had killed a deer out of season and was processing the hides in the cellar that stood adjacent to a small cluster of trailers in a remote part of the county. According to court documents, the DNR officer followed up on the call and met with a deputy from the county sheriff's department to begin an investigation. The DNR officer had been monitoring the individuals after receiving the tip, and had decided that they were possibly making methamphetamine. He based this observation on the behavior of those involved: they were walking in and out of the cellar at frequent intervals, and when they walked out, they rubbed their eyes as though they were irritated. Additionally, there appeared to be some white smoke rising from the door.

The deputy and the officer drove by the building in the officer's personal vehicle so as not to be detected. They observed what the DNR officer had seen: people coming in and out of the house and rubbing their eyes. They approached the building. There was a strong chemical smell and white smoke was pouring out, which appeared to be coming from a plastic soda bottle near the door. On the grass they found coffee filters, paper towels, plastic tubing, and a number of large jars and other containers with lithium AA batteries that had been disabled. Through the open cellar door, they saw a yellow, two- to four-gallon bucket. Inside the bucket, a white liquid substance was bubbling.

Within five hours the officers made their first arrest. The suspect, Jimmy Barker, lived in one of the trailers and knew about the meth lab because it was in the cellar behind his brother-in-law's trailer (his brother-in-law, Larry Messinger, was one of the other suspects). According to Jimmy, Donnie Grate (the third suspect in the case) had constructed the lab. Donnie's father lived in a trailer next to Jimmy's father-in-law. Jimmy saw Donnie in the cellar that morning and stopped by to say hello. He saw him tearing up batteries, mixing something in a yellow bucket and calling for Larry (Jimmy's brother-in-law) to bring down the jars he'd left outside. The officers asked Jimmy if Donnie had told him he was making meth. "No I just assumed," Jimmy replied. "I'm not real smart, but I figured it out. He was all the time talking about how he could make meth. How easy it was."

The next day, a special unit of the West Virginia State Police was called in to collect the materials surrounding the cellar. They collected the plastic soda bottle that had been emitting the white smoke and tubing containing an orangey-white paste (which later tested positive for hydrogen chloride); they collected the batteries, coffee filters, and paper towels as well. Inside they found a one-gallon can of Camp Fuel, a half-gallon jug of Roto Drain Opener, one three-pound box of kosher salt, one cooler containing a half-gallon of an unknown liquid, with condensation on the side and smoke coming through the spout (which tested positive for ammonia), a one-gallon glass jar with an unknown residue, and the contents of the plastic bucket. All of this was collected as evidence.

Jimmy, Larry, and Donnie were all arrested on charges for two crimes, "Operating a Clandestine Drug Laboratory" and "Conspiracy to Commit an Offense Against the State of West Virginia." Donnie waived his right to an indictment and agreed to a plea agreement with the state in which he pled guilty to the conspiracy charge. In return, the other charge was dropped. During the presentence investigation, Donnie made the following statement to the county probation officer:

> I was arrested for conspiring to commit a crime. I shared a recipe for meth with my family. I know what I did was wrong and I am sorry that I did it. For the first time in my life I am trying to get help with my drug problem and straighten up my life. I am trying to be a good father to my baby girl. After I was arrested I realized that my life is really messed up and I have been clean since the last time I was in court. . . . I only hope the court will give me a chance to continue to put my life back together.

Donnie was only twenty years old but claimed to have used drugs supplied by his family members since he was twelve, and at the time of his arrest he was engaged in "extreme methamphetamine use." He had used marijuana, cocaine, crack, inhalants, and amphetamines. Donnie managed to enter a private halfway house and undergo substance abuse and psychiatric counseling in Virginia. Because of this, he was allowed to serve his one-to-five-year sentence on probation, under the condition that he continued the therapeutic measures to resolve his addiction and continue in his newfound job as a janitor and maintenance worker at a home for the mentally disabled.

His was a fairly lenient sentence. At first it seemed the product solely of his plea agreement. I later discovered there was another reason. The prosecuting attorney gave me documents kept separate from Donnie's public case file. Contained in these documents was the transcript of an interview between two sheriff's deputies and Donnie, who was accompanied by his lawyer and the director of the halfway house where he resided. The interview took place roughly four months after Donnie's initial arrest. Donnie had already agreed to the plea agreement, and this interview was obviously one of its preconditions. The deputy conducting the interview stated for the record that Donnie had "full immunity from everything" as granted by the county's prosecuting attorney.

In this interview, Donnie painted a different picture of the events that led to his arrest with Jimmy and Larry. In his version of the story, Larry Messinger's father, Andy Messinger, had come home one day with a meth recipe and instructions on how to set up and operate a lab that he had obtained (presumably from a co-worker) at the poultry processing plant in Virginia where he worked. Donnie agreed to show him how to make meth, while Larry and Jimmy began gathering the necessary ingredients.

Jimmy, Donnie said, developed a technique to steal Sudafed from all the local stores that carried it: grocery stores, dollar stores, Wal-Mart, and the like. He would wear a camouflaged jacket, stuff the boxes of pills in his inside pocket, remove the pills from their boxes in the bathroom of the store, and walk out with the pills in his jacket. Both Jimmy and Larry were involved in obtaining the anhydrous ammonia, which they took from a large tank on a dairy farm in Virginia.

Donnie revealed that Jimmy's parents actually had a longer history of making meth, which they had done secretly for at least eight years. In fact, according to Donnie, there had been significantly more meth in their trailer than what was found by the police officer in their investigation of the meth lab, just a few hundred yards away. They made it for their own use, but also to sell to friends and acquaintances at the poultry processing plants in the area and other places in "the community." Just two months earlier, this small group of friends and relatives had manufactured two to three ounces of meth, which Donnie valued at between $4,000 and $6,000. This they used and sold. Donnie recalled a summer when he had gone to visit Jimmy and his family, and they had bricks of meth just sitting in their trailer.

Donnie had learned how to make meth from Jimmy's family but also from another small cluster of meth producers, the Stanley family, who had recently moved to the area from Indiana. In addition, Donnie named roughly a dozen friends, neighbors, and acquaintances that he knew personally were involved in the production and/or distribution of meth in the area.

The Stanley family disappeared before law enforcement officers could arrest them. And in the years that had passed since Donnie's arrest, none of those whom he'd named had been charged with anything. Members of law enforcement, the prosecuting attorney, and numerous members of the community complained extensively about how difficult it was to gain sufficient evidence to arrest such people, despite the fact that, as I often heard, "everybody knows they're selling drugs." Nevertheless, Donnie's story revealed an extensive network of local users and dealers who could obtain everything they needed to make methamphetamine in the local community. Indeed,

Jimmy, Larry, and Donnie were each second-generation meth users and cooks; in this case even family ties carried criminal potential. Thus, from a law enforcement perspective, Donnie's account confirmed the insidiousness of the methamphetamine threat and thus legitimized efforts to raise awareness about the chemicals used in clandestine methamphetamine production.

"Where Have All the Good People Gone?"

Policing methamphetamine through the signs of clandestine production enabled the detection of the meth lab. In Donnie's case, what began as a report of hunting out of season became, by virtue of the DNR officer's training, the detection and disruption of a local meth lab. This case would seem to illustrate, then, that greater awareness of the signs of meth production provides an effective means of policing methamphetamine. Yet, the acquisition of such knowledge was never a straightforward operation. Matt Keezle's efforts to police methamphetamine on state lands, for instance, were complicated by the financial disincentives accompanying the cleanup of former meth production sites. Additionally, one might wonder how willing citizens will be to participate in the Adopt-A-Highway program, once they know about the threats posed by methamphetamine. More significantly, however, greater awareness about the signs of methamphetamine production was, for many, an epistemic and existential burden. While it might aid in the detection of illicit producers, it also changed their everyday life in fundamental and challenging ways.

I experienced this dilemma firsthand while attempting to arrange an interview with a state trooper who spent two-and-a-half years working as part of a Federal Drug Task Force in the area. Most of this work had been undercover, so the trooper was surprised to receive my call. From the beginning he was suspicious of who I was and why I was interested in methamphetamine. He was particularly curious as to how I had gotten his number. After explaining that I'd been given his name and number from another police officer, and answering a series of questions about what I wanted to know and what I planned to do with the information, he eventually agreed to meet with me, but only reluctantly, and with no sense that I'd eased his suspicions. "I'm not gonna run a background check on you," he said with an uneasy smile I could hear through the telephone (a statement that made me assume he would be running a background check on me). Nevertheless, he took great care writing down my name and affiliation, and insisted that I bring two valid forms of identification to the interview because, as he put it, "you wouldn't believe what some people will do to get some inside information."

The officer was roughly my age (early thirties) and was predictably guarded during our conversation, signaling his discomfort with my writing anything down and refusing to answer any but the most basic of questions. Indeed, it was only months later, reading the court files on the meth lab discussed earlier, that I discovered he participated in its cleanup.

The officer provided little in the way of new information, and by the end of the interview I was ready to write off the encounter, attributing his disposition to the suspicion and secrecy required by his profession. But as he escorted me out of his office, he began to make comments that connected his suspicions of me to his experiences with methamphetamine. In addition to witnessing the extremes to which people would go in order to satisfy their addiction, he had had to come to terms with the extensiveness of the problem in his community—the sheer numbers of people who used the drug or were involved in making and selling it. He found all of this very challenging, particularly as he tried to lead a normal life outside of work. "It's hard," he said, "especially when you're out with your family. I can take you to any street anywhere in the area, including the dirt roads, and show you someone who's using or selling drugs. It makes you wonder, 'Where have all the good people gone?'"

I heard this as both an explanation of and apology for the suspicious way in which he'd treated me. More than that, it seemed to be a lament for the fact that we lived in a world in which such an exercise of suspicion was necessary. This sentiment was one I encountered a lot. Many people in the community, including police officers, addiction counselors, concerned citizens, and even addicts themselves, frequently figured their experience with methamphetamine as one of loss. What was being lost was their particular vision of the local community as they had once imagined it, a vision in which methamphetamine—and the problems that came with it—was not a factor. As the officer put it: "Sometimes I wish I was more naïve." In this way, while knowledge of methamphetamine implicitly placed new responsibilities on citizens to police the problem, it was also a kind of "poisonous knowledge" that residents adopted reluctantly (Das 2000).

Bearing this epistemic burden, however, did not obviate individuals from the policing responsibilities that came with greater awareness of clandestine meth production. Anti-meth measures included in state and federal legislation were predicated on, and thus sought to raise, public awareness about the signs of meth production and use, for in this way, citizens were drawn into the policing of methamphetamine. Even I was not immune to this. As I drove away from my meeting with the officer, I noticed a plastic Wal-Mart bag filled with what appeared to be garbage on the side of the road. I wondered, as I drove past, if it might not have something to do with meth.

3

"You Can Always Tell Who's Using Meth"

Late one evening in the spring of 2006, police officers set out to arrest Burt Culler and Mandy Swift at their home on the outskirts of Meadville. Over the past year numerous homes, businesses, and construction sites had been burglarized throughout Baker County, including the local mental health clinic, from which someone had stolen a computer. From other sites cash was stolen, as well as thousands of dollars worth of tools and building supplies. Police came to believe that the burglaries were linked, and Burt and Mandy, two known meth users in the community, were the primary suspects.

The stolen items turned up periodically in pawnshops or in the hands of unsuspecting workmen and contractors. Each described having been approached by a slightly scrawny twenty-something male, accompanied by an equally scrawny twenty-something female, who claimed to be "getting out of the construction business." This information led police to search for a couple; an unnamed local informant told them it was Mandy and Burt.

Mandy and Burt had been living together for just over a year when they were arrested. Mandy had moved in with Burt and his mother while his mother was dying of cancer. According to rumors that circulated through the community, Burt and Mandy had been poor caretakers, stealing Burt's mother's pain medication to use for their own enjoyment and to trade for methamphetamine.

Four police officers arrived at Burt and Mandy's apartment and Burt was immediately taken to the police station for questioning. Two officers stayed behind, searched the house for drugs (which they found), and questioned Mandy. Mandy was questioned for more than two hours, during which time she made no attempt to deny the allegations and even responded apologetically when she couldn't recall a particular incident. Mandy explained to the police officer that, although Burt had instigated the crimes, she had always helped. They had walkie-talkies and she served as lookout while he committed the burglaries. Mandy was standing watch, for instance, when Burt broke in to the mental health clinic to steal the computer, remaining there even when, in the midst of the burglary, he went into the clinic's kitchen and used the microwave to make a bowl of soup.

The interview focused on establishing Mandy's knowledge of the crimes and the whereabouts of the stolen items. But periodically the officer inquired into the motivation behind Burt's criminal behavior. Each time the officer asked, Mandy gave the same response: it was Burt's methamphetamine use, and his need to constantly find quick sources of cash to pay for more meth, that drove his criminality. This seemed to confirm the officers' suspicions, as did the meth found in Burt and Mandy's bedroom. It was the officer, then, who raised the possibility that Burt was an addict. This came out over the course of the interview, culminating with this exchange toward the end:

PO: Another thing to elaborate on that would kind of help me out maybe, ah, you made, you made a number of comments about that he [Burt], he is selling some of his stuff to obtain drugs. Ah, help me out on ah, he's not only a user? Would you, would you say that he's an addict?

MS: Yeah.

PO: How often does, how often are you aware of him using narcotics?

MS: Daily.

PO: Daily. What, what type of narcotics, ah, or drugs or anything does he use?

MS: Um, what do you call it? Meth? Crank? Crank.[1]

PO: And how, how many days, or how long have you known him?

MS: Um, Burt and I have been together since last September. So it's been approximately a year.

PS: And, and correct me if I'm wrong; you're saying that he used drugs everyday since you've known him?

MS: I can think of maybe three days of that amount of time that he hasn't.

Methamphetamine users like Mandy and Burt were increasingly the targets of enforcement efforts in Baker County, particularly with regard to property crimes such as breaking and entering and burglary where drug users were always the primary suspects. Viewed within the wider history of U.S. drug control, this development was hardly novel. Much of the work of contemporary criminal justice is focused on drug enforcement, the result of decades of criminalizing illicit drugs and their use. And while it has created challenges for the criminal justice system, such as addressing the medical complications associated with addiction in institutional environments poorly suited to this purpose, it has also provided a new grounding for members of the criminal justice system to rationalize their activities, generating new juridical techniques and resources in the process.

One effect of the focus on drug offenders has been the incorporation of knowledge about addiction into the everyday routines of criminal justice work. This has, in turn, provided the criminal justice system with new techniques and resources centered around addiction. The reorientation of criminal justice practice around addiction has been the most pronounced in three key areas: the explanation of crime, the identification of criminals, and the staging of interventions.

Knowledge of addiction has provided the criminal justice system with a working theory of criminal behavior. According to this theory, criminality is a symptom of addiction: drug users are driven by their addiction to commit acts of criminality in the constant and singular pursuit of more drugs. These crimes could include anything from property crimes to forgery to participation in the drug economy itself. Mandy's account of Burt's criminality fits neatly within this framework, given that she attributes all the crimes he committed to his habitual use of methamphetamine. Thus it is not surprising that the police officer was led to conclude that Burt was an addict, since identifying him as such provided the explanation and motivation for his crimes.

In addition to providing a means of explaining crime, knowledge of addiction has also served as a resource to assist in the identification of criminals. Members of the criminal justice system in Baker County often used the physical and behavioral symptoms of addiction as a lens through which to read the criminal body and to address what the sociologist David Garland has called "[t]he chimeral obscurity of criminal difference." (Garland 2002, 137). The symptoms of methamphetamine addiction provided a particularly robust resource in this regard, given the striking effects that methamphetamine use can have on the body. These included everything from scabs and missing teeth to psychosis and paranoia, even the "symptom" of criminality itself. Using the symptoms of addiction in this way fed into the long-standing desire within the criminal justice system—and popular culture more generally—to utilize scientific insights for forensic purposes, to uncover the signs of criminality on the very body of the criminal (Horn 2003; Valverde 2006).

Finally, addiction has provided a medium for the staging of interventions aimed at addressing criminality. Addiction is notable for the diverse range of interventions it supports. These include everything from investigation, arrest, and punishment to treatment, education, and prevention, as well as the broad array of practices aimed at "offender management." Taken as a whole, these techniques and practices make up a significant portion of the local drug enforcement apparatus, which is thus sustained by the common concern with addiction.

In this way, the profile of the methamphetamine addict functioned as a potent "figure of criminality" (Rafael 1999) in the local juridical imaginary. Anthropologists have noted the importance of such criminal figures in the making of contemporary social and political orders (Comaroff and Comaroff 2006; Parnell and Kane 2003; Rafael 1999; Siegel 1998). Such figures often become the object of collective anxieties, representing the intrusion of the dangerous, the threatening, the unknown, or the unexpected into every-day life. The potency of these profiles derives not only from their capacity to invoke law (they are, after all, *criminals*, and thus products of the legal order itself), but also because they test the limits of law's efficacy: it's powers of rec-ognition and retaliation, as well as its claims to legitimacy and to act in the name of collective opinion (Rafael 1999, 12–13; cf. Benjamin 1978). In this regard, they become the focus of collective action, the locus around which a common response may be carried out. Notably, although the specific outlines of criminality in question vary from time to time and from place to place, they seem nevertheless to be a common element in a diverse array of contempo-rary political regimes. As Jean and John Comaroff have written, "In sum, the figure of the archfelon, albeit culturally transposed, seems to be doing similar work in many places, serving as the ground on which a metaphysics of order, of the nation as a moral community guaranteed by the state, may be enter-tained, argued for, even demanded" (Comaroff and Comaroff 2006, 279).

The figure of the methamphetamine addict—and the drug addict more generally—was such a potent figure of criminality because it represented a dangerous conflation of moral, legal, and biological forms of deviance and difference. The use of the drug that began the addiction was construed as both an immoral and an illegal act that, in turn, set in motion the chronic, neurobiological condition of addiction. The addiction, then, embroiled the individual in further illegality, driving them into continued drug use and related criminal acts, eroding their physical and mental well-being in the process. The chronic character of addiction and high rates of relapse meant that the addict was viewed as perpetually inclined toward criminality, mak-ing him or her a constant threat (Garcia 2008).

This stereotypical understanding of the addict's life course fed into the popular representation of drugs as inherently criminogenic—a representa-tion that elided the historical role played by law in criminalizing drugs and drug use, thereby creating the conditions under which the figure of "the addict" has been constituted in criminal terms (Acker 2002; Goode 2006). Ultimately, however, the targeting of methamphetamine addicts provided members of the criminal justice system with a common medium to address perennial concerns, such as the explanation of criminality; the identification of criminals; and the retributive task of punishing past crimes and preventing future criminality. The emergence of this figure is thus a key feature of contemporary narcopolitics.

The specific effects of targeting methamphetamine offenders in this way is addressed elsewhere in more detail. Here, the focus is simply on showing the pervasiveness of addiction discourse in the criminal justice system, and the ways that this discourse gave rise to a particular construction of the methamphetamine addict as a criminal figure, shaping policing and other juridical practices in the process.

Pedagogies of Policing

Law enforcement's understanding of the link between drugs, crime, and addiction was most explicitly articulated during the public presentations given by police officers to various groups within the community. Officers regularly gave presentations on the dangers of methamphetamine and viewed this pedagogical work as part of their more general efforts at drug prevention, a sign of how contemporary police have been transformed into "knowledge workers" (Ericson and Haggerty 1997). In the presentations, the officers combined materials they received during training seminars with their own personal experience. The presentations frequently received local newspaper coverage, allowing them to reach a broader audience, which could indeed have a very tangible impact on police. For instance, upon hearing Daryl Montgomery's account of the methamphetamine problem, one resident donated $6,000 toward the purchase of a microphone to be used in undercover investigations.

Frank Fields was an officer who regularly gave presentations on methamphetamine to community groups. Frank was a state trooper who worked exclusively on drug cases. When I made arrangements to interview Frank, he offered to let me view his PowerPoint presentation. This move was, in part, to deflect attention away from the details of his police work, which he was somewhat reluctant to share with me, but it also reflected a sincere belief that the PowerPoint presentation contained the most relevant information for understanding methamphetamine.

Frank's presentation, which he had given to a variety of community organizations, employed a largely neuroscientific idiom to explain the experience of using methamphetamine and the eventual onset of addiction. "Methamphetamine is a powerful central nervous system stimulant," the presentation began, going on to describe the ease with which meth could be made, the pleasurable feelings it produced, and the "state of high agitation that in some individuals can lead to violent behavior." Another slide stated, "The rush and high are caused by the release of very high levels of the neurotransmitter dopamine into areas of the brain that regulate feelings of pleasure." Later slides continued in this vein, explaining the difficulty users experienced trying to stop their use of methamphetamine and the resulting high likelihood of relapse.

Frank said little as I clicked through the presentation, until I reached a slide titled "Physical Effects of Meth Use." "This one's pretty interesting," he said. The slide depicted the impact of methamphetamine use on the body, using graphic images to illustrate the effects of both short-term and long-term use. Short-term use was illustrated by a picture of an arm with severe open sores, the likely result of the person picking at imaginary "meth bugs" under their skin. Long-term use was illustrated with a series of mug shots depicting the physical decline of a woman who appeared relatively "normal" in 1998 and grossly disfigured by 2002, her hair thin and greasy, her face gaunt and pale, and her body covered with scabs and sores.

These images were the prelude to a more detailed explanation of long-term methamphetamine abuse in which addiction was explicitly defined:

> Long-term methamphetamine abuse results in many damaging effects, including addiction. Addiction is a chronic, relapsing disease, characterized by compulsive drug-seeking and drug use which is accompanied by functional and molecular changes in the brain. In addition to being addicted to methamphetamine, chronic methamphetamine abusers exhibit symptoms that can include violent behavior, anxiety, confusion, and insomnia. They also can display a number of psychotic features, including paranoia, auditory hallucinations, mood disturbances, and delusions (for example, the sensation of insects creeping on the skin, which is called "formication"). The paranoia can result in homicidal as well as suicidal thoughts.

This was the first of three slides explaining the long-term effects of methamphetamine use. Each slide used images of meth-ravaged bodies to illustrate the topic. On a slide picturing the arms of a man with open, bloody sores, the phenomenon of "tolerance" was discussed. It explained how excessive users must regularly increase their use of the drug to achieve the same effects. Use quickly became "chronic abuse," which "can lead to psychotic behavior, characterized by intense paranoia, visual and auditory hallucinations, and extremely violent behavior." The man's mangled arm was an illustration of this process. The next slide, showing a picture of a mouth missing most of its teeth (representing the condition known as "meth mouth"), further explained the symptoms that occurred when someone stopped using meth, including "depression, anxiety, fatigue, paranoia, aggression, and an intense craving for the drug."

The rest of the presentation continued in this vein, with slides addressing such topics as why people begin using methamphetamine, the signs of use, and the ways meth could be made. Methamphetamine's addictiveness was a recurring theme throughout:

Why is methamphetamine addictive?

All addictive drugs have two things in common: they produce an initial pleasurable effect, followed by a rebound unpleasant effect. Methamphetamine, through its stimulant effects, produces a positive feeling but later leaves a person feeling depressed. This is because it suppresses the normal production of dopamine, creating a chemical imbalance. The user physically demands more of the drug to return to normal. This pleasure/tension cycle leads to loss of control over the drug and addiction.

Though the presentation made frequent references to the negative effects associated with methamphetamine use, it was not until the very last slide that the presentation explicitly addressed the issue of the criminality. This slide was simply titled "CRIME" and stated the following:

Meth labs along with the selling of the drug can breed crime, including burglaries, thefts and even murder. Both teenagers and adults addicted to the drug and who have no income to pay for their habit may steal valuables from their own homes or even their friends' homes. High on meth, there's no telling what a person would do if provoked—people have been killed for not owning up to a drug payment or coming through on a transaction. This type of crime requires a great deal of attention from the police, for which a town may not have the funding or the resources to spare.

This last slide gave legal meaning to what had been up until then a strictly clinical account of the onset, effects, and symptoms of methamphetamine addiction. Rhetorically, the clinical framework served to connect the account of meth-induced addiction with the account of meth-related crime, the former serving as the foundation for the latter. This slide stated unequivocally that methamphetamine was a major source of crime, and that the majority of crimes were committed in order to appease the users' addiction. Moreover, it suggested that such addiction-induced criminality was a "type of crime [that] requires a great deal of attention from the police," but "for which a town may not have the funding or the resources to spare." Thus the detailed, neuroscientific account of methamphetamine addiction was marshaled in support of more funding for the police. This is a significant conclusion, given that such presentations played a large role in shaping the public's understanding of the methamphetamine problem and sense of appropriate response.

Cognitive Models of Crime and Addiction

The police were not the only members of the criminal justice system engaged in drug education. Administrators at the regional jail were likewise involved in a variety of pedagogical activities related to drugs, particularly methamphetamine. This educational work was but one technique that administrators had established to address the high rates of drug use and addiction among the inmate population. Other techniques, such as detoxification, were more common. Indeed, drug use was so extensive among inmates that detoxification was now a standard component of the intake procedure for every new inmate regardless of whether their crime was drug related.

Dealing with drug users on such a regular basis, jail officials became attentive to the signs of drug use in individuals. Different drugs produced different effects, and those jail administrators with more experience could often tell who was using what based on their physical appearance. "You can always tell who's using meth," said Bobby Lively, the warden at the jail. He described how meth users often looked decades older than they actually were. They were agitated and aggressive, "practically climbing the walls." As they underwent detox, they experienced nightmares, sweats, and would pace and dig at themselves. And they would beg for some kind of medication to help them sleep or feel less anxious or depressed. It was jail policy to refuse any request for medication. According to Bobby, they could never be sure what the person had taken, and worried that they might overdose. It often took a week or more of isolated detoxification before meth users were deemed "medically ready" to join the general population of the jail.

Shelly Carson, a licensed addiction counselor in charge of the jail's addiction treatment program, echoed Bobby's sense of the prevalence of drug problems at the jail and its deep ties to criminality. "[Their] crimes [are] usually committed under the influence of something," Shelly stated. The most common charges among women, for instance, were money-related charges such as fraud or writing bad checks. "Basically drugs," she said, explaining that these were crimes often committed by people in need of quick money to support their habit.

The treatment program at the jail that Shelly administered only served eight inmates at any given time, a strikingly low figure given that the jail was designed to hold two hundred inmates and was typically at or over capacity. These inmates lived in a separate area of the jail, away from the general population. There was a waiting list to participate in the program, and the selection process was competitive. Jail administrators determined admission based on an individual inmate's demonstrated desire and perceived ability to complete the program. Inmates had to have their problem recognized formally by jail administrators, attend the weekly Alcoholics Anonymous (AA) and Narcotics Anonymous (NA) meetings, remain well-behaved, and demonstrate a sincere willingness to take responsibility for their actions and to change their behavior. Thus, to gain admission into the program, inmates had to first conform to the behavioral expectations set forth by the institution.

Shelly's approach to addiction treatment emphasized cognitive-behavioral-therapy. She employed a curriculum developed by the Hazelden Foundation titled "Thinking About Your Thinking." It focused on changing an individual's *behavior* by changing their *thinking*. "Taking responsibility's the big thing," Shelly explained. Significant emphasis was placed on the idea that the inmate's situation was "nobody's fault but their own." As Shelly put it, "[The] only person you blame is the person you see in the mirror."

The emphasis on "taking responsibility" and restricting blame to "the person you see in the mirror" was understood to be therapeutically necessary and efficacious. But it was also completely in line with the larger juridical aims of the institution, which likewise emphasized taking responsibility for previous actions. Notably, however, this emphasis on the moral responsibility of those in the program was given a neurobiological grounding. That is, from the perspective of the treatment program, the addict's inability to take responsibility for their actions could be addressed as a cognitive problem. This offered a unique way of conceptualizing their criminality, as well as possibilities for direct intervention using a cognitive-behavioral approach to treat their addiction.

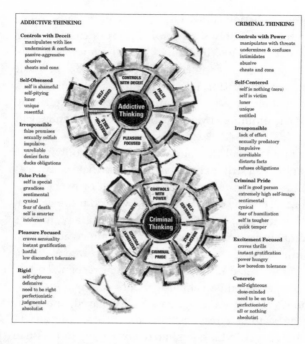

ADDICTIVE THINKING

Controls with Deceit
manipulates with lies
undermines & confuses
passive-aggressive
abusive
cheats and cons

Self-Obsessed
self is shameful
self-pitying
loner
unique
resentful

Irresponsible
false promises
sexually selfish
impulsive
unreliable
denies facts
ducks obligations

False Pride
self is special
grandiose
sentimental
cynical
fear of death
self is smarter
intolerant

Pleasure Focused
craves sensuality
instant gratification
lustful
low discomfort tolerance

Rigid
self-righteous
defensive
need to be right
perfectionistic
judgmental
absolutist

CRIMINAL THINKING

Controls with Power
manipulates with threats
undermines & confuses
intimidates
abusive
cheats and cons

Self-Centered
self is nothing (zero)
self is victim
loner
unique
entitled

Irresponsible
lack of effort
sexually predatory
impulsive
unreliable
distorts facts
refuses obligations

Criminal Pride
self is good person
extremely high self-image
sentimental
cynical
fear of humiliation
self is tougher
quick temper

Excitement Focused
craves thrills
instant gratification
power hungry
low boredom tolerance

Concrete
self-righteous
close-minded
need to be on top
perfectionistic
all or nothing
absolutist

"How Criminal and Addictive Thinking Drive Each Other." From: *A New Direction: A Cognitive Behavioral Treatment Curriculum Criminal and Addictive Thinking Longterm Workbook Parts 4-6* by The Minnesota Department of Corrections and the Hazelden Foundation. Used by permission.

According to Shelly, most of the inmates at the jail, even those who would never set foot in the treatment program, displayed both "criminal and addictive thinking." The two were closely correlated according to the treatment curriculum—the one, in fact, driving the other like two perfectly aligned gears (see fig. above). The prevalence of both criminal and addictive thinking among the inmate population was not surprising to Shelly, but it did underscore how detrimental the lack of addiction treatment resources in the jail was for the wider objectives of the institution.

Shelly explained the many ways in which criminal and addictive thinking were linked. For instance, thinking about theft—stealing something to support your addiction—was a classic example of criminal and addictive thinking working in tandem. The two forms of thinking were broken down in the program into sets of complementary traits and sub-traits. Thus, where addictive thinking "Controls with Deceit," criminal thinking "Controls with Power." Similarly, where addictive thinking is "Pleasure Focused," criminal thinking is "Excitement Focused." Both forms of thinking, according to the curriculum, display a tendency to be "Irresponsible."

Program participants were taught to recognize the various ways in which "criminal" and "addictive" thinking reinforced each other. They completed workbooks filled with tasks such as "List some crimes you committed to get drunk or high"; "List crimes you committed while you were drunk or high"; and answered questions such as "Are there crimes you believe you might not have committed if it weren't for your alcohol or drug use? List them." The cumulative effect of such tasks was to enable the inmate to start identifying their addictive thinking patterns. Identifying these patterns was part of a more general "Thinking Report" that participants generated over the course of the treatment experience.

Acknowledging and understanding this relationship between criminal and addictive thinking was the centerpiece of the treatment curriculum. And given that jail administrators had no control over the length of time inmates stayed in the program (those decisions were made by judges and prosecutors) the goal was simply to, as Bobby Lively put it, "pump as much information into them as possible and hope some of it sticks."

But the institutional significance of the jail's treatment program lay less in providing treatment to addicts than in creating an authoritative discourse to explain criminal behavior, one that represented the relationship between addiction and crime as a set of interlocking cognitive-behavioral processes. Like Frank Fields's PowerPoint presentation, the jail's treatment curriculum took the experiential, discursive, and political associations between drugs, crime, and addiction, and modeled them as a set of cognitive-behavioral processes. Addiction and criminality were so closely aligned, in fact, that they blurred into one single (bio)behavioral reality. Targeting the individual's addiction as the site of intervention in this context was thus a means of directly addressing the mechanism driving the inmate's criminal inclinations.

Targeting drug use and addiction in this way provided a key means through which the jail carried out its penal mandate. Every inmate went through detoxification and forced withdrawal as a kind of barebones treatment protocol. This was designed as a means of managing both the health and behavior of the inmate population, and as an initial intervention into the individual inmate's penchant for criminality. (One might also speculate that the suffering experienced by the individual inmate as he or she underwent forced withdrawal was institutionally tolerable given that the person was there to be punished).

A select few were allowed to enter the treatment program where they underwent more intensive therapeutic work, the aim of which was to continue to address their criminality through the medium of their addiction and vice versa. The small size of the program, which jail administrators lamented, was indicative of the state's reluctance to invest heavily in programs focused on rehabilitation. But administrators made strategic use of the program's small size to further manage the behavior of inmates in other, more indirect ways. For instance, the opportunity to participate in the treatment program was used as an incentive through which to induce compliance with behavioral expectations. Thus targeting drugs and addiction in the jail worked on multiple levels to assist administrators in dealing with the daily practicalities of managing the inmate population. It also provided the institution with options through which to pursue its more general penal mandate within the criminal justice system.

Addiction as a Police Matter

Police officers were quick to cite methamphetamine as a major source of crime in the county. They estimated that anywhere from 50 to 90 percent of the crime they dealt with was somehow drug-related.[2] These crimes, which included property crimes, passing bad checks, and participation in the drug economy itself, could all be traced back to methamphetamine's addictiveness.

The first police officer I interviewed (see chap. 1) was Daryl Montgomery, a deputy in the sheriff's department. In addition to his regular police duties, Daryl had served for two years working undercover as part of a Federal Drug Task Force focused on disrupting the methamphetamine traffic between Baker County and the Shenandoah Valley of Virginia. When I asked Daryl why methamphetamine was causing so many problems, he replied quickly, "It's so addictive." He underscored meth's addictiveness by contrasting it with marijuana, another common drug in the area. "With marijuana you're just gonna sit at home and eat chips or something," Daryl said with a smile. In fact, marijuana was of such little concern that local police had practically decriminalized it: they spent no time trying to locate marijuana users or dealers, nor did they suspect marijuana when a criminal offense was committed. While police did not ignore the illegal status of marijuana altogether, it was not a focus of their work.[3]

The same could not be said about methamphetamine. Meth's association with crime was so strong that police work was virtually unimaginable apart from it. Again, this link with criminality was articulated in terms of meth's addictiveness, which, Daryl explained, was driving the local drug economy itself, as users turned to dealing to support their addiction. This also made them distinct from marijuana users, who, according to Daryl, were rarely drawn into dealing or any other criminal activity to support their habit.

Deputy Casey Phillips expressed a similar view. He had returned to active police duty in 2000 after a brief stint in the military and had since witnessed the methamphetamine problem grow exponentially. Like Daryl, Casey attributed this to its addictiveness, as well as to the ease with which it could be made. The proof of meth's addictiveness was the fact that anyone was susceptible. "Meth is no respecter of person," he said. "It doesn't matter if you're high status or low class, living in a nice house or a trailer."

Casey went on to describe how methamphetamine had transformed policing in the community. As a small department, they had always had to function as a "one-stop shop" of police work. One day they might be doing routine traffic patrol, the next day answering a domestic disturbance call, and the next carrying out a criminal investigation. These activities had once seemed largely unrelated, but now there was a common denominator: methamphetamine. Routine traffic stops were increasingly producing methamphetamine or related paraphernalia, domestic disturbances were often meth-induced, and the vast majority of the crimes they investigated, property crimes in particular, were ultimately determined to be connected to methamphetamine.

Rose Hinkle, the probation officer for Baker County, likewise stated that drug offenders were a major focus of her work. In most cases, their criminality was rooted in their addiction. Indeed, Rose was consistently amazed by the lengths to which people would go to satiate their addiction, including the commission of crimes. "They'll sit right there and tell me about the urges," she said, gesturing toward the chair across from her desk typically occupied by probationers, the one in which I sat as I conducted the interview.

Rose saw the lack of viable treatment options in the area as part of the problem. The nearest inpatient treatment center was one hundred miles away. Being admitted as a patient was often difficult, either because the person's case was deemed insufficiently serious, or because their insurance (if they had it) would not cover the cost. This left most with outpatient options. In addition to the classes and counseling offered at the local mental health clinic, there were the AA and NA meetings that took place in the community. But none of this was adequate, in Rose's view, given that most drug offenders needed inpatient treatment with constant care and supervision.

The closest thing to inpatient treatment available to those ensnared in the criminal justice system was the program at the regional jail, but it served only eight inmates at a time, and access was competitive. Moreover, it only lasted as long as the person was incarcerated—the juridical rationale of the institution always trumped the rehabilitative efforts contained within. Thus by the time they reached Rose as a probationer, addicted inmates could no longer participate in the program. And all of this was overshadowed by the sad fact that one had to be arrested in order to gain access to the treatment program in the first place.

Rose was constantly frustrated by these contradictions and inadequacies within the system. Yet what she found most challenging—one might even say depressing—was the sheer magnitude of drug use and crime in the community. "I had no clue what went on [in Baker County] until I got this job," Rose said, noting that many of the people on probation were former classmates of hers from high school. "Its really hard to see people I know on drugs."

Seeing the Addict Like a State

The field of vision of these state officials was narrowed through the focus on methamphetamine addiction, its symptoms, and its links with criminality. In this section we will see how the state's targeting of methamphetamine addiction worked in practice through an examination of two cases in which methamphetamine addicts became the focus of the state's response to criminal activity. In each case, state officials invoked the discourse of addiction to understand the criminality of those they arrested. The accounts that follow are, by necessity, thin because they reflect the state's perspective on these individual's subjectivity, and thus are largely inattentive to broader aspects of their lived experience.[4]

Case 1: Dwight

In the spring of 2007, Dwight Hopper, a white working class man in his early forties, pled guilty to four counts of Grand Larceny. According to court documents, Dwight had committed numerous acts of breaking and entering and burglary over the course of the previous year. The event that brought about his arrest was his theft of the contents of a retired couple's summer home, everything from the coffee maker to the washer and dryer to the old tractor, which he used to haul the bigger items out of the house. The four counts of grand larceny to which Dwight plead guilty accounted for less than half of the crimes for which he had been indicted, all of which were dismissed as part of his plea agreement with the state, and represented only a fraction of the total number of crimes he was assumed to have committed in his lifetime. Indeed, this was not Dwight's first arrest but his third, each time on charges of breaking and entering and burglary.

Dwight was arrested after the owner of the house saw him riding her tractor around his own home. A state trooper came to investigate, and Dwight made no effort to deny what he had done. He openly admitted to having stolen the property and signed a written confession attesting to the crimes. When the state trooper asked why he had committed the crimes, Dwight replied obliquely, "I got in a bind, a financial bind. Picked a dumb way to try to make some money."

Awaiting sentencing at the regional jail, he elaborated on this explanation to the county probation officer:

> I was breaking into places to support my drug habit. I was using crystal meth everyday. I got to the point I didn't have anymore [sic] money. So the guy I was getting my meth from was trading me Meth for anything I could bring him. . . . It started out with little things and with time, my drug habit got worse. I wish I could turn back time and stay away from the drugs. . . . I'm not the same person when I'm not on drugs.[5]

Dwight's "drug habit" was common knowledge in Baker County. In citing it as the reason for his criminality, he simply made explicit what those in the community, including members of the criminal justice system, already knew. The secretary in the circuit clerk's office shook her head in pity when I asked to see Dwight's files. She told me that her husband, another lifetime resident, had grown up with Dwight and that he'd (Dwight) always struggled with drugs.

That Dwight's criminality was the result of his drug habit was widely acknowledged in the court proceedings as well: the probation officer mentioned it repeatedly during her presentence investigation, as did the judge during the conviction and sentencing hearings (largely perfunctory in light of Dwight's written confession). Both referred to Dwight as having a "severe drug addiction" and affirmed his need for treatment.

At no point, however, was Dwight's drug addiction taken to excuse his crimes. Nor was it seen to justify an alternative to incarceration. On the contrary, Dwight's "severe drug addiction" was cited specifically as reason to expedite his incarceration and deny consideration of any therapeutic alternatives (other than those he might receive while incarcerated). The probation officer, in her final report before Dwight's sentencing hearing, stated this explicitly:

> In talking with the Defendant regarding his crime he genuinely appears remorseful for his actions and is accepting [of] the fact that he has a severe drug problem. He also appears to understand what a problem his drug use has caused himself, his family, and his friends. . . . [T]he Defendant

acknowledges that he needs some type of treatment for his drug abuse and is willing to accept treatment. Based upon [this] information . . . , *the undersigned believes that the Defendant is not a good candidate for probation at this time due to his inability to keep clean from drugs. The undersigned believes that the Defendant would not be able to comply with the standard terms of probation* [emphasis added].

Acknowledging Dwight's "severe drug problem" and need for treatment, the probation officer recommended incarceration. Ironically, the severity of Dwight's addiction made him a poor candidate for the available treatment programs, which were outpatient programs administered in the context of probation. This was because they required a degree of self-monitoring and self-control that Dwight, as an addict, was seen to be incapable of managing. In particular, his inability to control his desire for meth made him likely to violate the key requirements of probation: obtaining and maintaining gainful employment, abstaining from any intoxicating substances including alcohol, refraining from any further criminality, and disassociation from other criminals.

Dwight had successfully completed probation for his previous convictions. But this had apparently been insufficient to prevent him from engaging in further criminality. Thus in Dwight's case, his addiction was recognized as the motivation for his crimes, yet it was then cited as a further justification for his incarceration, rather than a reason to consider any therapeutic alternatives. He was given a four- to forty-year sentence and immediately taken to the regional jail.

Dwight was paradigmatic of the addicted criminal. First, his crime—stealing to obtain money for drugs—was the most common offense associated with addiction in the local juridical imaginary.[6] Second, the chronic character of both his addiction and his criminality was affirmed by his repeated arrest for committing property crimes to obtain money to buy drugs. Notably, Dwight was a talented carpenter and, when he was able to find employment, regularly made more than $20 an hour. This simply reinforced the perceived power of the addiction to drive individuals into criminality, given that Dwight had had to steal to buy drugs even though he had a regular job. Third, no amount of treatment or punishment (such as were available) had been effective in preventing him from either continuing to use methamphetamine or committing more drug-related crimes. Thus we see what the state sees in Dwight's case: the recalcitrance of the addict and his chronic inclination toward criminality. The same themes recur in the case of Eddie Curtis.

Case 2: Eddie

Eddie Curtis was in his mid-twenties when he was arrested in the winter of 2005 on multiple counts of breaking and entering and burglary. During his interview with police, Eddie admitted to breaking into a dentist's office once, a local insurance company twice, and two private cabins multiple times. In each case he took whatever cash he could find, a sum totaling around $1,400. In the process of breaking into these homes and businesses, which typically involved kicking down a back door or breaking through a window, he caused close to $4,000 in damage. Police photographs revealed homes and businesses thrown into complete disarray by Eddie's apparently frantic search for cash.

Based on information provided to the police by an unnamed confidential informant, Eddie was taken into custody. Officers picked him up at his house and took him to the Sheriff's Department for questioning. Eddie was questioned specifically about the places he was suspected of burglarizing, and, like Dwight, he admitted to committing each crime. The police repeatedly asked Eddie, "What did you do with the money?" Each time, Eddie provided an answer that linked his criminality back to his drug use, "I spent it on methamphetamine."

After obtaining a detailed confession for each of the burglaries, and discovering that Eddie had spent all of his money on methamphetamine, the police queried Eddie about the motivations for his crimes.

"Why did you break into all these places?" Deputy Ted Thomas asked.

"For cash to buy drugs," Eddie replied. This led to an extended inquiry into Eddie's drug use, in which he admitted to a $300-a-week meth habit. And though he did not name names, Eddie also revealed the location of his dealer, providing directions to the trailer park where he lived.

Eddie's case bears a striking resemblance to Dwight's. Like Dwight, Eddie had committed a series of property crimes in order to obtain "cash to buy drugs." Additionally, these acts were part of a long history of proven and suspected criminality, much of which could be linked to chronic drug use. Though this was his first felony, Eddie had been arrested on several misdemeanors, including charges for domestic violence and possession of methamphetamine. Eddie was not incarcerated for these offenses but had incurred numerous fines.

Eddie, too, was seen to be a poor candidate for probation. Daniel Gardner wrote a letter to Eddie's court-appointed attorney to negotiate a plea agreement in which he stated, "The State will strongly oppose any probation or reconsideration of any sentence. It is the State's intent that the Defendant [Eddie Curtis] go to prison." He concluded the letter this way:

I have dealt with the Defendant for a number of years. . . . He has numerous cases which he has failed to pay. In fact, he would owe in excess of $6,500.00 to clear those cases. He was told many times that he needed to obtain employment and honor his responsibilities. He has shown no initiative in the past. Therefore, the State does not find him to be suitable for any leniency.

As a result of the plea agreement Eddie received a two- to twenty-five-year sentence. But Eddie was not satisfied with the outcome. He wrote a series of letters to the judge requesting a new attorney and contesting the state's narrow account of his subjectivity. Each letter also asked for a reconsideration of his sentence. Of the four he wrote, only one mentioned drug use, stating, "I know Also [sic] that I had a problem of drug abuse, and realize I do need treatment." Notably, Eddie made this statement in a letter complaining about the lack of treatment and other rehabilitative services available at the regional jail (due to overcrowding in the state penitentiary system, Eddie remained at the regional jail well beyond the time he was scheduled to be transferred). For Eddie, the lack of treatment services for a well-acknowledged problem justified a reconsideration of his sentence and reassignment (such as probation) that would allow him greater opportunity to seek treatment.

Letters such as these were familiar to administrators in the criminal justice system. These officials, however, tended to hold such efforts in low regard. Most saw them as insincere attempts to avoid punishment by trying to gain sympathy or convince those in power that they had changed. As such, these efforts were rarely taken seriously. Not surprisingly, Eddie's letters had no effect on the judge, who never reconsidered his sentence. Eddie's long history of domestic violence, combined with his criminal history, likely made his pleas to be released from prison for the sake of his family ring hollow.

Dwight and Eddie's cases illustrate in part why police focused their efforts on arresting meth offenders. Both were meth users who, by their own admission, committed a series of property crimes in support of a drug habit. By arresting them, the police saw themselves as not only responding to crimes that had been committed but also preventing future crimes from taking place, thereby fulfilling two fundamental police functions simultaneously. The opportunity to have such a broad impact through single arrests increased the incentive to focus on meth offenders. Similarly during prosecution, the prosecuting attorney (acting on behalf of "the State") cited Dwight and Eddie's addiction as reason to incarcerate them rather than pursue therapeutic alternatives (such as probation). This allowed the state to likewise fulfill the dual objective of punishing crimes committed and preventing (whether through deterrence, rehabilitation or incapacitation) the commission of future crimes. Thus there were strong institutional incentives for targeting methamphetamine users throughout the criminal justice system.

A Body on Drugs

The strong connection between drugs, addiction, and crime evident in all of the contexts surveyed thus far put a new premium on the identification of drug users in police work. But it also added a new complication. For if, as I was told repeatedly, meth's addictiveness meant that anyone was susceptible, then those old markers of difference long associated with drug use and criminality in U.S. culture (such as race and class) were of little use (Musto 1999). New methods and techniques for identifying drug users and other criminal offenders were needed.

In my interview with Deputy Casey Phillips, I asked him how he could tell who was using methamphetamine. Casey made reference to the physical symptoms associated with addiction and explained how easy it was to spot a meth user based on their physical appearance. He would see people on the street occasionally who had lost a lot of weight or just looked high. He'd stop and ask them if they were using meth ("Are you on the shit?"). Many admitted to using it. Some even requested to be taken to jail, according to Casey, so they could detox and try to beat their addiction. Similarly, seeing a crater or some other significant scab or wound (another common physical sign of methamphetamine use) on the face of a driver would provide enough "reasonable suspicion" to pull the person over and perform a search, particularly if they were also driving as though they were intoxicated (speeding, weaving, swerving, etc.). According to Casey, most were found to have drugs or drug paraphernalia on them.

Daryl Montgomery painted a similar picture. He regularly encountered people who displayed the symptoms of methamphetamine addiction. "They'll have open sores from digging at 'meth bugs,' their teeth will be falling out." Daryl explained that police would at times approach people in this condition and try to "bluff" them by threatening to arrest them unless they cooperated. This was part of a more general tactic of threatening low-level drug users with penal sanctions in order to "flip" them and turn them into

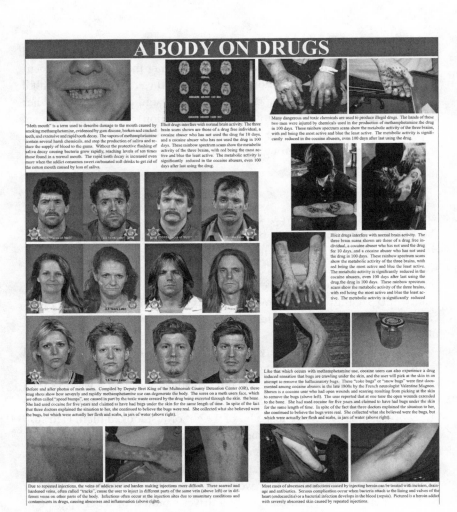

"A Body on Drugs." ©Amera-Chem, Inc. Used by permission.

confidential informants to aid in criminal investigations of other drug users and dealers. In this way, the symptoms of methamphetamine addiction were read by police officers as signs of criminal involvement, and were used to make arrests and/or coerce drug users to cooperate with police operations.

As I concluded my interview with Daryl and Casey, I walked with them back to the sheriff's office. The office was small, and the gray cinder-block walls were free of any decoration, except for a poster taped to the wall next to the entrance. The poster was large, white, and cluttered with text and images. The text was tiny and impossible to read from a distance, and the images were likewise difficult to make out from far away. Closer inspection revealed it to be composed of pictures of parts of bodies—arms, legs, hands, mouths, faces, and even brains—in various states of sickness, injury, and decay. The arms and legs had open sores, the hands were scabbed and bandaged, the mouth was missing teeth, the brains showed signs of malfunction, and the faces were prematurely aged. Small capital letters at the top of the poster stated its theme: a body on drugs (See fig. on facing page).

Here were all of the physical markers of drug use and addiction the deputy had just been describing. They were displayed on bodies of individuals whose pictures had been taken while in the custody of law enforcement, but the poster did not reveal their particular crimes. The facial portraits were obviously mug shots, but those of the other body parts carried no contextualizing details or explanations. What was important was not their specific crimes, it seemed, but that drugs had affected each of these individuals in the same way. In this way, the poster served the opposite function of the classic "Wanted" poster. Rather than drawing attention to an individual criminal wanted for particular crimes, this poster drew attention to a generic *type* of criminal and the signs by which they could be identified. Such a reading of the criminal body was made possible by understanding both their physical appearance and their criminality as symptoms of their addiction.

In its focus on the features of the criminal body, the poster was reminiscent of the catalogs of criminals from which the nineteenth-century criminologist Cesare Lombroso sought to discern the distinctive features of congenital criminality (Horn 2003). Though sharing this concern with general physical markers of criminality, the poster in the sheriff's office portrayed a different reading of the criminal body. In no way did it suggest that any of the individuals pictured were "born criminals." On the contrary, through its focus on the sudden and progressive deterioration of the subject's body and concomitant slide into criminality under the influence of drugs, it conveyed the opposite message: these were "normal" people, whose progressive physical and social deterioration had been set in motion by nothing other than their use of and inevitable addiction to methamphetamine.

This was particularly striking in the pictures of the faces—the "before and after" images bore witness to the social decline that accompanied the physical deterioration of the body in the course of the individual's addiction. In the space between the two images was an implied narrative of ever-deeper descent into both addiction and criminality evidenced by the person's dour facial expression, increasingly compromised physical appearance, and the fact that the police had multiple copies of their picture because of repeated police bookings.[7] Through these images the poster provided a concrete means of imagining the temporality of the relationship between drugs, addiction, and criminality. It was through such physical signs and symptoms, the poster implied, that drug users could be identified as criminals. In this way it also served a deterrent function, using the meth users' grotesque physical appearance to encourage members of the community not to use drugs.

But in its emphasis on the progressive deterioration of the body under the influence of drugs, the poster conveyed a more subtle but also more significant message, namely, that even though scabs, scars, missing teeth, and the like were the most obvious markers of methamphetamine addiction, these appeared only after an extended period of drug use. Until then, the signs were much more subtle or even nonexistent; as shown in the earlier pictures, the individuals looked very "normal." Thus, though the physical signs of meth use displayed by the poster provided leads to determining who was using, it also suggested that anyone could be a user, regardless of whether these physical signs were present. This theme has not only been a part of anti-drug media campaigns for a long time, but it has been taken to a new level of overtness in the case of meth.[8]

The poster was a topic of much discussion the following week at the meeting of the Substance Abuse Prevention Coalition. "Have any of you all been up to the sheriff's office to pay your taxes?" asked a brown-haired woman in her forties, whom I would later learn was the school guidance counselor. "There's a poster up there that shows what happens to you when you get addicted to meth." The woman went on to describe an encounter she had had with a young girl who was also looking at the poster. With a knowing smile she recounted their conversation: "She said, 'I know people who use meth and they don't look like that.' I looked at her and said, 'Yeah, *not yet* they don't.'" This brief exchange was a testimonial to the poster's effectiveness, indicating that it conveyed a particular vision of the temporality of drug use, criminality, and addiction, one that was progressive, deteriorative, and inevitable.

The guidance counselor went on to describe the program of which the posters were a part. Apparently, the sheriff's office had ordered a number of the posters and was planning on putting them up in various places throughout the community, including the hospital, the factories, and the schools. The hope was that the posters would make people more aware of the signs of methamphetamine use and that this, in turn, would enable them to both recognize drug users and keep them from drug use themselves.

The group saw the poster campaign as a positive development, particularly as they often complained that the police were not doing enough to deal

with the methamphetamine problem. The police were aware of these perceptions, arguing that the extensiveness of the problem exceeded their capacity
to address it. Without more funding or more officers they stood little chance
of doing more than containing it. This sense of being overwhelmed, of the
problem exceeding their capacity to address it, was due in part to the addic-
tion-centered approach. For instance, though focusing on the symptoms
of methamphetamine addiction helped in the identification of criminals, it
also suggested a high propensity for relapse/reoffending. Furthermore, the
recalcitrance of the addict in the face of the existing technologies of punishment and rehabilitation suggested that the state's efforts were inadequate to
address the problem.

These feelings of inadequacy revealed an underlying lack of faith in the
ability of the criminal justice system—and the state more generally—to
address drug problems through the punitive management of the addicted
offender population. They also pointed to the consequences of making
addicted criminals the target of police activity. While targeting addicted
criminals did provide a certain coherence to criminal justice work in Baker
County, it also threatened to undermine that work by making the problem
seem greater than state's abilities to manage it.

The next chapter examines efforts to identify drug users beyond the formal domains of the criminal justice system, including in families, factories,
and particularly in schools. Drug tests played a key role in this context. These
tests were able to address the problem noted above that, even though there
were specific physical signs associated with methamphetamine use and
addiction, addiction often set in before these physical signs become evident.
Even an enhanced understanding of the signs of addiction did not guaran-
tee that addicts would be identifiable within the general population. More
sophisticated technologies of drug detection were necessary that moved
from the surface of the body to the neurochemical processes going on within
it, and from the symptoms of drug use to the drug itself.

4

"The People You'd Never Suspect"

Emily Stevens was in chemistry class the day police came to search the high school for drugs. Word spread quickly among students when the officer arrived with the drug dog to do the search. In a panic, Emily tried to wash the marijuana she had with her down one of the sinks in the lab. Unfortunately, the sink did not actually work, so all she could do was stuff it down the drain and hope the police would not find it.

The police came through the classroom and left without incident, so she thought she was safe. But the next day she was called into the principal's office. An officer was waiting for her when she arrived. He claimed to have returned to the school and found the marijuana she'd hidden in the drain. Emily doubted the officer had discovered it on his own, however, given how little marijuana he recovered (she compared it with the head of the antenna on her cell phone). Rather, she suspected another student, not the drug dog, had told the police about the marijuana. "Someone narced me out," she said.[1]

But Emily's drug of choice at the time was not marijuana but methamphetamine. Her cousin introduced her to it, and by her second use she was hooked. Describing what it was like to use meth, Emily was unequivocal: "It was great." Methamphetamine gave her "amazing energy" and "the best rush." It also made her extremely productive. She was ahead in all of her classes, doing her homework at times weeks in advance. Her room was immaculate. Late at night, unable to sleep, she would focus obsessively on small tasks such as counting her change or organizing her socks. In a short story she wrote about the experience, Emily spoke of having "found the love of her life" in methamphetamine.

Emily's story had a profound effect on perceptions of the meth problem in Baker County. It legitimized a fear then traveling through the national media that white, middle-class youth were uniquely vulnerable to methamphetamine.[2] Emily fit this profile exactly. She was one of the "good kids" from the "good families." She was an honor roll student who participated in a variety of school activities, including Student Council, 4-H, and the swim team. Emily's social standing was actually reflected in her use of metham-phetamine as she channeled it toward such socially sanctioned ends as doing well in school and cleaning her room. It was not until other symptoms of use that were not so sanctioned began to manifest themselves, such as insomnia, dramatic weight loss, mood swings, and increasing involvement with boys reputed to be drug dealers that it became problematic.

Nor was Emily's an isolated experience, even though she was the only stu-dent to have been detected by a police drug search. Shortly after the inci-dent at the school, Emily entered an inpatient treatment program where four other students from the high school were already enrolled. The fact that Emily and others had become meth addicts despite their middle-class back-ground confirmed the fears of many in the community. In local terms, it was taken as proof that with methamphetamine, it was "the people you'd never suspect" to be using drugs who were, paradoxically, those most likely to be users. These were not the stereotypical "bad kids," whose drug use was part of a more general inclination toward deviance, but rather the "good kids" that were most likely to be involved with the drug.

This representation of the typical methamphetamine user altered the "rhetoric of drugs" in Baker County (Derrida 2003). To make sense of Emily's experience, drug use had to be decoupled from other types of deviance in the local imaginary. This was significant not only for administrators at institu-tions where drug use was a concern but also for parents, because they could no longer rely on their "stereotypic knowledge" of drugs and deviance to aid in the identification of drug users (Silverstein 2004). That is, an adolescent's appearance, academic performance, socioeconomic background, family and home life—all of which remain key sites of surveillance and risk assess-ment used across a range of institutional contexts in Baker County and else-where—could no longer be taken as sufficient measures for determining who among the local youth were using drugs. Emily's case was a testament to this fact, particularly given that she had become addicted to methamphetamine without immediately raising the suspicions of her parents or the school.

This theme—the prevalence of meth use among "the people you'd never suspect"—came up time and again in my interviews. It was used discursively as a substitute for the discussion of drugs and class, and allowed members of the community to articulate their fears about methamphetamine's impact on middle-class families. In and of itself, this was not particularly remarkable. The fear that a particular drug is creeping "up the socioeconomic ladder," as a *Newsweek* article on methamphetamine put it, is a recurring trope in the his-tory of U.S. drug scares (Goode 2006). Fears about the vulnerability of middle-class youth specifically have been particularly pronounced (Schneider 2008). Thus what was remarkable in this case was not the fear of middle-class vulnerability itself, but the institutional response that this fear generated.

The decoupling of drug use from other indices of deviance increased the felt need among administrators to thicken the system of surveillance within the school, a move that was hardly novel in the context of the U.S. public school system (Devine 1996). The logic was that if Emily was representative of the typical methamphetamine user, then traditional practices of risk assessment and surveillance were unreliable means of drug detection. New techniques were needed; and the general consensus among parents, community activists, teachers, administrators, and police was that drug detection technologies (such as the drug dog and the drug test) carried the greatest potential for meeting this need. These technologies held out the promise of locating drugs in places like pockets, bodies, lockers, cars, and other spaces that have typically been resistant to traditional forms of surveillance by dint of spatial, temporal, or legal obstacles. It was these technologies, then, that administrators felt should be at the center of this new system of drug surveillance.

The focus on drug detection technologies set in motion a deeper debate over the exercise of police power with respect to drug use in the community. The debate was between three institutions: the family, the uniformed police, and the school. All of these institutions carry particular powers and responsibilities with regard to the exercise of police power, specifically regarding the policing of youth. Following Foucault (1995), it has become common to view these institutions as pieces of a more general system of discipline and punishment—a unified surveillance apparatus for the administration of disciplinary power through which subjects move over the course of their life. But contrary to the unified system described by Foucault, the drug-centered surveillance system, then in formation in Baker County, was laden with breaks and fissures. Institutionally specific anxieties, which were rooted variously in law, politics, bureaucracy, culture, and class, stymied any effort to expand the use of drug-detection technologies into a common, transinstitutional system of drug surveillance.

This produced a striated, "nervous" (Taussig 1992) form of policing, the effect of which, ultimately, was to create a system in which certain meth users—particularly those of the middle class—were shielded from the threat of legal sanction and the force of law while others were subject to the public exercise of police power (Moore and Haggerty 2001). Thus the disjunctures in the local drug surveillance system were complicit with the reproduction and repetition of deeper divisions in the community. And although there were debates over a variety of drug-detection technologies, the focus here will be on that surrounding the implementation of a drug testing program at the school.

"It Doesn't Take a Long Time for Good Kids to Go Bad"

In August 2007 I attended my first meeting of the Substance Abuse Prevention Coalition. This group was composed of professionals from the education, mental health, and social service fields. They had formed when the local mental health clinic received a grant from the state to develop strategies for dealing with drug use in the area. Glenda Hutchins was hired to lead the group.

Roughly twenty-five people were at the meeting, and Glenda suggested a round of introductions. There were social workers, guidance counselors, and psychologists, as well as addiction counselors, representatives from state agencies such as the Department of Health and Human Resources, and two mothers with daughters who were addicted to meth. One of these girls, a senior at the local high school, had accompanied her mother to the meeting. After the introductions, which were made for my benefit, as the members of the group were all well known to each other, Glenda asked Marjorie Thompson to speak. Marjorie was one of two addiction counselors on staff at the mental health clinic. She spoke about the impact that the spike in methamphetamine use was having on the clinic. It seemed to be affecting everyone. Marjorie had worked with adolescents at the high school as well as employees at the poultry processing plant. The problem at the plant was particularly bad, so bad in fact that every employee now had to pass a drug test before they could be hired. This was in addition to the random drug tests that were carried out every two weeks. Just that week, the plant lost four employees as a result of testing for meth.[3]

Joan Staley, a social worker, spoke next. She had also seen a spike in methamphetamine use among the people she served. This was particularly true of the high school students. Of the twenty-six referrals she received that year, she estimated that methamphetamine was a factor in at least 80 percent of them. Joan was troubled to hear how extensive drug use was in their homes, and speculated that most had learned how to use drugs from their parents, as a normal means of "coping" in the family.

Nancy Daniels, the guidance counselor at the high school, said Joan had touched on "the heart of the matter." She, too, saw that drug use began at home as a component of "coping patterns"—an accepted but destructive way to deal with family dynamics. At the same time, however, she was seeing something different with regard to methamphetamine. "A lot of the people you'd never suspect were on it," she said. At the high school, most of the "preps" were heavier users than the lower-class kids. For instance, a popular, clean-cut kid had earned the nickname "Ice Man" because he was one of the most notorious dealers of methamphetamine in the area ("ice" being one of the nicknames for meth). Nancy concluded that, with methamphetamine, it "doesn't take a long time for good kids to go bad."

I had heard this before. Three months earlier I attended the meeting of a similar group composed of local professionals in a neighboring county. There I met Joan Bennett, a psychologist who worked both in the local hospital and at the high school. Half-jokingly she told me that if I wanted to see who was using meth, I should go to a meeting of the Fellowship of Christian Athletes, an organization, as the name implied, made up of all the "good" kids from the "good" families: the cheerleaders, football players, homecoming queens and prom kings, all of whom were equally active members of their local church. For some reason, which neither Joan nor her colleagues could figure out, these were the people most likely to be using methamphetamine.

Carla Smith, the head of the Department of Health and Human Resources in the area, echoed these sentiments, stating that the "people who you wouldn't suspect as drug users" were often the most likely to be involved with methamphetamine. In a phone interview she emphasized how this was changing her work. It was no longer just health-care workers that came seeking information about the signs of drug use in children, but parents asking what they needed to look for in their kids. Until recently, these were the parents that she would not have thought needed to worry about their children using drugs. Carla herself had become more aware of the prevalence of methamphetamine. One day as she was heading home from work, she stopped at a stoplight and noticed that the teenager driving the truck behind her was visibly agitated, in a way that suggested he was probably on meth.

But this ability to detect adolescent drug use through simple acts of informed observation was a skill with waning utility, according to those in the community. This was precisely because the "people who you wouldn't suspect as drug users," as Carla put it, were the most likely users of meth. The experience of Emily's mother, Nancy Stevens, drove this point home. Nancy in part blamed herself for what had happened with Emily because she had not noticed the signs of her methamphetamine use soon enough. And though Nancy had been aware that Emily had lost weight and was not sleeping much, she had been slow to attribute this to drug use.

Emily, for her part, was more sensitive to her mother's suspicions and assumed she was at least partially aware that something was going on even before the event at the school. I asked Emily what she thought caused her mother's suspicions. "I was bitchy, never at home, was down to 105 pounds, and the guys I was dating had a reputation for being drug dealers, [which was] good for me, [but] bad for them." Indeed, of the more than twelve numbers marked "VIP" in Emily's cell phone, all, Nancy eventually discovered, were drug dealers. Thus Emily felt her body and behavior made it "obvious" she was using, in the same way that it was "obvious" who the other meth users were at the high school ("the people who look like they've been up for two straight days"). At the same time, it took a while before Emily's mother considered that her daughter's changed appearance and behavior might be signs of drug use.

When Nancy did eventually confront Emily, she began by threatening her with drug tests, which she had access to through her job at the Department of Health and Human Resources (even though she could have just as easily purchased them at the local drug store). One night as Emily was getting ready to go out Nancy said, "I'm testing you when you get back." Emily had planned on using that night. Instead, she waited until she got home, took the drug test (which she passed) and then did the meth in her room. Still, the next morning Nancy greeted Emily accusingly, "Your car smells like meth."

Emily and Nancy's experience reveal some of the motivations that were driving the demand for greater use of drug detection in the school. Nancy's account begins with a lament that she did not pick up on the signs of her daughter's drug use soon enough, and an acknowledgment of her own resistance to the idea that Emily even had a problem. Once she did develop suspicions, she acted on them in part by her use of drug tests as a way to control her daughter's behavior. In this case, the drug test was not simply a surveillance technology. It held out the promise of remaking the tie between parent and child, a tie that had been threatened by drugs. For Nancy, it seemed capable of compensating for her own inability to fully recognize the signs of drug use in her child.

Development of a Drug Detection System

A system of drug detection was already in place in Baker County before methamphetamine became a serious concern. It was rooted in institutions, including the hospital, the poultry factory, the courthouse, and the regional jail. Drug detection was part of the standard operating procedures of these institutions, albeit at different levels and in different ways.[4] In addition, the practices of drug detection varied from institution to institution, involving the combination of drug education, drug testing, and the use of drug dogs in site-specific configurations. A partial list of the various ways institutions used one technology, the drug test, provides a sense of the extensiveness of drug surveillance in the community:

- At the poultry factory, workers had to pass a drug test as part of the application process and were subjected to regular random testing.
- At the obstetrician's office, drug tests were part of prenatal care for any expectant mother who arrived late in her pregnancy or was otherwise suspected of drug use.
- At the courthouse, anyone charged with a crime was subjected to a drug test on days they appeared in court, regardless of whether they had been convicted of a drug-related crime. Regular and random drug testing was also a component of probation for all offenders.
- At the mental health clinic, drug tests were often incorporated into outpatient treatment programs, particularly if participation in the program was court ordered.
- At the class for DUI offenders, participation in which was typically mandated by the court, participants had to pass a Breathalyzer test before each class meeting. Police officers also used Breathalyzers to police drunk driving. This included the administration of Breathalyzer tests during stops, as well as the mounting of electronically monitored Breathalyzers in the vehicles of offenders. The offender was required to blow into the Breathalyzer before operating the vehicle.
- At the hospital, drug tests were administered to anyone who arrived with suspicious injuries or symptoms.

The presence of this vast and varied drug surveillance system formed a backdrop to the discussions that took place between parents, teachers, administrators, community activists, and police regarding the implementation of drug searches and drug testing in the school. Many of those involved in the debates worked in professions such as health, social services, or criminal justice where drug surveillance was commonplace. The emphasis on drug surveillance as the key to responding to methamphetamine was rooted in the familiarity with this system as a standard component of daily operations at the institutions where they worked. Thus it was not a matter of implementing a new system, but of extending a system already in place to new contexts.

The presence of such a robust drug-detection system in Baker County reflects the more general increase in the use of drug-detection technologies in the United States that has taken place since the last quarter of the twentieth century. The most ubiquitous of these technologies is the urine-based drug test (Tunnell 2004). Until the 1960s, testing urine for drugs was a technique used almost exclusively in clinical settings, but by the late 1960s the technology had spread. The military was one of the first to adopt it amid reports that American soldiers in Vietnam were becoming addicted to heroin and other drugs. As soldiers returned from Vietnam, the Department of Defense developed drug-testing programs to identify heroin addicts and treat them.

By the late 1970s, police agencies had begun using urine testing in jails, not to identify addicts for treatment but to control and monitor the drug use of their incarcerated population (Simon 1993). Mass screening in the military did not take place until the early 1980s, enabled by the development and refinement of relatively inexpensive and efficient testing techniques that could detect a large number of drugs in a single urine specimen. In 1986, as part of his more general escalation of the War on Drugs, President Ronald Reagan extended the military's drug-testing program to nonmilitary government employees, further urging that "voluntary" drug testing be considered both in and out of the government. To underscore the point, President Reagan and Vice President George Bush themselves underwent urinalysis along with seventy-eight senior White House staff.

This was the prelude to the executive order signed two months later calling for broad testing of the government's 2.8 million civilian employees as part of Reagan's mandate to establish a "drug free federal workplace," and $56 million was earmarked for the first year of the program alone. The rules stipulated that employees in sensitive positions could be fired if they tested positive for illegal drugs; refusal to be tested was grounds enough to be fired. This was one of several acts, which created federal mandates for maintaining "drug free" institutional environments. With the new policy in place, by 1987 the level of drug testing doubled. Testing spread from federal agencies to local police and fire departments, with calls for the testing of judges and attorneys as well.[5]

The rise in popularity of testing led to a boom in the country's testing laboratories. Between 1980 and 1985 sales of drug-testing equipment grew from $25 to $73 million, a rate of 22 percent a year. By 1988 laboratories were processing between 15 and 20 million drug tests annually, evenly split between private corporations and prisons, police, and public drug-treatment programs (Ackerman 1991).

Drug testing remains widespread in the United States throughout industry, the military, health services, government, education, and criminal justice, and is used for a variety of purposes. Penalties for testing positive vary widely and range from denial of employment or worker's compensation to expulsion from school or extracurricular activities to incarceration. In addition, drug-testing kits are now available at the local drug store and are increasingly marketed toward parents—particularly middle-class parents—to use on their children (Moore and Haggerty 2001). The popularity of drug testing may be due in part to the fact that it is a distinctly modern solution to the distinctly modern problem of drugs. As the criminologist Kenneth D. Tunnell writes:

> The drug-testing industry is the quintessential example of modernity. Its profound faith in technology; its underlying philosophy of surveillance; its ability to process large numbers of people; and its confidence in science as a means of social control—each suggests modern strategies and ideologies for addressing complex social issues. (Tunnell 2004, 55)

This brief history explains, in part, the presence of a relatively robust drug testing apparatus in Baker County before methamphetamine became a concern. It also suggests why attempts to expand this apparatus were part of the initial response to meth. However, as we will see, the complexity of the methamphetamine problem in Baker County exceeded the capacity of drug tests and other drug detection technologies to serve successfully as a panacea. Efforts to expand the drug testing apparatus were stymied by a range of social, political, and legal concerns. Institutional administrators became reluctant to aggressively increase drug testing for fear of upsetting the local social order and the power relations that sustained it. This was nowhere more evident than in the school system.

The School: Drug Testing and the Will (Not to) Know

Although every institution felt besieged by increased levels of drug use, the school was the place where an increase in drug-detection technologies was most desired but also where their implementation was most contentious. Administrators at the high school were dealing with this in different ways. One strategy was to continue the emphasis on drug education. Education was what Wendell Albright, the school guidance counselor, had in mind when he brought the DEA officer from Baltimore to the school to speak about methamphetamine. The officer did a presentation during the school day for the students, but the real focus was on educating teachers and parents. It was assumed the students were already aware of most of what the officer would be telling them regarding methamphetamine's prevalence and the effects of its use.

Connie Dixon, a teacher at the high school, vividly remembered the DEA officer's presentation, which made her aware of the signs of methamphetamine use. This was helpful because teachers at the school were expected to report students they suspected of drug use to the guidance counselor. The guidance counselor would then address the issue with those students and their parents. Identifying students who were using drugs had always been a challenge. But after the DEA agents' presentation, Connie knew what to look for in students, particularly to see if they were using methamphetamine. Sometimes she would see kids who, over the course of a year or more, would lose a significant amount of weight, or whose face would start sinking in. All the teachers would comment, "Have you seen so-and-so? They're not looking so good."

Education alone, however, was insufficient to address drugs in the school, according to school officials. Despite her own increased awareness, Connie was certain that most student drug use took place unbeknown to school officials. This created the sense that the school needed to incorporate additional strategies that did not rely so heavily on teachers' direct observation of students.

A key strategy here was to have the police search the school periodically with the drug dog. Wendell explained that this was done randomly and without warning to either students or teachers. The principle would simply come over the school intercom and announce a "Code Red." The teachers would then lock the doors of their classrooms as the police officer did a "sweep" with the drug dog, focusing particularly on the lockers that lined the halls. The dog was then taken to every classroom; the students, who were required to leave all of their belongings in the classroom, would file out into the hallway, and the officer would go through the room and their belongings with the dog.

Drug searches like these typically happened once or twice a year. This was frustratingly infrequent for Wendell, who was a former probation officer. He had been under the impression when the school year began that the police would be conducting a drug search with the dog at least once a month, but that had not happened, and he was not sure why. "They have an open invitation," he said. All they had to do was give the school enough notice to get all the students into the classrooms. This was not just for the purposes of the search but also because, as he understood it, the drug dogs were also attack dogs, and they didn't want any of the kids to get hurt.

Not only were the searches too infrequent for administrators, they were often undermined when students got wind of what was happening. One teacher complained that officers were not careful enough when going to the school to do a search. She mentioned an incident in which the officer stopped at Annie's, a popular local restaurant in town, to get coffee before doing the search. Students passing by Annie's on their way to school saw the officer's patrol vehicle, which says "K9 Unit" on the side, and began to suspect that he might be on his way to the school. This frustrated school officials. "If you're gonna do a search," one teacher commented, "don't stop at Annie's on your way there to get coffee. Half of the town is gonna see you and so everyone will know."

A similar incident occurred earlier that year when a 911 operator told her son, who was a student at the high school, that the drug search was going to happen. She suggested that he not go to school. He, of course, told many of his friends, thereby eliminating the element of surprise that was crucial to the search's effectiveness. This was even more frustrating for teachers, because parents were colluding with students to thwart the efforts of the police and the school to detect drugs and users. School officials could not understand why a parent—and one involved with the police at that—would go so far as to tell her child not to go to school the day of the search. It seemed to them that she was enabling his drug use (if he was in fact a drug user). It was actions like these that caused many in the community to blame the rising drug problem on the parents themselves. When I asked a police officer what he thought should be done about the methamphetamine problem, he looked at me with a half-smile and said, "Make people take IQ tests before they have children." Similarly, the sheriff of Baker County, Michael Sheerer, evoked the idyllic rural environment of his youth when he stated, "I didn't have time to get into drugs; I was too busy working on the farm."

Wendell felt that having police officers in the schools was absolutely necessary because he assumed that the teachers did not know anything about drugs, or at least not enough to know what to look for in the students. He recalled an incident in which a teacher found a "bag of dope" on the floor and had no idea what it was—a fact which Wendell found both reassuring and disheartening. This was why the speaker from the DEA had been invited to speak, primarily so the teachers would become more informed. This was necessary because the school had both a legal and moral responsibility to maintain a drug-free environment. Doing drug searches with the dogs was the best means of meeting this obligation.

I asked Wendell if the school performed drug tests on students. He told me it was completely out of the question. For one, he was pretty sure it was illegal.[6] But even if it were not, there would be such protests from students and parents that the program could not last long. Part of the protest would be rooted in the invasion of privacy. But more deeply, Wendell felt that parents and others actually *did not want to know* the truth about their children, what they knew, or what they were doing. This was another explanation as to why the 911 operator had warned her son about the impending search of the school. Wendell implicated teachers in this will-not-to-know, as well. "As parents and educators," he said, "we don't want to know what they [students and children] know, or that they know." His experience as a guidance counselor had driven this point home. He continued to be shocked by the ability of parents to deny or rationalize their children's behaviors, thinking either that their kids were not really involved with drugs or that if they were, it was just a phase and would pass.

"Does that mean that parents don't care?" I asked.

"Absolutely not," he said. Their desire not to know, or to deny or rationalize their children's behavior, was indicative of the degree to which they *did* care about their children, to the point that they would rather imagine that their child was out of harm's way than confront the fact that they might actually be at risk. "Parents hate to feel inadequate and love their kids too much to believe that their children are doing bad things."

This explained, in part, the low turnout when the DEA agent offered an "info night" for parents the evening of his presentation at the school. Only about thirty parents attended the program, even though the school offered incentives to students, such as homework passes, if their parents attended the presentation. And at least twenty of those who attended were parents of what Connie called the "low risk kids"—low risk because the kids were involved in school and extracurricular activities, and parents were involved in their lives. The "high risk" kids were those whose parents were not particularly involved in their lives, and who were, in fact, the least likely to attend an event like the DEA agent's information session. "But then there's Emily's case." Connie said. Connie knew that Emily's mother had always been involved in her life, and that Emily herself was a "low risk kid." Nevertheless, she had become addicted to meth, and only the search of the school by police had detected her use.

Reasonable Suspicions

Despite Wendell's reservations, the school board maintained an interest in developing a drug program for the school. They asked the board president, Dana Matthews, to draft a policy that would govern the testing of students and/or employees. Dana agreed, and turned to the West Virginia Education Association for guidance. In a meeting chronicled by local media, the staff attorney Greg Casterman met with the local school board to discuss the legality and advisability of various drug-testing options. His presentation focused on the institutional risks associated with drug testing.

Greg addressed three possibilities: random drug testing, suspicion-based drug testing, and situation-based drug testing. Random drug testing, as the name indicated, involved randomly selecting students and employees to submit to a drug test. The possibility that anyone might be tested made the test seem equitable and provided a general deterrent for the entire school. However, Greg strongly discouraged the school board from taking this approach. This was not because such a program was strictly illegal, but because it would inevitably require long-time and well-respected employees to undergo a drug test. This would be an embarrassment to both the person tested and the school, and might generate public outrage, which would undermine the legitimacy of the program. "I just think it's legally dangerous for a governmental system to impose random drug testing on its employees," Greg stated.

Greg saw greater potential in suspicion-based drug testing, specifically, a program guided by the principle of "reasonable suspicion."[7] In this approach, any person about whom there was a reasonable suspicion of drug use could be tested. Such a program could be used for both teachers and students. And virtually anything could provide reasonable suspicion, including direct observation of a person using a drug, the exhibition of physical and behavioral symptoms associated with drug use, and/or displays of abnormal behavior.

But even this approach carried potential risks. Greg gave the hypothetical example of one employee who holds a grudge against another employee and turns them in for "suspicious activity." Greg stated, "You and I know there's a lot of suspicion in a community; people like to talk. There's people like that in every community; it's just the way it is." By providing a formal system of accusation based on minimal, subjective evidence, the drug-testing program could potentially amplify interpersonal conflicts and create problems for the school. There was also the issue of false positives. "If you eat a lemon muffin with poppy seeds, those poppy seeds give a false positive for opium," Greg stated. This meant that nondrug users could potentially return a positive test. In this situation a second, more reliable (and more expensive) test was required to determine whether the initial test gave a false positive. Sometimes legal proceedings were necessary to settle the issue. All of this could become very costly for the school and the county government that funded it.

A third option was to make drug tests situational. Tests could be incorporated into the application process for prospective employees, for instance, or required for current employees involved in accidents. Such an approach was legally sound and very effective in keeping drug users out of schools, according to Greg. Testing prospective employees as part of the application procedure was particularly effective. "It makes you Ivory Soap safe," Greg stated, "99 percent pure."[8] Dana Matthews mentioned that the school already required bus drivers to submit to a drug test if they were involved in an accident, and hypothesized that the policy could be expanded to include anyone involved in an accident while driving a school-owned vehicle. Greg encouraged the school board to pursue such an expansion of the policy, "Especially [for] anyone who is involved with the transportation of students."

One board member asked Greg about a program that only tested those students involved in athletics and other extracurricular activities. Again, he advised caution, less because of potential legal problems than because of the social and political risks should the "wrong people" be subjected to a test. Like testing employees, randomly drug-testing students was a fraught endeavor, involving the same serious risk of false positives and resentments from upstanding students and their families. Greg advised using the principle of "reasonable suspicion" as their guide. Some evidence that the student was involved in drugs, or, more concretely, "if you have an indication of [drug] abuse," then the drug-test requirement was legally sound and the social risk minimized. Dana concluded the meeting on a high note, thanking Greg and saying that he had given the administration "some wonderful tools to work with."

Greg's legal advice encouraged school administrators to use tacit systems of risk profiling, rather than a completely randomized approach, to implement drug testing for students and employees. This approach would inevitably shield some students and employees from scrutiny while targeting others. Furthermore, it created incentives for school administrators to continue developing the abilities of teachers and students to identify drug users within the school population through education and other means. A randomized drug-testing program would have been more equitable, but a program based on the principle of "reasonable suspicion" was less politically fraught, reducing the possibility that the "wrong people" would be subject to a test. Incorporating drug tests into administrative functions, such as application procedures and post-accident inquiries, held even greater potential as it targeted individuals who either did not yet work for the school or who had been involved in an incident requiring investigation.

This created a paradox: while it was the fear of drug use among white, middle-class students that had, in part, driven the demand for the expansion of drug testing in the school, Greg advocated for a drug testing program designed to shield such students from scrutiny. If school administrators followed Greg's advice, they would be limited to drug testing those students about whom there was a "reasonable suspicion" of drug use, which would be difficult in the case of methamphetamine, given that the typical methamphetamine users were thought to be "the people you'd never suspect." Reflecting on Greg's advice, I was reminded of a comment that Wendell Albright had made with regard to the challenge of drug testing in the schools: "Everyone wants rules," he said, "until it falls on their kid's neck."

From DARE to LEAD: "Giving Parents the Power"

While the school board sought legal advice in devising a drug-testing policy for its students and employees, another program went ahead with little discussion. This was LEAD, an acronym standing for both Law Enforcement Against Drugs *and* for Local Educators Against Drugs. It was a national program developed by the company Total Diagnostic Services, or TDS, a private, for-profit company based in Michigan. The company specialized in providing drug-testing services to the increasing number of institutions that use them in their everyday operations, including addiction centers, courts, police departments, businesses, construction sites and schools. According to their Web site, the company developed the LEAD program in 1999 in consultation with law enforcement officers. The program was launched in 2000.

Though originally conceived and marketed for law enforcement officers, the focus was always on controlling drug use in schools. Notably, the program was not designed to help law enforcement officers detect and arrest drug users but, rather, to transfer this responsibility to parents. The LEAD program actually brokers an exchange between parents and police in which the threat of formal legal sanction is removed. The criminologists Dawn Moore and Kevin Haggerty have drawn attention to this aspect of contemporary drug testing programs. "In exchange for becoming deputized agents in the anti-drug campaign," they write, "white, middle-class parents can divert their child from the state's official system of drug-regulation" (Moore and Haggerty 2001, 61). This is a key selling point of the program and is stated explicitly in the program's mission statement:

Law Enforcement Against Drugs provides law enforcement agencies with a comprehensive program that empowers parents to keep their children drug-free by offering information and convenient, affordable drug and alcohol tests. These tests produce immediate results in the privacy of the home. In the event of a positive result, LEAD directs them to appropriate community resources.[9]

Even though it was initially marketed toward police, the LEAD program quickly expanded to formally include schools. The mission statement for this branch of LEAD, referred to by the same acronym but standing for Local Educators Against Drugs, is virtually synonymous with that for the original LEAD program:

> *Local Educators Against Drugs* provides educators and community coali-
> tions with a comprehensive program that empowers parents to keep their
> children drug-free by offering information and convenient, affordable
> drug and alcohol tests. These tests produce immediate results in the pri-
> vacy of the home. In the event of a positive result, LEAD directs them to
> appropriate community resources.[10]

Despite being targeted toward educators and undefined "community coali-tions," the focus is again on encouraging (or, from the program's perspective, "empowering") parents to do the work of monitoring their child's drug use—away, of course, from the eyes of the police. In both of these mission state-ments, and in the more lengthy description of the LEAD program, the selling point is that the tests can be conducted privately, by the child's parents and in their home. This enables parents to avoid the embarrassment of having their child test positive for drugs in a public space such as the school. It also allows them to handle their child's drug use as they prefer, without the public inter-vention of either the school or the legal system. At their request, parents are given information on local drug treatment options. As Moore and Haggerty state, "It sends the clear message that while poor, minority parents continue to witness their children repeatedly coming into conflict with the law, white, middle-class parents should not, and need not, rely on the state to monitor and respond to their child's drug use. Furthermore, it implies that the state's strategy in the war on drugs—criminalization—is not the most effective, desirable, or appropriate way to govern this population of offenders" (ibid.).

The test is also marketed as a strategic intervention into contemporary American family life, which the LEAD program literature depicts as funda-mentally unmanageable. They appeal to parents' purported sense of disem-powerment, particularly in the area of raising children, suggesting that the frustration they experience with their children may be (unbeknown to them) rooted in drug and alcohol use. It states:

YOU'RE NOT ALONE

You're not alone; raising teenagers in today's world has become a challenge for even the most stable of families. At times, parents find themselves at their wits' end trying to interpret the different moods and behaviors of their children. Often they misinterpret the signs that their child's problem is far more serious than they would ever have suspected. Often the problem is drug and alcohol use. The shocking truth is that over sixty percent of young people use an illegal substance before leaving high school. Through LEAD, your school empowers parents by providing a simple way to detect a potential problem with anonymity before it becomes a police matter.

The program literature then provides a list of suspicious or frustrating behavioral changes that parents might have observed in their child, again suggesting the likelihood that these changes are related to unrecognized drug use.

HAVE YOU NOTICED A CHANGE?

Maybe you've noticed a change in your child's school performance, or his appearance or choice of friends. Perhaps they are more withdrawn or depressed, no longer interested in favorite activities. Your child may even be more aggressive, hostile to you or other members of the family. While there certainly could be another explanation, these are some of the same characteristics which often indicate drug or alcohol use.

Finally, the program literature encourages parents to act on any suspicions they already have that their child is involved in drugs, combining this suspicion with a sense of helplessness that the LEAD program is poised to remedy. It does this by providing parents with the "necessary tools to confirm their suspicions in the privacy and security of the home."

DO YOU SUSPECT A PROBLEM?

If you do suspect a problem, you may not know where to turn for help. This is precisely why the LEAD program was created. Through local educators, LEAD gives parents the necessary tools to confirm their suspicions in the privacy and security of the home and directs them to appropriate resources if alcohol or drug use is discovered. Easy-to-use test kits that give almost instantaneous results are available for a nominal fee. Whether the problem is drugs or alcohol, one simple urine or saliva test provides accurate results within three to eight minutes. The LEAD tests can also reduce peer pressure by providing kids with an "out" ("I can't because I might get tested.")[11]

The person who was working most diligently to bring the LEAD program into the local schools in Baker County was Ronnie McKinney, a sheriff's deputy who worked as the "resource officer" in the school system. Ronnie learned of the program at a conference, and he brought the idea to another officer, Lester Bottoms, who began implementing it in the school.

Lester lauded the program as providing drug control options to both parents and children. In an interview with a local reporter, Lester stated, "In the past, parents have asked to have their kids tested [by the police], and this will make it easier for them." He continued, repeating the information from the program practically verbatim. "[LEAD] is also good for kids who want to get tested to prove to their parents that they're not on drugs, and will aid them in dealing with peer pressure when they're at places like a party. It can give them an out because they can say, 'I can't drink because I might get tested.'" Thus, from Lester's perspective, the LEAD program offered parents a means of keeping their children off drugs by threatening them with a test, and it offered children a means of avoiding alcohol and drug use, allowing them to use the threat of the test as a reason not to drink or use drugs if pressured. It provided a less legally contentious avenue for implementing a school-based, drug-testing program because it was parents, and not the school, that performed the actual tests. In this regard, by eliminating the necessity of either the law or police to intervene in the situation, it also held out the promise of restoring a social relationship—that between parent and child—into its "proper" balance, countering the negative effects of modern life (including drug and alcohol use).

The LEAD program marked a departure from other anti-drug programs administered by law enforcement in schools. It was particularly different from the Drug Abuse Resistance Education, or DARE, program, which was, until that point, the primary anti-drug program that police officers implemented in the schools, and one that had had little effect on the drug problem in the area. As one police officer put it: "You've got three kinds of people: those that will never do drugs; those that will do drugs no matter what; and those that could go either way. The best we can hope for with education is to get those in the middle before they start using."

Developed and run by the nonprofit DARE America, the DARE program is now a ubiquitous component of the American education curriculum: DARE programs are currently implemented in 75 percent of American school districts.[12] Like LEAD, DARE is a national program. It was started in 1983 by police officers in Los Angeles. The DARE program sends law enforcement officers into schools to educate students about the perils of drug use—physical, social, legal—and to provide them with reasons and tools for avoiding drug use. The program has recently revamped its approach and curriculum: re-imagining law enforcement officers as "coaches" rather than teachers; underscoring the "scientific" foundation of their curriculum through an emphasis on "research-based refusal strategies" and the use of neuroimaging technologies that show the effects of drugs on the brain; and expanding the curriculum beyond drugs to include everything from school violence to terrorism. Nonetheless, the goal remains a pedagogical one: law enforcement officers are teachers drawing on their unique expertise to provide students with information that will prevent them from using drugs.[13]

Although LEAD resembles DARE in its emphasis on prevention and focus on students, education is not seen as the primary tool through which to achieve this end, nor are law enforcement officers positioned as those most qualified to implement the program. LEAD has only a small educational component, largely limited to informing parents about the signs of drug use, providing them with rudimentary information about common drugs of abuse (including alcohol), and alerting them to resources such as drug treatment programs in their area.

But none of this information is figured as useful in its own right. Rather, it is a kind of technical knowledge necessary for effectively using the drug tests provided by law enforcement through the LEAD program. Moreover, whereas DARE is a nonprofit organization, LEAD is a for-profit enterprise. By encouraging police departments and schools to adopt its program, Total Diagnostic Services has created a market for its drug tests. Although some departments have chosen to sponsor the program themselves and distribute the tests for free, and others have found community organizations to pay for the program (all strategies encouraged by TDS), most simply make the tests available to parents and/or students for a fee. In Baker County, tests for a single substance were five dollars and tests for multiple substances were thirteen dollars. Thus, the LEAD program was attractive to law enforcement officers because it allowed them to implement a drug-testing program in the school that avoided both the legal pitfalls surrounding school-based drug testing and the financial pitfalls involved with relying on the drug dog to perform drug searches. More significantly, it was a program in which police played a diminished role. Police made the tests available; it was up to parents to purchase and use them.

Here, too, the two programs differ. In the LEAD program it is not the police or the school administration that is doing the work of either education or surveillance, but the parents of the children. Indeed, a key selling point of the tests is that neither school nor police officials are involved. Parents have the ability to find out if their child is using drugs without having the public know about it. Conversely, law enforcement and school officials are relieved from part of the responsibility of keeping schools free from drugs by encouraging parents to do the work themselves. In this way, the schools avoid many of the thorny legal issues raised by drug testing, law enforcement officers can focus their efforts and resources on other areas, and parents are re-saddled with the responsibility to police their children. This is significant, given the frequency with which the household was identified as the key location of the drug problem.

A primary concern with methamphetamine was that unlike other drugs, it was appearing in those places and among those people "you wouldn't suspect" of using drugs. This perception drove concern over the presence of the drugs themselves and fueled the desire for an increased presence of drug detection technologies in institutions, particularly in the local schools. At the same time, legal officials—from state attorneys to local police—were advising caution in the institutional use of drug-detection technologies or, in the case of the LEAD program, attempting to transfer responsibility for performing such drug-detection work to other institutions, particularly the family.

But while this was going on, there were indicators that older dynamics of drug control were at work as well. At the end of the meeting of the Substance Abuse Prevention Coalition I attended, Glenda mentioned that even though meth seemed to affect "the people you'd never suspect," it was still "only the rednecks who go to jail"—a point she whispered to me even though we were the only two people in the room. This comment revealed a tacit perception of the way class structured the fates of those who became involved with drugs: the "good kids" like Emily going to a treatment facility (at great cost, both financial and emotional, to her family), and the "rednecks" (a derogatory term for poor whites) without such means becoming enmeshed in the criminal justice system. Thus, while the cultural representation of methamphetamine was fueling the desire to expand the use of drug-detection technologies in local institutions, it was doing so without necessarily altering the broader patterns of enforcement, which tended to focus on those without the means to shield themselves from the law.

5

"Against the Peace and Dignity of the State"

There was a sense of excitement in Baker County the day David Johnson was arrested. David was one of those people that "everybody knew" was selling drugs. In 2003 he was a recent high school graduate, a part-time gas station attendant, and a meth user. David began by buying small amounts of meth from local dealers but was soon driving to Virginia to purchase larger amounts. It was not long before David decided to go into business for himself, using part of the meth he purchased and selling the rest.

David's business grew quickly. After he made two high-priced (and therefore high-profile) purchases, rumors began to circulate that he might be doing more than just working at the gas station. The first purchase was an all-terrain vehicle (ATV), or four-wheeler; a few months later, he purchased a new pickup truck. It was not uncommon to see David driving through town in his truck, four-wheeler in the back, heading up the mountain to go ride around.

This caught the attention of the other residents, and it did not sit well. As one officer put it:

> You've got people here who've worked hard all their life. They'd like a new truck and a four-wheeler, but they just don't have the money. And here you've got this kid, been working a part time job for less than a year, and suddenly he's got two new vehicles? I think that made a lot of people mad.

The police began receiving telephone calls from people demanding David's arrest. The police told them that more convincing evidence was needed before an arrest could be made, and this angered the callers, which in turn angered the police, who were constantly frustrated with the way the community was involved with the policing of the drug problem. On the one hand, when police officers were looking for information on a suspect they could rarely find anyone willing to provide it. The fear of reprisal was strong enough (because of the fact that "everybody knows everybody") that residents were extremely reluctant to give any information that could be traced back to them. On the other hand, when the police did receive calls from residents it was in the form of demands that a particular person be immediately arrested because "everybody knows they're selling drugs."

This attitude bothered law enforcement officers deeply, as it reflected what they felt was an inaccurate view about how the law actually worked. As a sheriff's deputy with significant experience working on methamphetamine told me in an interview:

> People don't understand that the law just doesn't work that way. It may be true that this individual is selling drugs. I may even know for a fact that they are. But that doesn't mean that I can just go arrest them. We have to get proof that they are doing it. We have to catch them in the act. And that takes time and a lot of work. But people still think that we can just arrest someone because "everybody knows" they're selling drugs. There's more to it than that.

The opportunity to arrest David Johnson did not come until federal officials became involved. A Federal Drug Task Force was established in the area, the purpose of which was to disrupt the interstate methamphetamine traffic coming into West Virginia from the Shenandoah Valley of Virginia— the exact route David Johnson was using to maintain his supply of meth. The Task Force employed members of the Baker County Sheriff's Department as well as state police. David was one of the first people they targeted.

Members of the Task Force made a series of controlled buys of methamphetamine from David using a confidential informant. The individual who made the buys was a friend of David's, someone he had sold to before and had known for most of his life. This person had himself been arrested for possession of methamphetamine and had agreed to assist the police in obtaining evidence to convict David in exchange for the possibility of a lighter sentence. After making three separate buys of methamphetamine using the confidential informant, members of the Baker County Sheriff's Department arrested David Johnson.

The Task Force's efforts produced few "big time" arrests other than David, whose significance in any case was limited to Baker County; and only one individual was prosecuted on federal charges, a longtime meth cook discovered by accident when a deputy sheriff responded to a domestic disturbance call. The Task Force did, however, enable the indictment of dozens of individuals for methamphetamine-related crimes throughout the region. In Baker County, roughly a dozen criminal indictments were handed down. This was a significant number, given that there were rarely more than thirty criminal indictments over the course of a typical year in Baker County.

Those who were arrested and prosecuted were, like David, local users and dealers. Most worked in low-paying jobs or were unemployed. Most were poor. They were methamphetamine users who sold periodically to their family and friends in order to support their own habit or to generate a minimal supplemental income. Some of these individuals had been using and selling methamphetamine in this way for close to ten years. For others, their involvement with methamphetamine was more recent. In either case, the efforts of the Federal Drug Task Force made these individuals visible to the state in a way they would not have been just five years earlier, even though, according to local residents, methamphetamine was just as prevalent (if not more so) then. Indeed, by the mid-1990s, Meadville, the county seat of Baker County, had already earned the nickname "Speedville" owing to the prevalence of amphetamine use in the area. The most common form of "speed" in circulation at the time was "crank," a type of methamphetamine.

The prosecution of crimes and the meting out of punishment is one of the most basic political functions performed by the state. It is also a key means through which the state seeks to establish it legitimacy, particularly its claim to act in the name of collective opinion (Greenhouse 2003). In the United States, the state's efforts in this regard have been pursued increasingly through the prosecution of drug offenders, particularly since the declaration of the War on Drugs (see chap. 1). This raises the question: How is the state working to legitimize its authority when drug offenders are at the center of the politics of crime and punishment?

The focus in this chapter is on three cases that resulted from the Federal Drug Task Force's operation in the area. The individuals in each case were arrested and indicted for illegally selling methamphetamine. Such cases, referred to in legal terminology as "possession of a controlled substance with intent to deliver," but known more commonly as "drug dealing," are notable instances of how the state's prosecutorial practices perform to establish its legitimacy because the only recognized victim in the case is "the state" itself. Whereas in other kinds of criminal cases—murder, theft, assault, fraud, etc.—there is usually a citizen/victim on whose behalf the state is (at least purportedly) acting, in cases where the sole crime is drug dealing or possession, it is the state alone that is the victim.

The very language used in the documents that accompany the court proceedings underscores this point. Processing and maintaining these documents properly is at the heart of criminal procedure and plays a significant role in the wider semiotics of statecraft (Riles 2006; Hull 2003, 2008). These documents are kept in a file, which is managed by officials at the courthouse. Much of the work of prosecution is a matter of filing the proper paperwork. Each file has a cover page that lists the various crimes with which the accused individual has been charged. For every count there is a description of the crime, which ends with the phrase "against the peace and dignity of the State," as in one of the charges leveled against Christie and Justin Stokes. This is how their indictment on the charge of violating West Virginia Code 61-10-31, "Conspiracy To Commit An Offense Against The State of West Virginia," was recorded in their official court file:

THE GRAND JURY CHARGES:

That on or about the _____ day of _____ 2003, in Baker County, West Virginia, JUSTIN STOKES and CHRISTIE STOKES, committed the offense of "Conspiracy To Commit An Offense Against The State of West Virginia" by feloniously, knowingly, intentionally and unlawfully conspiring with each other to commit the offense of "Delivery Of A Schedule II Controlled Substance" in Baker County, West Virginia, and did in furtherance of said conspiracy commit an overt act to effect the object of the conspiracy, to-wit: they delivered methamphetamine, a Schedule II Controlled Substance, to Randy Reynolds for which they received remuneration, when they were not authorized by law to do so, *against the peace and dignity of the State* (italics added).

In this way, "the state" takes on a life of its own in the context of court proceedings. The state becomes present through the action taken to redress the violation of its "peace and dignity" (anthropomorphic properties attributed to the state by such legal documentation and proceedings). It is not "the state," of course, that carries out this redressive work, but people, practices, and things performing various tasks and duties as part of a wider bureaucratic machinery. The adjudication of criminality performs a particular kind of work in this context, enabling "the state" to be known and knowable in the world as an empirical entity.

But it is not simply through the semiotics of adjudication and other bureaucratic practices that the state makes itself known. It is also through the use of violence to punish those found to have violated the law. The prosecution of drug offenses provides a unique resource in this regard as well. A drug offense is a possession offense. The legal scholar Markus Dubber has detailed how the prosecution of possession offenses has become a favored tactic of the contemporary U.S. criminal justice system, the effects of which have been far-reaching. Dubber argues that the focus on possession offenses has transformed the practice of criminal justice in the United States, turning it into a "police regime" whose objective is not to redress harms but to proactively police threats. "Policing human threats is different from punishing persons," Dubber writes. "A police regime doesn't punish. It seeks to eliminate threats if possible, and to minimize them if necessary. Instead of punishing, a police regime disposes. It resembles environmental regulations of hazardous waste more than it does the criminal law of punishment" (Dubber 2001, 833).

In the cases that follow, there is evidence of the state taking the "waste disposal" approach Dubber describes in its prosecution of methamphetamine offenders. In each case, those who were prosecuted were figured abstractly as "drug dealers" who posed an imminent threat to "the community." This figuration of local meth dealers and users as categorically threatening played a significant role in their prosecution. In most cases it provided the foundation for public support of the state's efforts and the guiding rationale for the judge's sentencing decisions.

The extent to which those prosecuted were able to escape being depicted as threatening depended in part on the position they occupied in the community before their prosecution. Those who occupied a more favorable position (by dint of their family ties, for instance) were able to challenge the state's characterization of them as threats (a key component of criminal procedure in an adversarial system like that of the United States). This did not necessarily prevent them from being prosecuted, but it did provide a partial check on state power during sentencing and helped with their reentry into the community after their incarceration. Those individuals with stronger community ties were better able to make a case for themselves that through their punishment they had "learned their lesson" and no longer posed a threat to the community. David Johnson was the most prominent of those few who were in this position. In David's case, there was even a sentiment that he could have been released earlier than he was, a sentiment that subtly called into question the state's judgment if not its legitimacy.

Those who were already living on the margins even before their conviction, however, found themselves much less capable to challenge the state's depiction of them as threatening. Not only did their cases not go to trial (they were settled, instead, by plea agreement), but their prosecution further marginalized them. For these individuals, the public seemed content to let the state engage in its work without question or oversight. Indeed, no one second-guessed the state's prosecution of these individuals, their sentences, or the length of time they spent incarcerated (except, perhaps, to claim that the time spent incarcerated was insufficient). On the contrary, many in the community wrote letters thanking members of the criminal justice system for their work. In this way, the state seemed to be establishing its legitimacy by targeting those marginal members of the community who were demonstrably involved with the local drug economy. Such individuals were figured consistently by both members of the criminal justice system and the wider public as the appropriate recipients of the state's punitive powers.

At Court

The sheriff was serving as bailiff the first day I attended court in Baker County. Taking my seat on a bench outside the main doors, he promptly approached me to ask who I was. I explained my presence, even producing a business card to make it seem more legitimate. "You've got a right to sit in," he said, ambivalently. "We just like to keep track of who's here."

Several clusters of people sat in near silence on the benches and chairs around me as lawyers, police, clerks, social workers, probation officers, and others ran around the courthouse trying to locate clients, obtain paperwork, and meet briefly to address the particulars of those cases on the docket for that day. The suits and uniforms of these officials stood in stark contrast to the appearance of the accused who were dressed in work or casual clothes—old shirts, blue jeans, boots, sweatshirts, and weathered camouflage baseball caps. A police officer appeared at one point escorting three men from the regional jail dressed in orange jumpsuits with cuffs around their wrists and ankles.

An older woman who appeared to be in her seventies sat next to me accompanied by a couple in their twenties. They began angrily trying to guess who the confidential informant was that had "worn a wire" while (allegedly) purchasing methamphetamine from one of their relatives.

"Somebody's running their mouth about something that didn't happen," said the elderly woman, visibly agitated.

"We'll see who it was," the young woman with bleached-blonde hair replied. The man next to her just stared blankly ahead and said nothing.

"That's hearsay. That don't mean shit," the elderly woman continued. "I'll catch him. I might go to jail, but I'll catch him."

Baker County was like the rest of the United States in that most criminal cases ended not with a trial but with a plea agreement. After being indicted, and usually at the pretrial hearing, the prosecuting attorney would present the accused with the evidence against them, the maximum penalty he or she could receive if found guilty for their crimes, and the reduced sentence he would recommend if they would take a plea agreement instead of going to trial. Among police officers, there was deep resentment toward anyone who took their case to trial. Police officers viewed the plea agreement as an opportunity for offenders to admit their guilt and "take responsibility for their crime." But "if they wanna be a butthole about it" and take the case to trial, as one officer put it, then the prosecutors would typically "get them for everything to the fullest extent."

There were other pressures that encouraged plea agreements. A public defender whose practice included Baker County called it, "the most conservative place on earth." He disliked taking cases there because juries so willingly sided with the state. There was a general feeling there that, "if the prosecuting attorney said it, it must be true," which made it difficult to contest the claims of the state. Not surprisingly, most cases ended with a plea agreement and the admission of guilt on the part of the accused in the courtroom setting.

Once plea agreements were reached, there was a concluding event in which the accused was expected to stand up, confess his or her guilt, and express remorse for his or her crimes. This all occurred before the formal sentencing process, at a time when the specifics of the sentence remained undecided, the judge having no formal obligation to abide by the terms of the arrangement made between the accused and the state. Indeed, the judge emphasized that the court was by no means compelled to accept the plea that the prosecuting attorney had offered, and could in fact institute a harsher penalty.

The accused invariably maintained a look of shock, shame and/or bewilderment in the courtroom throughout the proceedings, but these sentiments became particularly acute during this procedure. Chronic self-consciousness and uncertainty seemed to pervade their every move. As the judge spoke to them, some showed expressions that indicated they were only too aware of their predicament, while for others, their faces indicated no sense of comprehension, rather they turned each time they were addressed to their attorney who provided them with the proper response to the judge's questions.

One man, accused and ultimately convicted on one count of possession of methamphetamine with intent to deliver, only once demonstrated an understanding of what was happening during the proceedings. The judge was explaining that as part of his plea he would serve a minimum of one year in jail and could serve as many as five years in jail. The first time the judge told him this and asked if he understood, the man gave a slight, wide-eyed vacant nod as he had to each of the previous questions, conveying only the most basic sense that something was being asked of him, but no indication that he comprehended what that was. The judge, suspicious, explained again in more straightforward terms the crime to which he was preparing to plead guilty and the possible penalties that would accompany it. Suddenly it became clear to the man that he would be spending at least one year of his life in jail—in this case, for selling methamphetamine to his nephew who was actually working with the police.

The man turned pleadingly to his attorney at this point, a sense of shock and betrayal on his face. The attorney simply nodded her head, indicating the man should answer yes to the judge's question. Suddenly all became clear to the man. He was admitting to being a criminal and was going to be treated as such. During the procedure a social worker sitting beside me just shook his head. "He's just a dumb old boy that lives out here on the mountain and doesn't know any better," he said. "There's somebody running a meth lab out there that they can't catch, so they're just arresting people to see if they'll tell them anything. His whole family's like that. I've known them a long time." As I looked around the courtroom I realized that his family included the people I'd overheard talking earlier that morning.

The social worker went on to say that the man and his family were "real Appalachians" with a reputation for violence. The police were, in fact, scared of the family and refused to arrest the man without being heavily armed. The man's mother—who'd described the evidence against her son as "hearsay" that "didn't mean shit"—reacted violently to the proceedings, yelling as she left the courthouse that she was going to go home, retrieve her gun, and come back and shoot the people responsible for her son's prosecution. At the next session, after stern warnings from police, she made a public apology to the judge and the court.

The Cases

The cases considered here were all the result of arrests made during an operation in 2003 when a Federal Drug Task Force, in conjunction with local law enforcement, targeted individuals involved in the illegal sale of methamphetamine in Baker County. In each case an informant was used to make what is known in law enforcement parlance as a "controlled buy," a purchase of a "controlled substance" such as methamphetamine overseen by law enforcement officers using a "confidential informant."

A different informant was used in each case, but the procedure they followed was roughly the same. The person was given money and outfitted with a concealed recording device. Then, while being monitored by the officers, the informant approached someone they knew to be a seller of methamphetamine (the target of the operation) to make a purchase. Having made the purchase, the informant then returned the money used and the substance purchased to the overseeing officer(s). These materials, plus the informant's testimony (including the audio recording from the concealed recording device worn during the operation), then became the key pieces of evidence used in the cases to prosecute the person accused of selling the illicit substance. The confidential informants in each case were individuals who had themselves been arrested on drug or alcohol charges (usually minor offenses such as "simple possession" or DUI) and agreed to work with law enforcement officials in the arrest of others in exchange for a reduced sentence. Defense attorneys often used this fact to call into question their credibility as witnesses.

David

The biggest arrest that came from the Drug Task Force's work in the area was that of David Johnson. As mentioned earlier, David had grown up in Baker County, and he and his parents were well known locally. His father owned a small construction company that did much of the work building and repairing houses in the area. His mother worked at Annie's, where one resident estimated that half of the town ate at least one meal on a daily basis. A search of David's residence turned up more than $10,000 in cash in a small safe, and a subsequent search of his truck revealed plastic bags containing a white substance, which laboratory analysis confirmed was methamphetamine.

This was the first major drug arrest in Baker County, and the news brought a strong reaction from the community. A petition was presented at the courthouse containing more than one hundred signatures demanding a harsh sentence:

> We the undersigned on the matter of illegal drugs (controlled substances) either selling or manufacturing, feel that any defendant that has been given due process of law, tried, and convicted by a jury of his peers should be prosecuted to the fullest extent of the law. This type of behavior creates a hazard to the community, which cannot and will not be tolerated!

The judge also received numerous letters. A formal letter from the Board of Education echoed the sentiment expressed in the petition:

> The Baker County Board of Education shares the community's concerns about drug abuse and supports the Law Enforcement officials in their efforts to address this problem. We accept the challenge to provide information and education that will allow our students to make good decisions. The Board believes that those who use illegal drugs need treatment, while those who deal in drugs that can destroy the lives of our young people should suffer the consequences of their behavior.

The courtroom was "standing room only" on the day David's trial began. David's court-appointed attorney raised questions about the way in which the evidence was gathered. Did the police get the permission of the owner to use his property to stage the buys? Was it lawful for one of the officers to hide in the vehicle? The lawyer also attempted to discredit the informant: Was he, a drug user and dealer himself who had made a deal with the sheriff's department, a reliable witness?

The county prosecutor maintained that there was nothing wrong with the way the evidence was gathered, and then charged that the defense attorney was trying to get the case thrown out on legal technicalities when "everyone knew" David was a drug dealer. As a drug dealer he was a threat to the community, and the community (represented by the jury) as well as the state (represented by the prosecutor and the judge) had to protect themselves by finding him guilty and imposing a harsh penalty, both as a punishment for the specific crimes committed and as a warning to other drug dealers in the area.

In his closing argument, the defense attorney again questioned the way in which the evidence was gathered (and by implication the federal, state, and local law enforcement officers involved) and the reliability of the informant (a local boy who had also been involved in dealing drugs and had turned against someone he had known and trusted all his life). He also pitted the community against the state by reminding the jury that it was the state's responsibility to prove David's guilt.

The prosecuting attorney countered these arguments by emphasizing the importance of the jury's decision for the protection of the community. The jury, he said, was in fact acting on behalf of the community, and to return a "not guilty" verdict would be to betray the work of the good citizens (like the members of the sheriff's department) and reward the bad (drug dealers like David):

This is an important case, ladies and gentlemen of the jury, very important, because when we leave here today, you're going to make a difference. It's going to make a difference as to what happens out in this community and that difference is going to be for the better or it's going to be for the worse. And we're going to know when we leave here . . . whether or not this evidence of this Defendant, who came in here with the drug money, the drugs . . . can be let off with that evidence against him. It is an important, important case, ladies and gentlemen. You've heard the evidence and [the defense attorney] gets up here and tries to chastise these officers, who did a good job. They were laying in the leaves in the middle of the night, who were hid in a vehicle, who were doing what it takes to keep this stuff off the streets. Keep this money that should be used to take care of kids for lunch money and other things that's important, keep it from being used for purchase of $900.00 worth of methamphetamine.

The jury returned a guilty verdict on three of the five counts for which David had been indicted: two felony charges of delivery of a Schedule II controlled substance, and possession of a controlled substance, a misdemeanor. Each of the felony convictions carried one-to-five-year sentence and a fine of up to $15,000.

David was not sentenced for another three months, during which time he was required to undergo a sixty-day psychological evaluation. In addition, the probation officer for the county had to conduct her own pre-sentence investigation. On the day of the sentencing hearing, David's attorney requested a probated sentence, based on time served and the sixty-day evaluation, as well as his client's willingness to undergo drug abuse counseling and anger-management training:

> I believe he has sincerely learned from his conviction and incarceration. I would tell the Court what he told me at one point . . . before he was convicted that after two or three days in the regional jail he could not understand why anyone would ever want to break a law, another law or anything, that was sufficient for him to never want to go back there.

The attorney asked further that if the court decided against granting probation, David be sent to a prison that could provide him with counseling.

The county prosecutor replied by submitting the petition and the letter from the Board of Education saying, "I filed that to show that there is community support for stiff punishment for these types of offenses."

Your Honor, I think the Court's aware of the problem that this community has had with methamphetamine in the past few years. . . . And the Court has been able to see that in the recent cases that's come before the Court; and the Court's well aware of the effect that we've had as a result of that. And the effect is you have individuals like [the informant] who buys methamphetamine from an individual like the Defendant in this case and then in—because of the high price and the fact that it's so addictive—he keeps some of it and sells it to somebody in order to pay and support his habit. So it's a pyramid, Your Honor, and it's a pyramid that keeps going on and on and on and due to the fact that it's very expensive there's only two ways to do it. You either sell to support your habit or you have to commit some type of criminal offense to support your habit.

David was at the top of the pyramid, he said, supplying individuals involved in other cases that had come before the court, as well as to "children" in the high school. He also questioned David's claim that he was legitimately employed at the time of his arrest, noting the absence of any documents to support the claim, and added that "working people don't have $10,000 in a safe."

And . . . he's going to be in here with . . . the same type of argument. "Well I've learned my lesson, I want probation" . . . . That's the type of argument, Judge, that the Court hears in every case, but the Court needs to take a look at . . . the significance of this case and impose a harsh penalty, it's called for.

The judge then turned to David and asked him if he had anything he would like to say "on his own behalf". "Not really," he replied.

Other than what my attorney's mentioned. Yeah. I do not—I mean, I've—I've learned—out of these five months [the time he had spent in jail] I've learned a lot. I want to change—change a lot of things and I've learnt my lesson. Would be—would like to have a second chance.
    "Anything further?" the judge asked.
    "No, Your Honor," David replied.

Then David's mother asked the judge if she could speak. The judge agreed and asked her to come forward.

I'm David's mother and I feel that David has learned a valuable lesson from this . . . [H]e knowed [sic] he has made a mistake and he has wrote and he has told me that he's made a mistake. That he took the wrong road and that if he would get a chance he would get a lot better.

She went on to cast doubt on the testimony that had been given by the prosecuting attorney. She noted that the "child" at the high school David had been accused of selling drugs to had been suspended for stealing the letters off the high school sign; that she had heard he might even have failed drug tests, too (although she admitted that that could just be hearsay); and that the confidential informant who made the buys off of David would "tell anything . . . to save his own skin because [he] was convicted too." She concluded by suggesting that the police spend their time finding more drug dealers instead of "trying to make my son look really bad . . . because I'm sure it wasn't my son who was just doing that [i.e., selling drugs]"

Then David's father spoke. He, too, leveled a retort to the prosecuting attorney, specifically addressing his claim that David had no proof that he had been working two jobs at the time of his arrest. And, in the same way as David's mother had done, he pledged his support for his son and described how he would contribute to his rehabilitation by providing him with steady, full-time employment:

Judge, I would just say that my son has not had a bad upbringing. He has not been a . . . a bad person. He's had . . .he's been brought up to know right from wrong. He knows he messed up and I know that he'll . . . I know that he'll do good. I know that he'll do what's right from here on out; and he has worked for me. I don't . . .[the prosecuting attorney] said that he had not seen nothing for the amount where . . . where he's worked for me, but he has worked for me; and I've got full-time employment for him and I would be more than glad to show him weekly payroll slips or whatever it's going to take because he needs the work. So I think he deserves a chance at probation. He . . . he is not a bad person and that's . . . he deserves a second chance. Thank you, your Honor.

The judge thanked David's parents and then turned back to David. "Mr. Johnson, once again you've now heard not only from your counsel, but from your mother and dad and I would ask you again, Is there anything further that you'd like to say?"

David replied, "Nothing further, Your Honor."

The judge began the sentencing by acknowledging the strong sentiment in the case both for and against David. Those against him were those who knew him only as a "drug dealer" in the abstract, or who were angry because of the money he was so obviously spending. They demanded that the state punish him with a harsh prison sentence. Those supporting him knew him personally and, in the judge's words, had "trust and faith" in him: his parents, relatives, and friends, and his employer. They wanted the state to grant him probation so that he could be returned to the supervision of the community. His father offered to look after him and provide him with a job; his mother offered to provide him with a home and keep him out of trouble and under control. After commenting on the division of opinion in the community, the judge stated that he based the sentence on four things: (1) the seriousness of the offense, (2) the pre-sentence investigation, (3) the sixty-day evaluation, and (4) "the defendant's response, or lack of response" during the trial. Ultimately it was David's lack of personal remorse—his inability to confess his guilt and express his remorse before the court and the community that was the deciding factor:

> My concern through this, this whole matter is the magnitude of the offense and probably more important than that, the lack of responsiveness from you. . . . You made a limited statement, but it's not what I was hoping to hear. . . . I can't take a vote on these matters and, and weigh how many people are for and how many people are against you.

David was given consecutive one-to-five-year sentences for the two felony convictions, and a six-month sentence for the possession conviction, to be served concurrently. No fine was imposed because of the $10,000 that had been confiscated.

The initial response to the decision from the community was positive. The judge received several letters commending him for the way in which the case was handled. With time, however, the community began to have second thoughts. Annie's was the scene of many conversations about the case. Within the year the court was presented with another petition. This one was started by David's mother. It had roughly three hundred signatures, three times that of the previous petition, and included many names that had appeared on the earlier document demanding the harshest possible sentence. The petition began with a paragraph summarizing the crimes for which David was indicted, those for which he was found guilty, and the results of the probation officer's pre-sentence investigation and sixty-day evaluation, both of which recommended probation rather than further incarceration. Noting that David had served 350 days of his sentence, the petition concluded:

We the undersigned feel that David Johnson has served the appropriate time for his crimes and request that his sentence be modified. We the undersigned request that David Johnson's sentences be modified to run concurrently giving David Johnson a sentence of one-to-five years, which will make him eligible for parole after serving one year of incarceration.

We base the request on the following:

1. This was his first offense and he is a young man;
2. He has served almost 1 year in jail and we believe he deserves a second chance;
3. We do not believe he is a threat to our community and Baker County

Having first demanded that the harshest possible sentence be given against this individual, this "drug dealer," an even larger number of community members now demanded that he be released. It is worth noting that the original petition and letters never used David's name but rather used abstract references such as "any defendant tried and convicted by a jury of his peers" or simply "the drug dealers." The second petition characterizes him as a child, in particular a son, a member of the community, someone who has "learned his lesson" and, because of his family's guidance, will likely not make the same mistakes again. The second petition uses David's first and last name in every sentence, a total of twelve times. He is transformed from a "drug dealer" into a person locatable in the community by his name, his age, and his relationships with others. *David* is "not a threat" to the community.

The petition failed to bring about a change in the sentence (one which those state officials involved in the case were always quick to say began with significant public support). David ultimately served two years in the regional jail before being released on parole. He completed his parole in 2007, and as of this writing has managed to successfully reintegrate himself into the community. He has taken up the offers made by his parents during his sentencing hearing: he is working for his father's construction company, living at home with his mother and, so far, "staying out of trouble."

David's trial has been presented in some detail not because it was typical but because it was unique. Of all the cases that resulted from the Federal Drug Task Force's efforts, only David's went to trial. Only David's garnered significant public attention. Only David's prompted the public to become involved, to feel as though they had a stake in the outcome of the proceedings. Thus, in addition to being the highest profile methamphetamine case in the county, it was the only one to generate debate regarding the exercise of state authority in the community. In the rest of the cases, including the next two to be discussed, there was no such public involvement. Nor were there trials. The cases were settled by plea agreement; and the individuals were sentenced amid neither praise nor protest from the public.

Mike and Wanda

Like David Johnson, Mike Auerbach had grown up in Baker County. He held several jobs in and outside of the county, but had trouble finding steady employment in the region. This was largely due to cycles in the regional poultry industry that led to the opening and closing of three different processing plants in a ten-year period. Thus he had never left a job voluntarily, but only when a plant closure caused him to be laid off.

Mike's primary occupation was driving trucks, and it was while he was working as a truck driver that he began using meth. He was divorced when he met Wanda, who was also divorced, and they began living together. Both were addicted to methamphetamine. Like David, they used their contacts in Virginia to supply them with enough meth to both use and sell, but they sold only enough to meet their living expenses and support their habits. They were both in their forties at the time of their arrest. Mike had few remaining family connections in the county, and Wanda, who was from Virginia, had none. They lived alone and isolated except for those with whom they sold and used meth.

Wanda did most of the selling. Their customers consisted of a small group of personal acquaintances. Mike occasionally drove Wanda to the sales and assisted in other ways at their home. During one of the buys arranged by the sheriff's department, Mike offered the buyer a twist tie for the baggie that contained the meth. When the buyer accepted, Mike took the bag from his hand, put a twist tie around it, and gave it back to him. This made him an accomplice, and he, like Wanda, was indicted for possession with intent to deliver.

Wanda and Mike opted for a plea agreement rather than going to trial. They agreed to plead guilty to two counts of Delivery of a Schedule II Controlled Substance. In exchange, the remaining charges were dropped. Sentencing, of course, was left up to the court.

The sentencing hearing took place roughly six months after the plea agreement was reached. During this time the two did everything they could to demonstrate to the court that they were trying to make changes in their lives. Within a month of their arraignment they were married. They began attending the local Seventh Day Adventist Church and became increasingly involved in its activities. Both attended Alcoholics Anonymous and Narcotics Anonymous meetings on a regular basis. Mike even began outpatient substance-abuse treatment at the local mental health clinic.

Their efforts yielded letters of support written to the judge from those who were working with them. Mike's AA sponsor and substance-abuse counselor both wrote brief letters describing how well he had done in their programs, emphasizing his willingness to take responsibility for his crimes and to make a positive change in his life. The pastor of the church Wanda and Mike attended also wrote a letter. This was particularly noteworthy, as religious leaders in the area were extremely reluctant to embrace any active or explicit role in dealing with drug-related issues. The pastor's letter noted this reluctance, emphasizing that his role was to protect his congregation from drugs and drug dealers, largely by supporting the state's efforts to put drug users and dealers in prison. However, he felt Mike and Wanda provided a unique opportunity that justified making an exception in their case:

> As the pastor of three congregations belonging to a church which promotes a healthy lifestyle free from drugs, alcohol and tobacco products, I would be among the first to suggest locking up people who would influence any of my parishioners or anyone in the community to use illegal substances. However, I see a great opportunity to take advantage of [Wanda and Mike's] own personal desires to be drug-free backed up by church support and governmental threat (probation). As only a small percentage of meth users manage to become freed from their addiction, those that do are quite valuable to our efforts to educate and empower people to remain free of such devastating chemicals.

The crowd at Mike and Wanda's sentencing hearing was substantially smaller than at David's. Since neither had any family or friends there to speak on their behalf, the burden fell on Mike and Wanda themselves to argue for a more lenient sentence. In their statements they noted the letters of support from their pastor and counselors. They emphasized that the addiction with which they both struggled was at the root of their crimes, and drew attention to the significant progress they had made toward recovery through their AA and NA participation, as well as their newfound religious conviction. And if David had too little to say at the time of his sentencing, it appears Wanda had too much, offering an overly "extravagant" (Boon 1999) account of her experience since being arrested. Her remarks to the judge were impassioned and extensive:

While I was first incarcerated . . . I got ahold of this book. This book is written by a guy named Steve Box from Missouri. The title is, "Meth Equals Sorcery, Know the Truth." He himself was addicted to meth and went through so many of the same things I went through. To read this book was almost a reflection of myself in the mirror. I realized how important this book was too. I contacted the author directly and at first I tried to get this book through Books-A-Million. They—three months they couldn't get it—so finally I contacted the author himself, who then started shipping me them twenty at a time. I have handed out thirty-six. I still have four left. I've handed out two to the public library here in town, two to the high school library, two to the counselors at the high school, one to the Sheriff's Office, one to the Probation Office here at the courthouse. I'm going to go ahead and let my attorneys take this one, that's how important I think this book is to further anyone else who may be in my situation in the future. This book has been one of the first stepping-stones to my recovery.

She continued her statement for some time, coming at last to the role played by her involvement in a twelve-step program in her personal transformation:

At first I thought the twelve-step program would be steps you do and be done with it. You get through those twelve steps and you're healed and you're cured. Well it's not the fact. The fact of the matter is that NA, the twelve-step program, is a way of life. The twelve steps are a way of life and I intend from this day forward and one day at a time to live my life as a twelve-step program.

Although the themes were somewhat different than those which David's parents used in his defense, the emphasis was still the same: the law has served its purpose, and the proper action at this point is for the accused to be released to the care and instruction of nonlegal institutional domains.

The prosecuting attorney, however, was reluctant to acknowledge such arguments, and his response was significantly more concise. He simply reminded the court of the original offense that had been committed, noting that, "When people sell methamphetamine it's being bought and the result's the same, whether it's to support their habit or whether it's for financial gain; and most of the time it is to support people's habits." This statement echoed the view often expressed by sheriff's deputies and police officers on the subject of treatment versus incarceration in the case of methamphetamine use.

For most the question was irrelevant because, as one deputy put it, "In the eyes of the law the crime's the same: the motivation behind it doesn't make a difference."

After questioning the relevance of Wanda's addiction to the sentencing process, the prosecutor then went on to call into question the sincerity of Wanda's confession, saying that she had pled guilty to possession of meth-amphetamine three years earlier in another state, a charge which she had not revealed either to the court, the state or her attorneys. This prompted a long, heated response from Wanda's attorneys, in which they stated that this was the first time they had heard this information and that it was irrelevant to the matter at hand, which was focused on more recent charges in a differ-ent state. One attorney went on to criticize the state's position as "everybody ought to be locked up."

But the attorneys' efforts, as well as Wanda and Mike's own work at per-sonal transformation through religious, familial, and psychological means was ultimately to no avail. The judge put significant weight on the fact that Wanda had not revealed her previous charge and that, irrespective of their current efforts, both had admitted to being guilty of selling methamphet-amine. That offense required punishment. He denied the request for proba-tion, summarizing the reasoning behind the sentence in this way:

> The nature of the offense, the pervasiveness of drugs in our society, and the *protection of our society*; and I would also say, since the Bible has been quoted here today—and I think improperly—if I am throwing stones at her, then so be it. But I would say to you that Paul [the apostle] was incar-cerated, but yet he was free and so when you say that you're responsible for what you've done, don't say that you're responsible "if I get probation." The responsibility goes further than that. The Statute by our legislature indi-cates what the sentence is to be for someone who commits the crime that you have and *I'm just enforcing the statute*. (emphasis added)

Mike received the same prison sentence that David did—two one-to-five-year terms, to run consecutively. Wanda, because of her previous conviction, received a longer sentence.

Ties to the community had much less impact for Mike and Wanda than for David Johnson. The only members of the community that wrote or peti-tioned the court on their behalf were those they sought out through their own personal efforts, and they were professional people and religious leaders who had their own special place in the local culture. The judge had no community sentiment to take into account in this instance except for the general concern about meth use. He chose to make his decision on the basis of the law ("I'm just enforcing the statute") *and* his perception of the threat posed by methamphetamine to the community ("the pervasiveness of drugs in our society, and the protection of our society"). He therefore did not have to pass judgment on whether Mike and Wanda were sincere in their efforts to change their lives, or would be able to do so. He was merely the dispassionate instrument of the impersonal state, and there was no crowd of people from the community watching carefully to second-guess his decision.

While the results of the two legal proceedings appear to be similar, the post-incarceration stories are not. Unlike David, Mike and Wanda had no social network to lean on as they attempted to put their lives back together. Mike was eventually released on probation. In the regular appearances he had to make to the probation officer at the courthouse he slowly gained a certain degree of respect from those who worked there. He continued to emphasize his addiction and the difficulties it presented, but also the significant personal work—both religious and therapeutic—in which he remained engaged as he learned to live with it. Thus it was only through a full identification with his addiction after having served time for the crimes related to it that Mike was able to begin to make a place for himself in the community. However, the desirability of occupying that place—an ex-convict and a drug addict—in a community as small as Baker County remains an open question.

Wanda's future was even more uncertain. She hoped to eventually be released on probation, and planned to return to Baker County to live with Mike. She, like Mike, remained deeply religious. Whether this was enough to secure a place for her in the community was difficult to predict.

Justin and Christie

The same themes run through a third case, that of Justin and Christie Stokes. Christie and Justin were both in their late twenties when they were arrested for possession of methamphetamine with intent to deliver. As with Wanda and Mike Auerbach, it was Justin who was selling methamphetamine, while Christie was a user and essentially tacit accomplice. They were arrested as part of the same Federal Drug Task Force operation that had netted David, Mike, and Wanda. As with the other two cases, a confidential informant wore a wire and made a series of controlled buys of methamphetamine from Justin. During one of the buys, Christie handed the baggie containing the meth to the informant, thereby implicating her directly in the crime. They were arrested, indicted, and tried as co-defendants. They were charged with one count of possession of methamphetamine with intent to deliver, and one count of conspiracy to commit an offense against the state of West Virginia. The confidential informant in the case was Christie's cousin.

Christie was a relative outsider in the community. She was born in Virginia but lived in multiple states with her mother, who moved frequently. She moved to Baker County from Maryland with her mother when she was a teenager. In her late twenties she married Justin, an old friend from high school. This was her second marriage and third significant relationship. At the time she had four children, two with her first husband, and two with a man she lived with for a number of years but never married.

Justin and Christie had both been using methamphetamine regularly when they were married. Like many men his age, Justin worked in the poultry plants that provided the primary employment opportunity in the area. He worked in various areas of the plant, on the "live hang" floor where (in this case) chickens were hung upside down by their feet on a conveyer belt-like apparatus to be sent through the machine that slaughtered them; in the food preparation area where processed chickens were partially cooked so that consumers could simply reheat them; and as a truck driver, making trips from the plant to various distribution centers in the area. It was in the context of working at the plant, often for long hours at tasks that were to different degrees tedious, repetitive, and unpleasant, that Justin was introduced to methamphetamine.

Justin, like many others who began using meth at work, described the plant as a haven for drug use of all kinds. Most of the people with whom he worked used some kind of substance and meth was particularly popular. He told stories of female employees who would "turn tricks" in the factory parking lot to get it, as well as a time when a manager caught him using but instead of punishing him, simply made Justin share with him. According to Justin the administrators were well aware of how prevalent drugs were at the plant, but turned a blind eye because drug use—particularly methamphetamine use—enhanced productivity. Indeed, much of the initial attractiveness of meth to men and women in Justin's situation was that it actually increased their productivity: it made them more alert and energetic, able to work extra shifts, and thereby earn more money. At the same time, the pleasurable sensation meth produced provided a distraction from the feelings of boredom and disgust that often accompanied work at the plant, while also masking the physical pain that could result from frequent performance of repetitive, difficult, and dangerous duties.

Like many users of methamphetamine, Justin quickly became involved with its distribution and circulation. This he did as a means of generating extra income to offset the cost of his own habit. From contacts he made in the poultry processing plant where he worked, as well as by making it on his own, Justin began selling on a small scale. Most of the selling he did was to people he knew in Virginia and West Virginia—family members and close friends primarily. In this way Justin was able to cut the cost of his own use, while likewise providing a service to his close acquaintances.

Justin continued using and selling in this manner for a number of years. As selling methamphetamine was never his primary means of generating income, Justin was able to keep his operation small. Christie began using with Justin. Like Mike Auerbach, she only tacitly colluded in Justin's small-scale operation. And much of this was simply because she shared an apartment with Justin and was often around when he would make sales. This is precisely what happened the night the confidential informant met up with Justin and Christie to make what would ultimately come to be the purchase that led to their arrest and prosecution.

The confidential informant in this case was Christie's cousin, Randy. Unbeknown to either Justin or Christie, he had been arrested on a DUI charge, his second. This carried a minimum sentence of six months in jail. To avoid being incarcerated, Randy agreed to assist police in gathering evidence against his methamphetamine dealer (in this case, Justin). Following standard procedure Randy wore the concealed recording device, met with Christie and Justin, and purchased an incriminating amount of methamphetamine.

On their own, Justin and Christie were already outsiders in the community, and their marriage only seemed to reinforce this status. While Justin and his family were longtime residents of the community ("Stokes" is a common last name in the area), their family was not well regarded. Justin attributed this to the fact that he and his family were "colored," one of the few African American families in the entire county. The fact that they were relatively poor, known to be heavy drinkers, and rumored to be involved in the drug trade only served to further alienate them. Moreover, it belied the fact that Justin was, by his own account, such a hard worker, a point that was a great source of pride and the central characteristic of his own sense of self.

Christie had no close family connections in the community beyond her mother, with whom she no longer had a relationship, and distant cousins, one of whom aided the police in her arrest. She had trouble in high school and ultimately dropped out to get married to her first husband. She had known Justin at the time, but the two did not become involved until after Christie's two other relationships ended. The men in each case obtained custody of the children, the one moving to Texas with the two older children, the other moving to Virginia with the two younger. Thus Christie was alone when she married Justin, with all of her immediate family members other than her mother living in other parts of the country.

As with Wanda and Mike, no one wrote letters on either Justin or Christie's behalf. The poor light in which their families were viewed made them more liabilities than assets in the context of the court proceedings. Unable to afford bond, both went to the regional jail where they remained for the duration of their trial. During this time they had no access to treatment resources other than the weekly AA meeting. Incarcerated and in different parts of the jail, they were unable to make the kinds of institutional connections, such as with church groups or counseling facilities, that Mike and Wanda were able to. Thus as they went to trial, they had nothing with which to identify themselves in the context of the community that would stand in the way of the state's attempts to define them as criminals. Even Justin's status as a hard and reliable worker at the poultry plant was compromised because it was at work that his use of methamphetamine had begun.

Both Justin and Christie agreed to plead guilty to one count of possession of methamphetamine with intent to deliver. In exchange, the conspiracy charge was dropped. Both returned to the regional jail for a number of months before being transferred to different state prisons. Working toward obtaining probation, Christie's lawyer recommended that she get a divorce from Justin, stating that this would help her case. The fact that she was white and he was black bothered people, according to the lawyer. Plus, she could make a pretty good case that Justin was the one doing all of the selling whereas she was just there. Divorcing Justin would thus also show that she was trying to distance herself from drugs. This recommendation resonated with the psychological evaluation carried out at the regional jail that concluded: "We believe [Christie's] chance of success on probation is poor if she remains in a relationship with her husband."

For these and other reasons Christie filed for divorce from Justin from the regional jail six months into her sentence. Ultimately her request for probation was granted after she had served nine months of her one-to-five-year sentence. In an interview, Christie said she remembered the judge seeming pleased when she told him that she had gotten a divorce from Justin and no longer carried the last name of Stokes. Christie successfully served the rest of her sentence on probation.

Justin was also eventually released on probation. He expressed sadness and anger that Christie had filed for divorce while they were both in jail. Still, he continued to work in the poultry industry in the area. He worked as much as possible, just as before. And though he claimed that he had neither used nor sold methamphetamine since he was arrested, there was deep suspicion among employees at the courthouse, as well as with Christie, that he was using again, largely because Justin had lost a significant amount of weight since his release from prison. Justin was aware of these rumors, but shrugged them off saying that his weight loss was just the result of a new healthy lifestyle he had adopted where he drank only water or tea, and ate only salads or yogurt. Also the fact that he worked all the time and lifted weights at home helped. "You can drop a lot of weight like that," he told me.

Justin and Christie were extending significant effort to return to their marginal place in the community, a situation that was hardly improved by the stigma of having been convicted of a crime. Justin worked as much as possible and rarely left the house he lived in by himself on top of the mountain. Christie developed a relationship with a new man. They began living together, first in a trailer and then in a house in another part of the county. Her criminal record made it nearly impossible to find work, as no one wanted to hire someone who had been convicted of a felony and spent time incarcerated, especially on a drug violation. Health problems kept her from working at the poultry plant—one of the few employers willing to take on ex-convicts—but were not significant enough to earn her disability status with the state. She earned money by working informally in the underground economy cleaning houses and performing other chores for neighbors. She was also taking classes on-line to get a college degree (having earned her GED while incarcerated). Ironically, from her perspective, she had chosen to major in criminal justice.

The three cases considered here demonstrate how the state used the prosecution of methamphetamine offenders as part of the effort to establish its own legitimacy. The reactions to David Johnson's arrest demonstrate the strong negative feelings toward "drug dealers" that were present in the community. When David's case was framed abstractly, as the prosecution of a drug dealer, it enjoyed significant public support. However, David's deep local ties cast a shadow over the proceedings and ultimately provided the means through which to challenge the state's sentence—and thus, by extension, the legitimacy of its authority.

The prosecution of Wanda and Mike Auerbach and Christie and Justin Stokes did not spark the same kind of public debate over the state's prosecution of drug dealers. Like David Johnson, there was significant public approval of using strong punitive sanctions, given their status as dealers of methamphetamine, and their prosecution went unchallenged by the public, thereby giving tacit recognition of legitimacy for the state's actions. Furthermore, the punishment of these marginal members of the community simply worked to reinforce their marginality. Here we see an example of how the state uses possession offenses to legitimize its authority and activities. Drug dealers are figures for whom there is little if any public sympathy, whose actions are typically seen as destructive and threatening. As such, they may be prosecuted with little protest. The prosecution of drug dealers who are also marginal members of their communities generates even less debate. Strong institutional incentives have developed, therefore, to target these types of offenders, as their prosecution is very effective in establishing the state's legitimacy in the public eye. The impact of this practice on the lives of those prosecuted is the subject of the next chapter.

6

"What Do You Do with Them?"

A striking feature of my research was the pessimistic light in which those given the task of dealing directly with the methamphetamine problem (police, probation officers, public health workers, judges, etc.) viewed their efforts. I asked Frank Fields, a state trooper who spent two years working exclusively on drug-related cases, if he thought what he and his fellow officers were doing was having any effect. He smiled slightly and shook his head no. "All we can do is try and contain it," he said. "But we'll never get rid of it."

Daryl Montgomery, a sheriff's deputy who had carried out undercover drug investigations for two years as part of a Federal Drug Task Force, echoed this sentiment. After explaining in detail all he had done to locate and arrest local methamphetamine dealers, he sighed, and with a slight grin wistfully concluded, "Yeah, but we'll never win the war. We're just a nation of drug users."

Perhaps the most telling comment came during an early interview I conducted with Rose Hinkle, a probation officer whose caseload had doubled with the rise of methamphetamine use in the area. She lamented meth's availability and addictiveness, describing person after person who had ended up sitting in her office because of their involvement with meth. "Meth is impossible," she said, shaking her head wearily. "*What do you do with them?*"

Comments such as these occurred every time I spoke with someone whose job involved dealing directly with methamphetamine. For them the enormity of the drug problem, and the failure of existing policies and practices to adequately address it, was not a matter of opinion but experience. And yet, something had to be and was being done with meth users who became embroiled in the criminal justice system.

On the surface, what was being done appeared rather straightforward: low-level users and dealers, such as those targeted by the Federal Drug Task Force, were arrested for crimes related to their methamphetamine use. Most pled guilty to their crimes as part of a plea agreement and were sent to jail where they served the minimum time the legal statute would allow (typically between one and four years, depending on the charges). They were then released on probation, where they would remain until they completed their sentence (five to ten years or more), or violated their probation and were returned to jail.

The straightforwardness of this process (and the consistent pattern of enforcement) masked a deeper ambiguity at the heart of its administration, however: What was it *for*? What was the objective in processing convicted meth offenders this way? Were convicted meth offenders simply being punished for their crimes as required by the dictates of legal statutes? Were they there to be changed through programs aimed at their rehabilitation? Or were they simply being sequestered for the protection of the rest of the population?

The uncertainty surrounding contemporary punishment practices has become endemic to the U.S. criminal justice system and has received significant academic attention (Garland 2001; Simon 1993). Notably, this uncertainty has arisen as state and federal prison systems have undergone decades of unprecedented expansion. Thus it would seem that the perceived need for punishment, particularly through incarceration, has grown as its meaning and purpose have become more ambiguous.

As a means of mitigating this ambiguity, contemporary criminal justice administrators have come to rely heavily on clinical knowledge from the psychological, criminological, and social work fields. This clinical knowledge generates information about the particular risks an individual offender poses, as well as their specific needs for rehabilitation, and provides recommendations (or at least scenarios) about how a particular subject would likely respond to different forms of punishment.

Drug offenders are primary candidates for this kind of clinically infused form of punishment. Most drug offenders are considered addicts and are understood to suffer from a disease that drives their criminality. They are likewise understood to be embroiled in pathological milieus, and involved in problematic relationships with individuals who have a higher propensity toward criminality. This clinical knowledge about the nature of drug use and addiction takes on forensic significance in the case of detection and prosecution. It is then re-clinicalized for purposes of sentencing, and considered as one factor among many in the subject's broader "risk/needs" profile (Hannah-Moffat 2005). Punishment finds, if not its meaning, then at least its justification in its use as part of a more general intervention strategy intended to transform the subject through targeted interventions into various aspects of their life, most of which have only an indirect relationship to the crime for which they were arrested and convicted.

This scenario has much in common with that described by Michel Foucault in *Discipline and Punish*. Foucault analyzed the transformation of the European juridical system as it moved progressively from a focus on the crime as the object of concern to a focus on the criminal. In particular, he charts the gradual process by which, in order to establish the "truth of the crime," it increasingly became necessary to establish the "truth" of the criminal. "[J]udges," Foucault writes, "have gradually, by means of a process that goes back very far indeed, taken to judging something other than crimes, namely, the 'soul' of the criminal" (Foucault 1995, 19).

To this end Foucault notes how the modern judge is "not alone in judging." Rather, the judge is merely one node in a wider "scientifico-legal complex" that cumulatively determines the fate of the condemned. He states:

> Throughout the penal procedure and the implementation of the sentence there swarms a whole series of subsidiary authorities. Small-scale legal systems and parallel judges have multiplied around the principal judgment: psychiatric or psychological experts, magistrates concerned with the implementation of sentences, educationalists, members of the prison service, all fragment the legal power to punish. . . . The whole machinery that has been developing for years around the implementation of sentences, and their adjustment to individuals, creates a proliferation of the authorities of judicial decision-making, and extends its power of decision well beyond the sentence. (Foucault 1995, 21)

For Foucault the emergence of these "parallel judges," whose expert authority is grounded not in the law but in science, have become not simply a supplement to but the foundation of the juridical system. "Today," he writes, "criminal justice functions and justifies itself only by this perpetual reference to something other than itself, by this unceasing reinscription in non-juridical systems" (ibid., 22). This shift has fundamentally altered the application of punishment such that the objective is no longer "to punish the offence, but to supervise the individual, to neutralize his dangerous state of mind, to alter his criminal tendencies, and to continue even when this change has been achieved" (ibid., 18).

On the surface, the use of clinical knowledge in the sentencing and punishment of meth offenders would seem to reflect precisely Foucault's account of the shift in punishment from the crime to the criminal, the offense to the offender. Certainly the use of scientific and clinical knowledge and practice factors heavily into the sentencing process, determining in many ways the particular punishment that the individual receives (Rose 2007; Rhodes 2004; Simon 1993). There are two significant differences, however. The first has to do with the profound lack of confidence that judges and other members of the criminal justice system had in the ability of these techniques to produce the kind of "docile body" that Foucault describes (Foucault 1995). At best, what these clinical evaluations revealed was the inability of available disciplinary technologies to effect the moral comportment of the addicted criminal. That is, the "soul" of the criminal revealed by these evaluations appeared to be more than the juridical system could handle. Thus, while psychological evaluations might indeed reveal the "truth" of the criminal, this revelation did more to confound the juridical system than embolden it, for it further dimmed the prospects that any kind of punishment would be effective in relieving the individual of their addiction or preventing them from engaging in any future criminality.

The second reason has to do with the effect of such punishment practices on meth offenders themselves. In Foucault's account, the endpoint of modern punishment is "normalization" (Foucault 1995, 20–21). But it was hardly normalization that was taking place here. As legal professionals were quick to tell me, the system rarely worked for drug offenders, whose addiction was such that they inevitably re-offended and were returned to jail or prison. For those who were able to manage themselves in such a way as to avoid re-incarceration, their prosecution continued to have lingering effects that maintained their marginalization even as they conformed to the dictates of their punishment. This was because their prosecution—and the series of evaluations that went with it—fundamentally altered the narrative conditions under which they could give an account of themselves, a transformation that likewise tended to marginalize them within the local community (Butler 1995).

The clinical evaluations used by the criminal justice system fed into this predicament as they created both a catalog and a narrative of criminal identity with which the subject was to identify. Although this identification was never complete, the person had to at least nominally inhabit this identity if they were to have any kind of success in the system. This created a "can't win" scenario for the convicted person. While acquiescing to this narrative was necessary for their rehabilitation, the wider effect was to deepen their marginalization.

Thus, pace Foucault, we might think of this as the process of "abnormalization." This process takes place when faith in clinical diagnostics becomes decoupled from faith in clinical treatment. That is, while clinical techniques are still understood to be capable of generating authoritative knowledge about the subject, clinical treatments are viewed pessimistically as incapable of curing the subject—of doing the work of "normalization." In the contemporary criminal justice system, this loss of faith in the power of clinical treatments to cure (i.e., "normalize") offenders has simply deepened the ambiguous meaning of punishment, particularly for drug offenders. In short, it is not normalization but abnormalization that is taking place through the incorporation of clinical knowledge into the juridical task of punishment.

"The Experts Aren't Even Sure What to Do": Efforts at "Habilitation"

Arthur Cravens had been the judge for Baker County for the past thirty years. When we spoke about methamphetamine, he echoed the prevailing sentiments at the courthouse. Methamphetamine was everywhere; and as a result meth-related cases were fixtures in his courtroom. Much of this was to be blamed on meth's addictiveness. "I thought heroin was the most addictive [drug]," he reflected, "But they say meth is even more addictive, that you can be hooked after trying it just once." He paused before adding, with a slight smile, "But then that's what they said about heroin."

Judge Cravens went on to call methamphetamine the "new kid on the block." He compared its rise to that of sex offenders, another criminal type that was flooding the dockets. "Are we seeing more of it only because there are laws against it, so we know to look for it?" he asked thoughtfully.

I asked Judge Cravens if he ever pursued treatment instead of incarceration for drug offenders. "It's not possible for me to sentence someone to treatment," he said, suggesting I was asking the wrong question. The most he could do was delay the actual sentencing so that the person could undergo treatment. Likewise, he could (and often did) require treatment as part of someone's probation even if this amounted to attending a certain number of Alcoholics Anonymous (AA) or Narcotics Anonymous (NA) meetings every week. But even these few options were still difficult to utilize because the local treatment resources beyond the twelve-step programs were limited and expensive. Most of those prosecuted in his court could not even afford their own counsel, much less a treatment program. Thus, even if the judge could sentence someone to treatment, it would ultimately be a pointless gesture in the absence of public funds, which could be used to pay for the individual's participation in the program.

"But even then there are problems," Judge Cravens continued. The primary one was that that existing treatment programs rarely worked. Of those cases he'd overseen in which the offender had been able to participate in some kind of drug treatment program, only a few had successfully stopped using drugs. "Even with the best treatment, people still can't quit," he stated, slightly exasperated. "The experts aren't even sure what to do."

The challenges of dealing with drug offenders on a routine basis, and with little positive result, left Judge Cravens susceptible to the same feelings of pessimism that others at the courthouse felt. "I'd like to think of myself as a grandfather, showing people the right way," Judge Cravens reflected. "But I know that's probably not the case." Part of the problem was that those who appeared in his courtroom had so many problems in their lives it was hard to know where to begin. In drug cases, for instance, the people involved often lived in poverty, were poorly educated, had histories of abuse (mental, physical, sexual), had troubled relationships, were in poor health, and were unemployed or had few job prospects. This made any kind of rehabilitation of the person seem almost impossible. "'Rehabilitation' is probably the wrong word," Judge Cravens continued. "It's really more like 'habilitation'"

Judge Cravens's situation with regard to sentencing drug users was a common but difficult one. He did not have the power legally to sentence anyone to treatment. Nor did he have any publicly funded programs to which he could send someone who needed treatment but could not afford it. On top of that, his own experience requiring offenders to participate in treatment as a condition of their probation was that these programs largely did not work, as the majority of those he required to undergo drug treatment ended up falling back into drug use. This relapse was due in part to the challenges of drug addiction itself, but also because addiction was usually one of many problems the individual was facing, making the challenge of rehabilitating—or in the judge's term "habilitating"—offenders an extremely difficult procedure.

And yet, in making sentencing decisions the judge still openly viewed his role as a kind of wider intervention into the individual offender's life. Thus the purpose of punishment as the judge discussed it was a therapeutic one, aimed less at punishing offenders for the specific crimes they committed than using the individual's prosecution as the pretext for a more general intervention into their life—an effort at "habilitation" or "turning their life around."

Notably, the issue of punishing individuals for their crimes, or protecting the public from criminals, never surfaced in our conversation. In practice, however, these latter concerns inevitably came to the fore, as Judge Cravens had to assume his role, not as a grandfather showing people the right way but as a judge, administering state statutes. To this end, the efforts at "habilitation" Judge Cravens described were re-inscribed in the juridical system as efforts at crime control, a way to prevent the individual from engaging in future criminality.

In determining sentences for convicted offenders, the judge relied heavily on clinical knowledge and practice provided by professionals such as psychologists, probation officers, and counselors. We will explore the formal generation of this clinical knowledge about offenders and its use in punishment in the following section, but first we will examine another context—in my interviews with methamphetamine offenders themselves—in which I encountered such knowledge and its importance in the punishment of drug offenders.

Methamphetamine Addicts and the Limits of "Person-Centered" Interviewing

Over the course of my research I conducted extensive "person-centered" ethnographic interviews with a small cohort of recovering meth users. Through various channels, I was put in contact with individuals in this situation. The cohort was small because most of those I contacted were uninterested in speaking with me. They declined my offer outright or agreed to meet and then never arrived. Follow-up phone calls were rarely returned. The few who did agree to meet would usually only do so once; then they, too, became unreachable.

My experience with Ken Burdette was typical. Ken and I met one Saturday morning in February 2007. A mutual friend, who knew both Ken's story and my research interest in methamphetamine, had introduced us. This was one of the many connections I was able to make only after I had been a resident of the community for an extended period of time. Our friend gave Ken my number, and Ken, generously, called me to set up a time to meet.

Ken arrived in his pickup truck and parked across the street. While Ken and I chatted, I noticed that all of his bottom teeth were missing. I began by explaining that I was an anthropologist doing research on methamphetamine. I emphasized that a crucial element of my research was spending time with people familiar with meth to get their perspective. "So you're living with the monkeys," Ken responded, smiling, but with a hint of derision.

Ken was in his early forties. He had been using methamphetamine for twenty years, and amphetamines (Benzedrine and other forms of speed that have moved in and out of legality for the past century) for even longer. He had worked as a truck driver for most of his life, just like his father. It was through this work that Ken began using amphetamines (again, just like his father). When we met, Ken was working toward recovery. It had been almost a year since he'd used methamphetamine. His alcohol use had increased in that time, such that he now considered himself an alcoholic, too. When we met, it had been almost a month since he'd stopped drinking.

When Ken was thirteen years old, his father died. This event still loomed large in his life, as evidenced by the privileged place it occupied in his narrative. It was the second thing he told me when we began the interview, the first being the fact he'd been born and raised in the area. By his own account he had been "raised in a good Christian family with good work ethics." Ken graduated from high school at eighteen and married the same year. He also bought a house. To support his new wife, pay for his new house, and assume his place as an adult, Ken "pursued the occupation of driving a truck." From the beginning there were "long hours, long trips, long weeks." To cope, Ken started "using bennies [Benzedrine] or pills or whatever to stay awake." Ken had first learned to use pills from his father, in response to the demands of the job. "My dad drove a truck and I seen him, you know, take a few pills every now and then."

Within five years Ken was making weekly runs to California. He was working for one of the poultry processing plants in the area surrounding Baker County. He would leave the plant on Friday evening, drive to California, and return to West Virginia on the following Friday. He would do this two to three times a month, and on the "so-called week off," as Ken put it, he would pick up extra shifts driving short routes within the region (Atlanta, Chattanooga, and other points south). This was the mid-1980s and, as Ken put it, "nobody'd ever even heard the word 'meth.'" But just as Ken was starting to run the California route, the amphetamines he'd become accustomed to using were becoming hard to come by. Methamphetamine was already prominent in California and other parts of the West Coast. Ken was exposed to it on these trips ("there's always something bigger and better") and incorporated it into his existing regimen of amphetamine use. Running this route for close to a decade, Ken witnessed and participated in meth's spread east.

In 1994 Ken caught his wife having an affair with another man, and they divorced. Ken's five-year-old son continued to live with his now ex-wife, and Ken moved in with his mother ("In the same bedroom I growed up in with the same bed and same dresser."). He increased his pace of work to cover the $500 in child support he was now paying, as well as the "$100,000 in negative assets" he acquired when his wife stopped paying the mortgage and accumulated a significant amount of credit card debt. Ken then started hauling cattle from Virginia to Amarillo, Texas. His use of methamphetamine at this time increased, not only to cope with the heavier workload but also to deal with his new predicament. "I was on it bad after my divorce. I used it to do my job, but then it was also due to depression, you know, here you've worked all your life and had that mortgage since you was eighteen. Now you're twenty-eight. I only had five more years [on the mortgage] . . . and come to realize she run up five credit cards and was three months late on the house payment. . . . She has this boyfriend that she's taking care of, so you go and it's become a depression drug."

Ken remarried and assumed more debt to pay for a house that also required a significant amount of work, which he had to do himself. He continued using meth. He would quit periodically, when he got into trouble at work or when his wife threatened to leave, but otherwise he continued with regularity, at times spending between $300 and $500 a week. To pay for this habit he began to "move a bit" on his routes, transporting from west to east. Finally his wife threatened to leave him and she did, for two days. At that point he decided to seek treatment. He turned to the drug treatment program he'd seen advertised at work. "So I walked in [and] told the manager, I said, I told him right to his face, 'I have a drug problem. According to the sign out here on the wall you can get me help and me not lose my job.'"

The company enrolled Ken in substance-abuse counseling at a state mental health clinic in a neighboring county. He was drug tested at least four times a week and had to attend at least two AA meetings a week. He had to receive proof of his attendance at the meetings by getting the director to sign a paper. "[Y]ou needed the initiative, you need to have that little pressure on you, and it was the kind of pressure my wife couldn't give me, you know what I mean? It was a different pressure."

But even though he saw the pressure it placed on him as necessary part of entering recovery, he acknowledged it came at a price. "[O]nce you acknowledge yourself as a user," Ken said, "to me its been like a scarlet letter. . . . [Y]ou seem to always be marked." Ken had even quit his job just a month before our conversation. "I just got, I been a test subject for the big industry which, I kept my job, but I got tired of being a subject." In other words, the prevalence of drug testing soured him to the treatment experience.

This experience recurred again and again. Ken had actually attempted to enter treatment on his own, outside of the work program. He had inquired at the local mental health clinic, which was a strictly outpatient facility, as to where or how he could receive drug treatment. He went three different times and was told that he needed to go to the emergency room of the hospital and be admitted. A doctor would need to evaluate him and then he would need to call the sheriff.

Ken bristled at the whole scenario. He was understandably reticent to involve the sheriff, given that his drug habit was an illegal activity. But he was also resentful of having to go to the hospital and be evaluated. "I'm not crazy. *I got a drug problem. . . .* You want my evaluation? I'm spending $300 to $500 a week on methamphetamines. Now, *do I have a drug problem?* I'm a month behind on my mortgage because I used my mortgage payment to buy meth. Now, *do I have a drug problem?* I got people calling me or sitting at my house, midnight to two o'clock in the morning we're doing lines off my bar. Do I need to see a doctor, pay him thousands of dollars emergency room visit?"

Ken eventually did enroll in an outpatient treatment program at the mental health clinic after he had done a more extensive inpatient program. But he still found this experience frustrating. He was particularly critical of one of the counselors there, a woman named Shirley Williams.

> "Now what about your experience down at the mental health center? You said that wasn't too good," I asked.
> "Yeah, they give you little papers to take home and do," Ken responded. "Ms. Williams discussed things with me, *sort of like you are, psychoanalyzing, probing me.*"

Ken's comment at this point in the interview revealed the structural similarity between my own person-centered ethnographic interviewing ("psychoanalyzing, probing") and the clinical interviews he had undergone as part of his forays into the world of addiction therapeutics. In other words, I was not the first professional to ask Ken to give an account of himself as an addict, to lay bare his history of drug use. My desire to know the intimate details of his addiction and its place in his wider personal milieu was expressed through my questions about his family, his work, his history of meth use, and so forth. Such questions deeply resembled the kind of clinical interviews that I later learned Ken and others were subject to as part of their participation in addiction treatment programs. For Ken, participating in these programs meant rehearsing details of his life and assigning them a certain value, either as a positive or negative factor relative to his addiction (cf. Carr n.d.).

Ken had no criminal record, but his experiences with methamphetamine had nevertheless made him feel as if he were a criminal:

> "I never was caught, I've never been convicted. [But] I should have been."
> "Why's that?" I asked.

"Oh, there's been times I've been searched and just squeezed out, you know what I mean. . . . It's just in like Arkansas or other states you'd pass through, get caught for speeding, you know, and there's probable cause. And of course when you're riding 80 in a 65 in a tractor and trailer, it just draws suspicion. Or it'd be snowing outside and 10 degrees and [the police officer would ask,] 'Why are you in a T-shirt?' you know; you don't realize it."

Thus Ken's experiences with methamphetamine had created a sense of criminal identity that existed apart from any actual arrest or prosecution—the feeling that he *should have been* convicted, even though he wasn't. This feeling of guilt, in both its legal and affective registers, was part of a more general sense of stigmatization. "[O]nce you acknowledge yourself as a user," Ken said, "to me its been like a scarlet letter. . . . [Y]ou seem to always be marked." Ironically, the emphasis in addiction treatment on acknowledging the history of use seemed to further this sense of marginalization, even as it held out the promise of therapeutic effect. Ken himself struggled with this, as his attempt to "accept responsibility" for his drug addiction was consistently dogged by his awareness of the numerous people in his life who knew about his drug problem and did nothing but look down on him. "I'm not looking for a pat on the back or a party," Ken said, "I just wanna be treated equal. You know what I mean?"

Ken's exposure to the world of addiction therapeutics came through his own initiative. But those who encountered it through the criminal justice system experienced the same sense of marginalization. Indeed, even before they received "treatment" (in the form of counseling, etc.) for addiction, drug offenders underwent an in-depth clinical inquiry. Clinical information, ranging from basic biographical data such as family history to more technical psychological testing, was systematically collected about any offender the judge deemed in need of an evaluation before sentencing. Probation officers, psychologists, and others conducted the interviews and administered an array of psychological tests. Based on this information, these professionals would make formal evaluations of the person's overall health and well-being. To this they would add a sentencing recommendation. These evaluations were sent to the judge, who took it under consideration as he made his own decision regarding the punishment the person should receive for their crime.

The legal code set certain parameters to guide the judge in making a sentencing decision based on the criminal act that the person had committed. The clinical information allowed the judge to make a sentencing decision within these parameters, and tailor it to fit not only the crime but, more importantly, the criminal. This was not simply a therapeutic intervention, or even an example of what has been called "therapeutic justice" (Nolan 2004). This is because the logic and purpose here was still juridical: to neutralize criminals and prevent future crime from happening.

Christie

The experience of Christie Terry provided further insight into how this approach worked. As discussed in the preceding chapter, Christie was prosecuted with her then-husband, Justin Stokes, on methamphetamine charges. By the time I met Christie, she and Justin were divorced. Christie was no longer using his last name (Stokes), but was once again using her maiden name, Terry.

Christie was one of the few recovering methamphetamine users with whom I was able to maintain any form of consistent contact, though even she became withdrawn and unreachable at times. When I first met her it was January and she was recently single. The man with whom she had been living had left her shortly before Christmas to return to his wife and teenage daughter in Alabama. Christie told me later that the day he left, she had attempted to kill herself, a fact which she let fall so casually in our conversation it took a moment for the meaning of her words to register. I assumed at the time that the frankness and nonchalance with which she informed me of her suicide attempt was her way of being dramatic. But I wonder now if it had more to do with the assumption that I would not be surprised or would not care.

The first time I met Christie was at the courthouse in Baker County. I was there examining court records when the probation officer, Rose Hinkle, came by and said, "There's someone here that you should meet." A small woman with long brown hair wearing jeans, glasses, and a bright blue sweatshirt was standing somewhat shyly behind her. She extended her hand and introduced herself. The terms of Christie's probation required that she meet monthly with the county probation officer, where she would go over the status of her case. At these meetings, conversations focused on Christie's efforts to maintain compliance with the terms of her probation. She discussed her ongoing efforts to find work in the area, provided proof she was attending AA meetings, made payments (such as she could afford) toward the outstanding balance on her court fees, and took a drug test (which she was required to pay for) to show she was not using alcohol or illegal drugs. In addition, she discussed what was happening in her personal life, being careful to omit any details that might cause the probation officer to revoke her probation.

Christie enjoyed speaking with the probation officer and considered her a friend (the two had actually gone to high school together). However, she resented having to make the monthly trips to the courthouse. Her driver's license had been revoked for failure to pay child support in Pennsylvania three years previously, and so she had to find someone to drive her to the courthouse. She consistently had trouble finding employment ("no one wants to hire a felon"), and so each meeting held the possibility that she would be returned to prison for violation of her probation. Finally, there was the cost and embarrassment of having to take the drug test, and the possibility that it might come back positive—even though Christie was no longer using illegal drugs—triggered by some other substance in her system or by a malfunction of the test itself.

Despite these frustrations, since being released from prison Christie had embraced her situation as a convicted felon, (recovering) addict, and probationer. She began to speak regularly at the high school, sharing her story with students in the health education class. Christie felt it was important for people to hear from someone who had actually gone through (and was still going through) drug addiction and its consequences. Indeed, Christie felt a certain calling to share her story with as many people as possible. It was this conviction that brought Rose to introduce Christie to me.

Rose returned to her office, and Christie sat down across from me at the table. Stacks of file folders sat between us. Christie had been on her way out to smoke, and she continued to hold onto her cigarette, rolling it back and forth in her hands. I explained a little bit about my research and my interest in hearing her story. Christie nodded. She began by telling me that this visit to the probation officer was not her normal monthly visit. She had had to make a special trip so that the probation officer could do an additional drug test. Christie had started a new job at the poultry processing plant in a neighboring county (roughly an hour from where Christie lived). She had had to take a drug test as part of her application for employment. The test came back positive for PCP (a substance Christie claimed never to have used). The plant would not hire Christie until she passed her drug test. They offered to send her urine sample to a lab where a more detailed test could be conducted, but that would cost Christie $100. The probation officer could do it for $30, and that was why she was there.

Christie then began to tell me her recovery story. She said she came from an alcoholic family and started using alcohol herself at an early age. She switched to drugs, meth specifically, when she was twenty-seven. Christie said she became addicted to meth after the first time she used it. I asked why she thought she had become addicted so quickly. Christie said it was because of the energy meth gave her, and the fact that it made all of her cares go away. As a result of her addiction, Christie's meth use increased quickly, from half an ounce per day to two- to three "8-balls" a day (an 8-ball typically equals one-eighth of an ounce). Her use was such that, eventually, she would not get out of bed unless she was high.

Meth was a terrible drug, according to Christie; it had had a devastating impact on her life. Besides her incarceration, she expressed the deepest amount of regret for the impact it had on her children (she has four boys who were, at the time, ages fifteen, thirteen, ten, and seven). Once, she told me, she stayed up four to five days on meth. She fell asleep while she was driving, with her kids in the car. She woke up to the sound of the gravel under her wheels as her car began to veer off the road. Despite such experiences, Christie prided herself on having never used meth in front of her kids. She was thirty-three and had been sober for three years.

Christie said that her involvement in AA had been a significant help. Most importantly it had shown her the need to change her "people, places, and things." She had embraced this directive wholeheartedly. Christie moved from the town where she was living at the time of her arrest to a small trailer in the country. She made new friends, many of whom were also in recovery. Christie had also learned to deal with her daily cravings for meth by avoiding her "triggers" including aluminum foil and ballpoint pens, both of which could be used to smoke meth.

Christie mentioned how much she enjoyed going into the high school every year to tell her story. She had had the idea of sharing her story with kids while she was incarcerated. Christie offered to type up a copy of the presentation. She gave me her telephone number and I promised to be in touch.

Pre-Sentence Evaluations

I was already familiar with Christie's case from my work in the archives at the courthouse. Christie's case file contained information about her crime and conviction, detailed biographical information, and a series of clinical evaluations conducted by officials within the criminal justice system, including the probation officer and two psychologists. I did not approach this case file as providing the truth of Christie's condition, but rather as a bureaucratic technology containing the state's account of her subjectivity and experience (cf. Biehl 2005). It was this account that the judge and other officials in the criminal justice system used to understand Christie and determine her punishment. As such, it was essential that I consider it alongside the various contexts in which she was asked to give an account of herself as a drug user and criminal. This included her interviews with me, the interviews conducted three and four years earlier with probation officers, psychologists, and correctional facility administrators contained in her case file, and her work in the local school system telling the story of her experience with methamphetamine to high schoolers. The latter was part of the school's drug prevention curriculum and counted toward Christie's community service requirement.

Before examining the evaluations contained in Christie's case file, it will be useful to review her arrest and conviction. Christie was arrested in June 2003. Bond was set at $25,000. To have remained free, she would have had to pay the court 10 percent of the bond. Christie could not afford that, so she remained incarcerated at the regional jail as her case was processed. She was not sentenced until March 2004, so for roughly eight months she was incarcerated before receiving her sentence.

Like most of those who had been arrested in the Federal Drug Task Force's operation, Christie entered into a plea agreement with the state rather than going to trial. Christie and Justin had been indicted on two charges: one for the actual act of selling the methamphetamine to a confidential informant, the other for "conspiring" to commit the act. Christie and her then-husband Justin agreed to plead guilty to the charge of selling the methamphetamine, and the prosecutor agreed to drop the conspiracy charge.

This means of prosecuting was extremely common. Those arrested for a drug crime were usually indicted on at least two charges, sometimes more, related to their crime. Prosecutors would then present those arrested with the maximum penalty the crimes carried. In Christie and Justin's case, both of the crimes with which they were charged carried a sentence of between one and five years incarcerated and up to a $15,000 fine. The prosecutor would usually tell them that if they chose to go to trial, he would seek the maximum penalty in the case. Were they to be found guilty by a jury, they would thus be incarcerated for ten years and fined $30,000. Faced with this grim possibility, Christie and Justin, like most, agreed to forego the trial and plead guilty to one of the crimes with which they were charged. All that remained for the court to decide was their sentence.

Sentencing was done in each case by the judge for the county, in this case Judge Cravens. But the judge did not make his decisions in a vacuum. Rather, he took into account a range of factors, from the state legal statutes that set the possible punishments for the particular crimes to the individual criminal's personal history. Though legal statutes were easily accessible, the more personalized factors took some time to compile. Thus, after Christie and Justin entered their guilty pleas, they were subject to a series of evaluations carried out by other members of the criminal justice system.

The report process that Christie underwent was for the "Pre-sentence Investigation Report." This was compiled by the probation officer for the county, Rose Hinkle, and consisted of an individual evaluation of the offender and a report gauging "community sentiment" in the case. Rose interviewed Christie using the standard questionnaire for the evaluation. It began with basic biographical information, including her name and address, height and weight, sex and race, citizenship and marital status, occupation and religion, social security number, and education. Very little attention was given to the actual crimes committed, or even the circumstances surrounding the crime. Instead, the evaluation focused largely on Christie's personal history and present life.

The Pre-sentence Evaluation focused on twelve points of interest for determining Christie's sentence: the offense committed, adult arrest record, personal and family background, marital status, home and neighborhood environment, education, religion, interests and activities (including drug and alcohol use), military history, health (both physical and mental), employment/economic status, and community sentiment. Again, in this list the crime committed is but one factor in a wider profile. In the context of the evaluation, it took on clinical rather than juridical significance.

The results of the probation officer's investigations were summarized on a four-page form, which was placed in her file and used by the judge to determine the sentence in her case. There were only two pieces of direct speech taken from Christie. This was in the offense section, under "Defendant's Statement and Attitude." It had a two-sentence quote from Christie, which stated simply "I was there with my husband when the buy went down. I wasen't [sic] really paying attention. I didn't even know the informant had given my husband the money." The rest of the form was summary information providing a personalized profile of Christie.

The picture of Christie that emerged from the investigation was one of constant instability. Her parents divorced a year after Christie was born. Shortly after her parents divorced she and her older sister were taken into custody by the state. Her sister was eventually adopted by another family. Christie went back to live with her mother. At the time of the interview she had not seen her father for a year, but knew he was living in Ohio and was in poor health as a result of hepatitis C. Her mother lived nearby in West Virginia, but, according to Christie, she had no contact with her.

Christie had been married twice. Her most recent marriage was to Justin, her co-defendant in the case. Before that she had been married for eight years to a man named Jerry, whom she left because he was physically abusive. She was also in a long-term relationship with a man named Dean. From these three relationships she had four children, none of whom at the time lived with her. The two oldest lived in Oklahoma with the parents of Jerry, her abusive ex-husband. The kids lived with his parents because Jerry was himself incarcerated after being convicted on an assault charge. Her two other children lived with Dean and his wife in Pennsylvania.

The evaluation described Christie's home, a two-bedroom house that she shared with her husband and a roommate. It listed her education, noting that she dropped out of high school in the eleventh grade to get married and had been working on obtaining her General Education Diploma (GED) since being incarcerated. The evaluation noted the importance Christie placed on religion, mentioning that she was Pentecostal and had attended church and Bible studies at the jail. It provided an abbreviated list of her interests and activities. The first was alcohol and drug use, noting that she began drinking and smoking at age thirteen and using drugs (cocaine and amphetamines) at twenty-seven. It also mentioned that family members supplied her with drugs and used drugs themselves. The report stated that she did not think she had a drug problem, but was undergoing counseling at the regional jail. "Other" interests were brief, limited only to "spending time with her husband."

After noting that she had never served in the military, the evaluation moved on to her health. Under physical health, she experienced anxiety and migraines, and had undergone several operations. She was taking a variety of medications, including Risperdal, Inderal, Tylenol, and "something for her migraines." Under mental health, the evaluation noted that she saw a local psychologist for her migraines, anger management, anxiety, and general counseling. The evaluation concluded with a description of her employment history and economic status, noting that until her arrest, she had worked at the local chicken processing plant making between $100 and $150 a week, and that her husband, Justin, worked at the same plant making $350 to $375 a week. She was required to pay $450 a month for child support and had hospital bills totaling $1,000; she was behind on her payments and had been turned over to a collection agency.

A supplemental report was attached to the evaluation that described "community sentiment" regarding Christie's case. The report was somewhat confusing, as it was ambiguous whether the report referred to Christie, Justin, or both.

After talking with several people within the community, on September 19, 2003, the majority of the people would recommend that the defendant be placed in the custody of the Department of Corrections to serve his time. The defendant is known in the Baker County area. Several of the individuals interviewed felt that the defendant made a mistake and that she was not a bad person.

The evaluation concluded with a summary and analysis:

The defendant, Christie Stokes, a thirty (30) year-old female, plead (guilty) to the indictment charging her with the offence of one (1) count of "Delivery of a Schedule II Controlled Substance." After reviewing my interviewing notes and all the information I have received, this probation officer would recommend that the defendant be placed in the custody of the Department of Corrections.

Prison Evaluations

The second evaluation Christie underwent was at the Carterville Correctional Facility, the facility within the West Virginia prison system with the most diverse range of psychological resources. This took place five months after the Pre-sentence Evaluation conducted by the probation officer. It was listed as both a "psychological evaluation" and "diagnostic evaluation." Its structure was almost identical to the evaluation conducted by the probation officer. It began with the offense, offering Christie more room to explain it in her own words. The report stated:

When asked about the circumstances of the instance offense Ms Stokes [she was still married to Justin at the time] gave the following account:
    "My husband (Justin Stokes) and I were at the bowling alley, he asked me if I wanted to go with him to meet a guy. I said yes, my husband and I were close and did things together. My husband and Randy met and my husband gave him crank and Randy gave him money. I wasn't paying much attention to them and did not see the actual deal go down."

When asked why then she pled guilty to this charge, she stated that Randy (who was a confidential informant) reported that she had handed him the drugs. Justin Stokes also pled guilty to a delivery charge. He has completed a court ordered diagnostic evaluation at the Donaldson Correctional Center. He is currently housed at [the regional jail] awaiting sentencing.

After noting that Christie had no prior criminal record, the evaluation went on to discuss Christie's social history. This covered the same aspects of her home life and early upbringing that were covered in the Pre-sentencing Evaluation, but with some additional material. The Correctional Center evaluation included more details about her marriages and children, the age of her first sexual relationship, and an expanded summary of her medical history, including a seizure disorder that was not mentioned in the other report. More information was provided about Christie's mental health as well, noting that she had undergone counseling for close to ten years for "issues involving her mother and the loss of custody of her children." Finally, the Correctional Center report identified Christie officially as an addict, stating that at twenty-seven "she became addicted to crank" and had been a "heavy user" of drugs for three years prior to her arrest.

In addition to the clinical interviews, Christie was given a number of psychological tests. The purpose of these, according to the evaluation, was to "assess the subject's intellectual, academic, and personality traits." Tests included the Wechsler Adult Intelligence Scale-Revised (WAIS-R), which measured her verbal, performance and full-scale IQ; the Adult Basic Learning Examination (ABLE) that tested her grade-level equivalencies in reading skills and problem solving; the McAndrews Alcoholism Scale; and the Minnesota Multiphasic Personality Inventory-2 (MMPI-2), which assessed her personality. The evaluation provided a summary of this test's findings:

The subject's profile indicates that she tried to present in a positive and optimistic way, yet still reported feeling significant anxiety, self-doubts, and social alienation. This is a woman whose behavior is often impulsive and irresponsible and whose relationships are shallow and superficial. When stressed or intoxicated she may become volatile and act out. She had difficulty trusting other people and usually feels uncomfortable and uneasy in social situations. Her self-esteem is extremely low. She appears to be conflicted emotionally and psychologically and often struggles with feelings of insecurity and dependency and her distrust of others.

The evaluation concluded:

The subject has a long history of problems in her relationships and life. She has limited insight into the lifestyle she has evolved. She grew up with an alcoholic/drug addicted mother [and] has had many short and abusive relationships with men. She married early herself, failed to complete high school, and has had a succession of pathological relationships with men. Each of her children may have a different father. She claims to have only started drug use at the age of twenty-seven (27) years old. Ms Stokes lost custody of her first two children to her first husband in 1995 in a court action in Pennsylvania. She lost custody of her second two children in 2001 to her ex-boyfriend, Dean Pike. She reported that her mother who had been helping her with the children after she returned to WV in 2000 turned against her due to her relationship with her current husband, Justin Stokes, and likely due to her drug use. She reported that her husband is "my best friend," that they don't argue or fight, and that he is not abusive.

Ms Stokes seemed rational in her thinking, but of low average intelligence. If her report of employment is accurate, she has considerable experience in working the poultry business. Her weakness seems to be linked to growing up in a chaotic household, lack of adult nurturing or guidance, seeking to achieve independence through relationships with men, failing to develop her own personal identity and resources to support herself so that she could avoid dependence on sociopathic or domineering men.

The report used all of this information to make recommendations regarding the type of sentence the judge should give her. It described Christie as a "fair at best" candidate for probation or non-incarceration alternative, breaking down the decision as a divergence between "positive" and "negative" factors in her life. Positive factors included the fact that Christie did not have a prior criminal record and that she was able, until her arrest, to maintain employment. The negative factors were much more numerous. They included:

(1) her pattern of unstable relationships and lifestyle, (2) her significant illicit drug use, (3) her lack of family support, (4) her husband's (and co-defendant) involvement in selling illegal drugs, (5) her husband's family's reported involvement in illegal drug trafficking and manufacture, (6) her personal dependency and insecurity, and (7) her probable lack of strength to maintain her position that she will only continue the relationship if her husband gives up drugs.

After listing the positive and negative factors, the report gave its "final recommendation":

The final recommendation in Ms Stoke's case is a recommendation for probation if adequate supervision is possible and she can withstand the influence of her husband/co-defendant. We believe her chance of success on probation is poor if she remains in a relationship with her husband. However, the court may have additional information that suggests a course of action different from that above.

Though the evaluation reluctantly recommended probation, the conditions under which she would be successful involved a significant amount of supervision and surveillance. For instance, she would need to remain separate from her husband and his family, be tested frequently for drugs, remain employed, participate (and make progress) in a substance-abuse treatment program, attend Narcotics Anonymous meetings, undergo personal counseling as well as "monitoring of her home situation and her relationships with men," and live with a relative who could provide "a stable home environment" and can "exercise some supervision and be counted on to provide accurate reports to authorities."

On the other hand, the report noted the many benefits of incarceration, including the likelihood that Christie would become "a model inmate." While incarcerated she would be able to avail herself of educational and rehabilitative resources, including substance abuse education, basic adult education, vocational training, work experience (in the prison food service and elsewhere), and take a limited number of college courses. She would also be able to participate in a number of "social rehabilitation" programs, including group substance-abuse treatment, "life skills" programs, including parenting, anger management, and counseling, mental health services, and training in "victim empathy."

What is Punishment For?

It is notable that these evaluations spend little time discussing the actual crime for which Christie was convicted. Indeed, from a certain jurisprudential perspective, the clinical information gathered in preparation for Christie's sentencing has no legal significance. Why should it matter, for instance, what Christie's IQ is, or the results of her personality test? What bearing does it have on the fact that she pled guilty to a charge of dealing drugs?

The sentencing recommendations provided by these reports were based on clinical evaluations, which provide information that would likely never emerge in the context of a criminal investigation or trial. This information was presented as both a set of mitigating factors that explained Christie's criminality as well as a portfolio of risk factors at work in her life. The judge had this information in front of him when he sentenced Christie. He examined it in light of the legal statutes that set the parameters for her punishment. Thus the judge's role in the sentencing process was to take the clinical information gathered by the other members of the criminal justice system and give it legal significance.

Do the judge's actions still constitute punishment at this point given that he is being asked to recommend state intervention into a person's life based largely on clinical information? The classical jurisprudential task of appropriately calibrating punishment to the crime committed appears to have been superseded by,(1) the epidemiological task of determining where the subject should be placed within the population and under what conditions, and (2) the clinical task of determining the best intervention into the person's life so as to bring about a rehabilitative effect. Of course, in the case of drug offenders like Christie, judges had to make their sentencing decisions on the assumption that rehabilitation was improbable under the circumstances. This, at least, was the conventional wisdom.

*　*　*

A week later I visited Christie in her home. She lived in the shadow of a mountain off a secluded state highway. It took me a long time to find the place, and I was half an hour late when I arrived. She lived in a cozy double-wide trailer between a locus tree and an elegant yet neglected white house that appeared abandoned. The trailer was one of about a dozen nestled in a small valley between the state highway and the mountain. Roughly half of the trailers had full-time residents. The others were rented to tourists—everyone from the bikers who enjoyed riding the area's winding mountain roads to the church groups that would hold week-long retreats in the summer. I parked next to a rusty white van, as Christie had instructed, and approached the front door of the trailer. There were two fishing poles and an empty coffee can on the front porch. I knocked on the metal screen door and heard a muffled voice shout, "Come in."

Entering the trailer, I was struck immediately by the unmistakable aroma of cigarettes and upholstered furniture. A young girl with long, brown hair and wearing pink pajamas was sitting in the middle of the living room floor, watching cartoons. Christie sat at her computer, her back to me as I entered and took off my boots. I stood in the small entryway that separated the living room from the kitchen. I peered down at my tube-socked feet. They seemed inappropriately white on the thick brown carpet. I glanced at the kitchen where I saw two bare feet peering out from below the open refrigerator door. "Hello," the female voice belonging to the feet called out, her head somewhere inside the refrigerator. Though neither of us knew it at the time, within a year she would be back in prison on her third charge of forgery.

"Have a seat," Christie called from the other side of the room. She continued typing on her computer. I made my way to a thickly padded gray armchair. The chair was soft. As I sat down I sank deeply into the cushion. My arms perched awkwardly on the armrests that grew ever taller as I sank deeper into the folds of the chair. The smell of cigarettes became stronger; I realized I was still wearing my jacket.

The woman who'd greeted me from behind the refrigerator closed the door and walked across the room. I smiled and nodded. "That's Sandy," Christie said as the woman sat down on a couch across from me. "And that's Jani. She's like a daughter to me." Christie gestured toward the girl on the floor with a backwards nod of her head. Jani squirmed slightly at the mention of her name but kept her eyes fixed on the television.

Christie's eyes never left the computer screen. "I'm almost finished," she said, the blue-white glow of the monitor reflecting in her glasses.

"Finished with what?" I asked.

"My presentation."

Obtaining a copy of the presentation that Christie would do at the high school in three months was the official reason for my visit. The presentation was on her experience with methamphetamine. The health teacher arranged the presentation, usually toward the end of the school year. Like Christie, the teacher thought it was important for the students to hear about the dangers of drugs like methamphetamine from someone who had "been there, done that."

Pages began emerging from the printer on the floor next to Christie's computer. As each page emerged, Christie placed it on my lap. Christie explained that, in addition to the presentation, she was giving me a copy of her "book," an autobiographical account of her life, which she had been working on ever since her boyfriend left her and she attempted suicide.

Sandy talked while Christie worked. Like Christie, she had had a series of bad experiences with the criminal justice system. Sandy had a deep resentment of the system. "Its all who you know and how much money you have," she said, expressing a sentiment I often heard. Something else I heard repeatedly was that prominent members of the criminal justice system, as well as local politicos, were themselves involved with drugs. "I've seen the prosecuting attorney do a line of cocaine off the hood of a car," she exclaimed, bewildered at the hypocrisy that such a person could then turn around and prosecute others for drug offenses.

Christie echoed Sandy's grievances about the state of injustice in the criminal justice system. She felt it was unfair that some people got arrested and others didn't, and that people convicted of the same crime often received different sentences. Christie was particularly resentful of her own conviction. She thought it was unfair that she and Justin had been tried together and received the same sentence since he was the one who did the majority of the drug dealing. She also resented the fact that her cousin, Randy, had worked with the police to get her arrested, particularly since his motivation was keeping himself out of prison.

At the same time, Christie credited her arrest and incarceration with saving her life. She underscored this belief with a story she told me the first day we met and often thereafter. One day when she was making her monthly report to her probation officer at the courthouse, she encountered Randy in the hallway. As Christie told the story, when she encountered Randy he was already shrinking away from her, bracing to experience the brunt of her anger. Instead, she stopped and thanked him for saving her life. If he hadn't done what he did, she told him, she would never have gotten off of drugs and turned her life around. Randy listened to her silently, his head down, unable to meet her gaze. Christie noted that everyone at the courthouse was surprised by the way she'd handled the situation. She said she'd even surprised herself a little.

Randy's actions had enabled Christie to establish a different trajectory for her life. She made new friendships, obtained her GED, and became involved with Alcoholics Anonymous—all achievements in which she took great pride. Christie was also taking classes online, working toward a degree in criminal justice. Christie relished the irony that she, a convicted felon, was pursuing a degree in criminal justice. But, as with her work speaking at the high school, she felt her experience gave her a kind of expertise that the majority of her classmates and teachers were lacking. Christie took what pride she could in this experience-based expertise, and the unique position in which it placed her.

Still, she was painfully aware that numerous doors had been closed for her by her conviction. The most difficult of these was the near impossibility of finding a job. Finding and maintaining gainful employment was a condition of her probation. However, the few businesses in the area with jobs available were unwilling to hire someone with a felony conviction, particularly for drugs. Christie applied at the local supermarket and the Dollar General

Store. She applied to be a secretary at a small real estate company and at similar businesses. Every letter of rejection she received was a minor defeat, prolonging the possibility that her inability to find employment would land her back in prison. The only business willing to hire her was the poultry processing plant. This was where most of the people in her position eventually found employment. Ironically, this is where many began using methamphetamine in the first place. The plant was located more than an hour away. After she exhausted all of her other options, and under pressure from her probation officer, Christie filled out an application. She was required to take a drug test as part of the application, and, as noted earlier, it came back positive for PCP. This was why Christie was at the courthouse the day we met, attempting to resolve the issue through a more precise lab-based test. Once that issue was resolved (the laboratory analysis came back negative) she was hired to work overnight on the live kill line—hanging live chickens by their feet on conveyer belts to go through the machine that slaughtered them.

Christie's employment at the chicken plant did not last long, however. The first night she worked she had a seizure and had to be taken to the emergency room at the hospital. In a state of delirium in the back of the ambulance, she vaguely remembered yelling *"Just let me die, just let me die!"* She attempted two additional times to return to the plant to work but each time had to leave because she began experiencing seizures. She went to the doctor for an examination. Her doctor wrote a note to the administrators at the plant and her probation officer explaining that she could not do the work required of her at the chicken plant. As a result of this diagnosis, she had begun the long bureaucratic process of gaining permanent disability status from the state, which, if granted, would provide her with a regular income and eliminate the pressure to find employment.

Targeted Interventions: Divorcing Justin

While incarcerated, Christie's lawyer told her that she would need to get a divorce if she wanted to have any hope of getting her sentence reconsidered. The lawyer's reasoning, according to Christie, was that the prosecuting attorney in the case was against interracial marriage (Christie was white, Justin was black). This may certainly have been the case, but as Christie's case files indicated, her relationship with her husband was cited as a key risk factor in her life. It had led directly to both her criminality and her elevated drug use. Thus, from the state's perspective, to end the relationship would significantly reduce the likelihood that Christie would engage in future criminality. It would also likely lead to improvements in Christie's overall well-being, and would be necessary if she were going to have any chance at success on probation.

This was not the first time the law had asked Christie to make a hard decision about her family relationships. In 2001 she had terminated her rights to her two youngest children. She did so because she had accumulated a debt of $25,000 in unpaid child support. The only way to keep the amount from growing was to give up her rights—and therefore her financial responsibility—to her children. This did not eliminate her responsibility to pay the $25,000 she already owed, however. Nor did it keep interest from accruing on the debt. Nor did it shield her from prosecution from unpaid child support, which almost happened in the spring of 2008. What it did was to keep any new debts from accruing. Christie ultimately decided to terminate her rights to the two children, allowing them to remain in the custody of her ex-boyfriend and his wife. But the decision haunted her, in part because it resonated so deeply with her own experience of feeling abandoned by her mother.

The circumstances that led Christie to divorce Justin began with their arrest and prosecution as co-defendants. From the beginning, Christie insisted that she was a victim of circumstance. Justin had done the selling, and she was simply there when it happened, largely oblivious to what was going on. The confidential informant (her cousin, Randy)– had accused her of handing him the meth. Christie continued to deny that she had been involved, even after she entered a plea of guilty to the charge.

This insistence that Justin was the truly guilty party and she barely even an accomplice appeared on both the probation officer's Pre-sentence Evaluation and the correctional center's Psychological Evaluation. These statements were taken to represent her "attitude" at the time of the evaluation. Although the various administrators conducting the tests did not affirm Christie's perspective that she had been unjustly prosecuted, they did agree with her perception that Justin had played a significant role in creating the circumstances that led to her arrest. Thus Christie's relationship with Justin was quickly flagged as a key criminogenic risk factor in her life and a target for intervention.

Of the seven "Negative Factors" listed in the Correctional Center's Psychological Evaluation, Justin was named explicitly in three of them and was implicitly implicated in the rest. The basic point of the report was that Christie was involved in a pathological domestic life. Only by intervening drastically in that life would rehabilitation become possible.

It is unclear how this message was communicated to Christie. She claimed that her lawyer told her that she needed to divorce Justin before the judge would reconsider her sentence. This was the case, so the lawyer claimed, because of the prosecuting attorney's bias against interracial marriage. But all of the legal authorities involved, including the judge, Christie's lawyer and the prosecuting attorney would have read the probation officer and Correctional Center's evaluations. They seem to have agreed with the Correctional Center's explicit statement, "We believe her chance of success on probation is poor if she remains in a relationship with her husband." Moreover, the implication of Justin in essentially all of Christie's risk factors made their relationship a particularly promising site for a kind of therapeutic intervention. By ending the relationship, Christie's risk/needs profile was fundamentally altered, thus opening up the possibility of a more thoroughgoing intervention into Christie's life.

Christie initially resisted the idea of divorce. But eventually she did request the necessary paperwork to initiate the divorce proceedings while she and Justin were still incarcerated. It went through just before she went before the judge to have her sentence reconsidered. Her sentence was changed and she was released from jail and put on probation.

Christie's relationship to Justin was at the center of the terms of her probation as well. Christie was explicitly forbidden from having any contact with Justin. Any contact would be treated as a violation of her probation, and she would be returned to jail. This requirement complemented the others, including finding gainful employment and refraining from consuming any intoxicating substances. Separating from Justin also enabled another requirement of Christie's probation: living with her grandmother. Christie initially liked the arrangement but quickly began to chafe, saying that her grandmother treated her basically as "a slave" requiring her to constantly get up early and do work around the house.

The divorce also provided her with some relief because her case was now separate from Justin's. Because they were no longer married, they could no longer be treated as co-defendants. This was fortuitous for Christie. In the spring of 2008, Christie called me to tell me the news that Justin was sent back to jail for violating the terms of his probation. Sheriff's deputies had discovered that he had guns at his house, which, as both a convicted felon and probationer, he was not allowed to possess. Justin claimed that he needed the guns to protect his dogs from the coyotes that roamed the mountains around his home. Christie suspected that the police, prosecuting attorney, and probation officer didn't actually care about the guns. They had simply used them as an excuse to "violate" him because they suspected him of using methamphetamine again. They had tried to catch him using—giving him surprise drug tests and the like—but had not been able to get any conclusive evidence. The guns charge allowed them to go after Justin a different way. Christie thought it was strange that Justin had only been sentenced to thirty days in jail. This was very short, in her opinion, and meant that he had probably made a deal with the prosecuting attorney to cooperate with the police. Christie said she would know if that was true when the next round of indictments came out. Based on the names, she would know whether Justin had assisted the police.

Christie assured me that she didn't get divorced just to get her sentence reconsidered, that other factors had prompted it as well. And the relief she felt no longer having her fate tied to Justin's was palpable. Still, I asked her once, months after our first meeting, if she thought she would still be married to Justin if they hadn't gotten arrested. "Absolutely," she said, without hesitation.

An Example to Others

In the clinical model of targeted punishment surveyed above, the various factors in Christie's life that led to her crime were given values as indices of risk and need. These were then used to develop a targeted punishment program for her within the criminal justice system. As her life changed—most notably through her divorce from her co-defendant/husband—so did her risk/needs profile and, by extension, her punishment.

The teacher at the high school would not allow me to sit in on her class the day Christie gave her presentation (she wasn't comfortable with strangers coming into her class, according to Christie). I provided Christie with a digital voice recorder, which she used to record her presentation. The teacher (Ms. Ivy) began the class by introducing Christie. She mentioned that Christie had attended that very same high school fifteen years earlier. As a sophomore, Christie had taken this same health class that they were in now; she (Ms. Ivy) had even been her teacher.

Ms. Ivy complemented Christie for her willingness to share her life's story with the class, particularly since it involved some things that "are not really pleasant for her to tell about. She's telling about some *failures*. I admire her to be able to do that and I think you will admire her to be able to do that." Ms. Ivy went on to underscore the importance of what Christie was doing for the students. "It's a really good thing for you guys to hear this story from her, *because she was you*, at one time."

Christie began this way:

I'm not gonna lecture. I'm not gonna do anything that your parents would do. I just give advice. I tell my story. I tell where I've been, where you could be. Because where you all are sitting now is where I was, like Ms. Ivy said. I said the same thing, "No, not me."

I'm 33 years old. I'll be 34 in June. Yes, I did go to this high school. . . . I have four children, two bad marriages. And went down the wrong road. My parents were drug addict-alcoholics; [I] was raised around that. All sorts of abuse—emotional, mental, physical, sexual, everything. [I've] been down that road.

In 2003 I was arrested for drugs, for meth. And, um, it's not a fun road. Its really not. And I swore, like Ms. Ivy said, in high school, "Nope, not me. My parents do it. Nope, not me." But I did. I went down that road. I was arrested. I lost everything. I lost my house. I lost my kids. I lost my job. I lost everything. Everything I had, I lost.

Christie began by affirming Ms. Ivy's characterization of her experience. In a very literal sense she had been where they were—same school, same class, same teacher—and so stood plausibly as an example of what they could become. But Christie proffered an alternative rendering of her personal history. Though she claimed she "went down the wrong road," her narrative locates the origins of this fate in her family milieu. Christie's first exposure to drug use and crime came from her parents. At their hands Christie suffered a range of abuses ("emotional, mental, physical, sexual, everything"). These actions prefigured her rendezvous with drug use and criminality later in life. The final injury they inflicted on her was, perhaps, the fact that she ended up becoming just like them ("drug addict-alcoholics"), despite her conscious commitment not to. Thus the "wrong road" that Christie eventually went down is the one of abuse and addiction laid down by her parents.

Christie likewise was assigned a different value to this experience than Ms. Ivy. She characterized it less in terms of *failure* than in terms of *loss*. "I lost everything," she said. "My house, my kids, my job—everything I had, I lost." This loss was prefigured in her parent's drug use and the abuse she suffered at their hands. It was actualized in her cousin's betrayal, and the state's zealous prosecution.

Having established this biographical foundation, Christie spent the rest of her presentation describing in detail her experience of arrest, prosecution, and incarceration. "When you go to jail, they don't care," she said, describing how she had had to strip naked upon her arrival at the jail while the guards watched. They sprayed her with "bug spray" to de-lice her and examined her thoroughly to make sure she was not trying to smuggle anything in to the jail. They took her clothes and belongings, and gave her an orange jumpsuit to wear. "You lose all the dignity you have," she said.

Christie went on to catalog the various indignities she suffered while incarcerated. Women were not allowed to talk to the men. Those who did, or committed any other infraction, were put into "lock down" and forced to stay in their cells for all but one hour of every day, for as much as thirty days. Meal times were strictly limited to half an hour. Those who were still eating at the end of the meal period did not get to finish. Phone calls were monitored ("They record everything that you say"). Visitations were frustratingly short—limited to anywhere between fifteen and forty-five minutes—and physical touch was kept to a strict minimum, a brief embrace at the beginning and end of the visit was usually the maximum allowed.

Travel outside of the jail was equally humiliating. When Christie traveled to court, she had to wear the orange jumpsuit, handcuffs around her wrists, and shackles around her ankles. She described the discomfort and embarrassment of having to come back into town for court dressed in prisoner garb, absorbing the stares of all those around her. "They don't care who sees you. And trust me, in Baker County, in Meadville, everybody sees everything." Moreover, when she saw someone she knew—family member, friend, etc.—she was not allowed to acknowledge them.

Christie then went on to give the facts of her arrest and conviction. She mentioned specifically that it was her cousin who served as the confidential informant in the case. Christie acknowledged that she had a lot of anger toward him, but then reiterated her story that the last time she saw him she thanked him for what he did. Still, she couldn't resist mentioning that things had not worked out for him as he hoped they would. "The confidential informant, it's come back to bite him for what he did. He had gotten into some trouble. He thought by wearing a wire, it would get him out of the trouble that he was in, and in actuality, it didn't."

Christie then returned to her experience in the criminal justice system, describing her time on probation. Again she emphasized the loss of dignity and freedom. "You have to go [to the courthouse] and report every month. You have to take random drug tests. [The probation officer] can come to your house any time, day or night, it doesn't matter. You better be there. If you're not, you better tell her." Christie resented the constant monitoring and restriction of movement that accompanied probation, and the fact that she could not leave the state without getting a travel permit.

Christie then went on to describe her transfer from the regional jail to the state penitentiary. Again, her attention to detail was absolute. Every restriction, humiliation, indignity, and abuse she could remember she described, invoking scenes of incarceration comparable to those discussed earlier in her presentation. This continued focus on the experience of her punishment made clear that for Christie, the danger in drug use lay less in the substance itself than in the possibility of getting caught and becoming subject to the punitive arm of the state. She stated this explicitly toward the end of her presentation, "If you get caught, it will ruin your life. It's been three years and I'm still labeled in Meadville that I'm a drug pusher. And I'm not." Thus it is the humiliations and indignities of punishment, and the stigma associated with her criminal conviction, that ruined Christie's life, and not her drug use per se.

At this point, Ms. Ivy broke in and attempted to redirect Christie's narrative away from her experience of punishment and back to her development into a drug user. She posed a number of questions focused explicitly on Christie's drug use: When she had started using drugs; the amount of meth she was using at the height of her addiction; and the cost (financial and otherwise) of maintaining her addiction. Ms. Ivy also asked Christie to talk about her children (none of whom she had seen in almost a decade) and to emphasize to the students how addictive meth was. Christie answered these questions dutifully. If at any point Christie returned to her experience of incarceration, Ms. Ivy would just as dutifully guide her back to her experience of drug use and addiction.

Christie concluded her presentation on a hopeful note, mentioning those aspects of her current life in which she took the most pride. She mentioned that she had a trip planned to see two of her children (she had last seen them when they were two and four; they were, at the time of the presentation, fourteen and sixteen), that she was writing a book about her life, and that she was, "God willing," going to complete a degree in criminal justice in the next two years. Both Christie and Ms. Ivy laughed at the irony that Christie had chosen to pursue a degree in criminal justice.

Christie earned the admiration of people like Ms. Ivy by sharing her story with others. The subtle conflicts over the meaning of this story that emerged at the beginning and end of Christie's presentation, however, reveal that in order to earn this admiration, Christie had to present her story (at least nominally) as one of failure rather than loss; justice rather than injustice; and redemption rather than resentment. Christie was certainly aware of these expectations. The fact that she continued to center her story around her experience of punishment reflects a reluctance to inhabit the stigmatized position that the various authorities in her life—from her parents to the community to the criminal justice system—would have her assume. In other words, Christie insisted throughout her punishment, and continues to insist and believe, that she is a victim of circumstances that were beyond her control. Why should she be punished for what her husband was doing? Or for her cousin's betrayal? Or for what her mother did?

Christie's experience demonstrates how punishment has been refigured in the U.S. criminal justice system around and through clinical knowledge about the criminal. Punishment is still occasioned by the commission of a crime, but its purpose extends beyond any strictly juridical considerations. Punishment is today treated as a means of intervening broadly into an offender's life. For this, clinical information is deemed necessary. The strictly juridical approach to punishment, which finds its justification solely within the law itself, is treated in this context as a last resort for those unwilling or unresponsive to the state's efforts to intervene therapeutically into their life.

Christie was widely touted as a success story, an example of how this approach to punishment could bring about positive change in offenders' lives. Christie shared this vision of herself and was justifiably proud of her achievements since being arrested. And yet, though this targeted intervention did promote what she perceived as positive change, it likewise undermined her capacity to live as anything other than a marginal member of the community. This is evident, of course, in her futile attempts to find employment in the area, none of which were successful due to her criminal record (and at the poultry processing plant, it was her body itself that rebelled). The only viable options she saw for herself ultimately were "exits" from the system either through school or disability.

But the more subtle impact of this approach to punishment can be seen in Christie's school presentation. As mentioned above, this was an event that Christie looked forward to every year. She even imagined a future for herself in which she toured the country giving presentations about her experience. In doing the presentation she'd gained respect from Ms. Ivy. In fact, Ms. Ivy became one of her strongest advocates, writing letters of support when needed for a court hearing and using her contacts to open doors at other schools where Christie might be able to do her presentation. At the same time, the presentation was part of her community service requirement and thus was technically part of her punishment. As such, the success of the presentation was predicated on Christie first identifying with the state's narrative about the course, then on the meaning and significance of her experience as a drug addict and criminal.

The narrative Ms. Ivy wanted to hear (and wanted the class to hear) was one of personal failure. She did not want to hear the narrative with which

Christie identified, which was one of abuse, injustice, and resentment. Indeed, so much of Christie's ability to succeed on probation, in AA and elsewhere, hinged on her being able to "accept responsibility" for her actions. Christie's reentry into the community was thus predicated, paradoxically, on the extent of her identification with a particular criminalized, stigmatized identity, which would itself continue to marginalize her in the community. It is this narrative—the state's narrative—of her experience with which she was expected to identify. In other words, Christie was trapped: the only position made available to her in the community was that which would further reinforce her marginalization.

And perhaps this is part of the reason behind the legal officials' (the judge, the probation officer, the state trooper, etc.) pessimism about the effectiveness of the criminal justice system in dealing with drugs and drug offenders. In addition to the numerous "failures" of the system to prevent the convicted from using drugs and committing more crimes, these individuals recognize that the system rarely helps those it processes to reenter the community, as their "debt to society" seems never fully paid.

Epilogue

"A Lot Happens in a Little Town"

This book has examined the response to methamphetamine in one rural American community in order to shed light on broader aspects of American political culture as it has taken shape around the issue of illicit drugs (i.e., "narcotics"). In Baker County, the response to methamphetamine involved the repetition of many practices developed to address previous drug threats, but it also enabled the introduction of new practices into the field of drug enforcement. Each chapter focused on a different context in which the response to methamphetamine was taking place. These included several sites within the criminal justice system, but also sites outside this system, including schools, homes, families, stores, and factories, just to name a few.

The fact that responding to the methamphetamine problem could mobilize such a broad swath of the local community underscores the power that the concern with narcotics has in American political life. Indeed, one of the most striking aspects of this research was the range of individuals, institutions, and groups whose very sense of identity and purpose was tied to the concern with narcotics. In this regard the issue of narcotics is political in the broadest sense: it is vital in sustaining particular forms and ways of life. The concept of narcopolitics was introduced to draw attention to this aspect of narcotics, and to underscore the central place it occupies in contemporary approaches to governance.

It would be going against the grain of this project to conclude with a set of policy recommendations that would somehow improve the system as it stands. Indeed, if there is a policy implication to be derived from this study, it is simply that the issue of illicit drugs is so deeply engrained in American political culture that one can hardly imagine political life in the United States without it. This is particularly true in the domains of law and police practice, where significant resources are devoted to dealing with drug-related issues and offenses. To imagine a significant policy change, such as recasting the problem of illicit drugs as a matter of public health, would require much more than simply convincing the public that addiction is a disease deserving of treatment. It would require addressing the fact that the workings of law and the exercise of police power are now in many ways dependent on having illicit narcotics as a target. And so to drastically change U.S. drug policy, the very organization and orientation of the legal order, and particularly the criminal justice system, would have to be re-imagined. Dismantling and reorganization the present "narco-enforcement bureaucracy," as it has been called, would be no small project (Bertram et al. 1996).

Nevertheless, there appear to be fissures in the contemporary narcopolitical apparatus, evidence of which emerged during my fieldwork. The first of these was the air of pessimism that hung over administrators and officials in the criminal justice system as they carried out the work of drug enforcement. There was a uniform feeling of frustration bordering on cynicism among these individuals regarding the intractability of the current drug problem and the inefficacy of current drug laws in addressing it. While there was still widespread support for the prosecutorial focus on drug offenders, as well as a stated preference for taking a punitive approach, there was also little sense of accomplishment that seemed to come with carrying out this work. Most of those officials involved directly with the prosecution of drug offenders viewed it as, at best, a managerial task—an exercise in containment. They did not see themselves as fighting a battle that could be won. Indeed, the "unwinnable" aspect of the drug war, which at least one officer mentioned specifically, speaks to the frustration I witnessed. It also suggests a possible openness to other approaches, in addition to or instead of the current punitive approach. This is a possibility that would-be reformers might highlight and embrace.

The second fissure in the system I witnessed was the cost. Nationally, the punitive approach has led to the now well-known prison population explosion over the past twenty years. Maintaining this rate of incarceration has placed a significant financial strain on governments. It is expensive to incarcerate someone, particularly for long periods of time, and so governments are being forced to entertain alternatives to the punitive approach out of financial considerations alone. This was certainly the case in Baker County, where county officials were constantly looking for ways to cut costs incurred through incarceration. Thus, it appeared that state officials were being forced to face the fact that the current punitive approach, which relies on enforcement and imprisonment to address narcotics, was not economically sustainable. The era of "carceral 'big government'" (Wacquant 2009a) may truly be over.

The third fissure, related to the first two, has to do with the effects of the focus on narcotics on juridical institutions, and particularly those focused on punishment. As demonstrated throughout the book, and particularly in chapter 5, there are numerous political incentives for states to target drug offenders. Drug offenders constitute a category of criminal for which the public has little sympathy. In fact the public seems quite willing to see drug offenders prosecuted and punished by the state. Pursuing such prosecutions is thus an attractive means for the state to pursue and ground its own legitimacy.

But there is a cost in taking this approach. This is particularly true, again, with regard to incarceration. With rehabilitation officially abandoned as an explicit goal of incarceration, and a lingering sense that "nothing works" still hanging over the criminal justice system as a whole, the question of why the United States continues to punish criminals the way it does seems increasingly in need of justification beyond the simple act of temporary incapacitation. It may be that the United States is still attempting to balance both the moral impulse to punish and the administrative need to manage the offender population. The targeting of drug offenders has worked as a kind of stopgap solution to this problem, given that their prosecution can be justified on both punitive and actuarial grounds. However, the poor "fit," one might say, between the crimes drug offenders commit and the punishments they receive—particularly when one factors in the various social circumstances, including addiction, that drive this form of criminality and are rarely addressed in an adequate fashion within the criminal justice system—does little to bring clarity to the state's wider purpose in pursuing particular approaches to punishment.

This brings us back to the issues of policing, law, and politics with which the book began. What this book has attempted to show is just how central the issue of narcotics is to law and the exercise of contemporary police power as they are utilized to achieve "the well-regulated society" in the contemporary United States. To imagine a future in which narcotics do not play such a prominent role in this pursuit means rethinking, not just the issue of narcotics but the relationship between law, police, and politics itself.

*   *   *

Leaving the field is never easy. One of the last people I spoke to as I prepared to go was Rose Hinkle, the probation officer for Baker County. I had returned to the courthouse for one last round of photocopying case files. She generously allowed me to use her copying machine, which would save me both time and money. As I photocopied page after page, Rose's phone never stopped ringing. Each call represented another case she was in the midst of managing. Some calls were from probationers, explaining why they could not make it to a scheduled appointment, or why they needed to leave the state. Others were from lawyers, with questions about the status of paperwork for a particular client. Rose seemed tired; and I understood, on a deeper level, the sense of frustration that she and others in the local criminal justice system felt as they carried out their work.

I gathered the stack of papers I had produced and prepared to leave. I interrupted Rose long enough to thank her for all that she had done assisting me with my research. She told the person she was talking to on the phone to hold on. "A lot happens in a little town, doesn't it?" she said, her lips curving into a slight smile.

I nodded; but before I could say more, she was already talking to the person on the other end of the phone again. The smile on her face had faded.

Notes

NOTES TO INTRODUCTION

1. "President Signs USA PATRIOT Improvement and Reauthorization Act." Retrieved on February 11, 2006, from http://www.whitehouse.gov/news/releases/2006/03/20060309-4.html.

2. The legislation in the PATRIOT Act authorizes $99 million per year over the next five years to train state and local law enforcement in "meth hot spots." This is by far the biggest block expenditure, dwarfing other emphases, such as the $20 million allocated to help children affected by meth, available only for one year and administered as grants; the paltry $4 million geared toward stopping the importation of meth from Mexico, which the DEA estimates is the source of 80 percent of the meth currently in the United States; or the undisclosed amount (I would assume it is less than $4 million) allocated to help pregnant and parenting female drug offenders, which organizations must compete for through grant applications. No money has been allocated in the PATRIOT Act bill to fund environmental clean up of meth labs.

3. I am indebted to Michel Foucault's discussion of "biopolitics" in my development of the narcopolitics concept. See Foucault 1997.

4. http://www.usdoj.gov/dea/concern/meth.html#8.

5. Walter Benjamin's experiments with hashish were part of his more general efforts to understand modernity at the level of sensory experience and thus were of a piece with his investigations of art, architecture, and the urban landscape (Benjamin 2006).

6. The names of all people and places are pseudonyms used to protect the privacy of those who generously agreed to participate in this research.

7. West Virginia is one of the most rural states in the United States. As of the last census, West Virginia had a population of 1.8 million over an area of 24,077 sq mi. (62,359 sq km). By contrast, the borough of Brooklyn, New York, had a population of 2.5 million over an area of 71 sq mi (184 sq km). Thus almost one million more people live in one borough of New York City than in the entire state of West Virginia. West Virginia is also one of the most homogenous states. Ninety-five percent of the population is white. Only 1.1 percent of the population is foreign born. And only 2.7 percent of the population speaks a language other than English at home. (http://quickfacts.census.gov/qfd/states/54000.html).

8. http://www.census.gov/compendia/statab/rankings.html.

9. http://www.usdoj.gov/dea/pubs/states/westvirginia.html.

10. The location of the research in West Virginia is significant for another reason. West Virginia is the only state in the United States to be located entirely in the Appalachian region. This region has long been considered the epicenter of social problems in the rural United States. As such, there is a slightly different history at work here than in other rural areas. Most significant in this regard is a deep ambivalence at the local level about any organization or program—particularly federal—that comes to the area for the sole purpose of fixing social problems. This ambivalence is part and parcel of an even wider uncertainty about the state and what its appropriate role should be vis-à-vis the local community. I was sensitive to such historically and culturally coded ambivalences about the state as I examined the way methamphetamine was addressed. However, the attitudes toward law I encountered were remarkably consistent with those documented by anthropologists in rural and small town areas outside the Appalachian region (Greenhouse et al. 1994). In the final analysis, I could find nothing exceptional or uniquely "Appalachian" about the response to the methamphetamine problem in the area where I conducted my research. Of more significance seemed to be the area's proximity to drug trafficking routes spanning from Mexico through Texas into the southeastern United States and onto the eastern seaboard. The presence of numerous poultry processing plants was also significant, as meth use was rumored to be rampant in these plants. These plants were also a place where the "homemade" and Mexican methamphetamine economies overlapped.

NOTES TO CHAPTER 1

1. See, for instance, the reports issued by the National Institute on Drug Abuse (NIDA 2006) and the Mayo Clinic (Lineberry and Bostwick 2006).

2. Since 2004 more than forty states have passed anti-meth legislation. At the federal level, the reauthorized USA PATRIOT Act includes the "Combat Methamphetamine Epidemic Act"—a multimillion dollar package that, like the state legislation on which it is based, focuses on increasing the criminal penalties for making, taking, or circulating meth. Federal prosecuting priorities shifted in anticipation of this new legislation. According to the DEA, the number of federal meth prosecutions *tripled* in the year before the anti-meth legislation went into effect. http://www.usdoj.gov/dea/concern/meth. html#8

3. The legislation in the PATRIOT Act authorizes $99 million per year over the next five years to train state and local law enforcement in "meth hot spots." This is by far the biggest block expenditure, dwarfing other emphases, such as the $20 million allocated to help children affected by meth, available only for one year and administered as grants; the paltry $4 million geared toward stopping the importation of meth from Mexico, which the DEA estimates is the source of 80 percent of the meth currently in the United States; or the undisclosed amount (I would assume it is less than $4 million) allocated to help pregnant and parenting female drug offenders, which organizations must compete for through grant applications. No money has been allocated in the PATRIOT Act bill to fund environmental cleanup of meth labs.

4. http://www.npr.org/templates/story/story.php?storyId=9252490.

5. Unless otherwise stated, all figures presented in this section are taken from the most recent edition of the U.S. Department of Justice, Bureau of Justice Statistics report, *Drugs*

and Crime Facts (U.S. Department of Justice, Bureau of Justice Statistics [2007]). A copy of this report may be found at http://www.ojp.usdoj.gov/bjs/pub/pdf/dcf.pdf, as well as http://www.ojp.usdoj.gov/bjs/dcf/contents.htm. This report is not paginated. I refer the reader to the original document for information about specific figures.

6. "Drug abuse violations" are defined by the Federal Bureau of Investigation Uniform Crime Report as: "State and/or local offenses relating to the unlawful possession, sale, use, growing, manufacturing, and making of narcotic drugs including opium or cocaine and their derivatives, marijuana, synthetic narcotics, and dangerous nonnarcotic drugs such as barbiturates." See http://www.ojp.usdoj.gov/bjs/dcf/enforce.htm.

NOTES TO CHAPTER 2

1. http://www.triethniccenter.colostate.edu/communityreadiness.shtml.

2. For more information on the "Meth Watch" program see http://www.methwatch.com/index.aspx.

NOTES TO CHAPTER 3

1. "Crank" is another name for methamphetamine and often refers to a particular kind of meth that is generally of lower purity than others, such as "Crystal."

2. It was impossible to quantify the exact percentage of local crimes that were drug related. This was because drug use was not always accounted for in the actual criminal charges. Moreover, police officer perceptions were based on the full gamut of their on-the-job experience. This included not just formal arrests but also informal practices such as surveillance, investigations, on-the-street encounters, and interventions in which no arrest was made. The important point is that the perception that methamphetamine was behind at least 50 percent of crime in the county was a common one that shaped the actions of police and other members of the criminal justice system.

3. They often used minor offenses such as marijuana possession as a means through which to pressure individuals to serve as confidential informants. Their assumption was if they knew where to get marijuana, they probably also knew where to get meth.

4. There is a striking similarity here to the form of biomedical perception described by Arthur Kleinman, which focuses on signs of disease to the neglect of the experience of illness (Kleinman 1995).

5. This quote and those that follow are taken from court documents. In the interest of protecting the anonymity of those involved in the cases to which I refer, citations have been omitted.

6. This association has national resonances as well. By the early 1990s the prominent legal historian Lawrence M. Friedman could write, "Many people [in the United States] sincerely believe that addicts are responsible for most of our violent crime: they rob to get money for a high; and on this high they rape and rob and kill, wantonly, cruelly (Friedman 1993, 356–57).

7. See also the "Faces of Meth" Program on the Partnership for a Drug Free America Web site http://www.drugfree.org/Portal/DrugIssue/MethResources/faces/index.html. The pictures on the poster were taken from this program, which was initially developed

by the Multnomah County (Oregon) Sheriff's Department, and has been used in other anti-meth ad campaigns.

8. See, for instance, the anti-meth campaign developed by the Montana Meth Project www.montanameth.org. The ads developed by the organization provide graphic portrayals of middle-class white teenagers sliding ever deeper into a life of drugs, addiction, and criminality. One of the most striking ads is titled "Laundromat," which shows a young male who bursts into a laundromat and assaults and robs the people inside. The ad ends with the boy confronting himself in the laundromat and screaming, "This wasn't supposed to be your life!" What is striking is that drugs are never specifically mentioned in the ad: the boy's behavior and appearance are seen to be sufficient to indicate that he is a drug addict. Notably the theme of the ad campaign is "Not Even Once," which plays on the idea that certain substances are "instantly addictive." For a discussion of this idea see Morgan and Zimmer 1997.

NOTES TO CHAPTER 4

1. If Emily was correct in her analysis of the event, then this indicates the indirect ways in which drug searches may be carried out. The search using the drug dog did not actually detect the drug or its user. However, it created an environment in which a deeper investigation for drugs could take place, one involving less sophisticated policing technologies such as questioning, intimidation, and threat. Thus the use of sophisticated technologies may simply offer a pretext or provide a context for undertaking an investigation.

2. Methamphetamine has been represented as a uniquely "white" drug (at least in its use) in national media and popular culture. At the level of class, the representation is not so homogenous. The association between methamphetamine and rural America—particularly poor, rural America—remains strong in both media and policy literature (NACo). But there is also a significant strain within the media that depicts methamphetamine as a white, middle-class drug. Indeed, a *Newsweek* article titled "America's Most Dangerous Drug," published while I was living in Baker County, stated that a shift was occurring. "Once derided as 'poor man's cocaine,'" the article states, "popular mainly in rural areas and on the West Coast, meth has seeped into the mainstream in its steady march across the United States." The ads produced by the Montana Meth Project present the most graphic association between methamphetamine use and white, middle-class youth.

3. In addition, the plant followed standard industry practice by testing any employee involved in an accident for drugs. This was to determine both the company's liability and the employee's compensation if the employee was injured. Both were diminished significantly if the employee involved in the accident tested positive for drugs.

4. The degree to which drug detection was emphasized in each institution varied, at times considerably. Thus, while passing a drug test was required in order to be employed and maintain employment at the chicken processing plant, no such requirement existed at the school for teachers or for students. Perhaps the most diversity could be observed in families, where the degree and kind of drug testing ranged from parents acting on (or ignoring) suspicions of drug use in their children to threatening them with drug tests.

5. A concomitant spread of drug testing in the private sector occurred at the time. It began in the 1960s in professional sports and then migrated into business. Between 1985

and 1986 use of drug testing in America's Fortune 500 companies increased 25 percent as a way to screen applicants and deter drug use among employees.

6. The issue of legality is a complicated one. Although drug testing of students in public schools is not inherently illegal, it is dogged by a host of legal and political complications, which mitigate against its implementation. Currently, random drug testing is permitted only among students participating in extracurricular activities. Alternatively, if enough "reasonable suspicion" exists that a student has been using drugs, it is lawful for school officials to ask them to submit to a drug test.

7. Though he did not name it as such, "reasonable suspicion" is a legal principle that developed with specific reference to Fourth Amendment concerns regarding police procedure. It is now a recognized legal term that refers to certain police practices, which use the perception of various indicators that a person might be engaged in or about to engage in some form of criminal activity as justification for intervention. As a legal concept it exists in the gray area between a "hunch" and the "probable cause" required for police to perform search and seizure under the Constitution's Fourth Amendment. The term was originally developed in the case of *Terry v. Ohio* (1968), in which the Supreme Court ruled that it was constitutional for police officers to detain and search someone whom they suspected was going to commit a crime, but did not have enough evidence to claim probable cause. The principle was then extended to schools in 1985 through the decision in the case of *New Jersey v. TLO*. In this case, two girls were accused of smoking in the bathroom. One, referred to only by her initials T.L.O, denied ever having smoked. The vice principal at the school searched her purse for cigarettes and in the process discovered drug paraphernalia, marijuana, and a list of names, which he read as a sign that she was selling drugs. The Supreme Court ruled that the vice principal's actions were constitutional under the principle of reasonable suspicion.

8. Drug testing of employees and potential employees has grown in popularity since the 1980s, despite the fact that they do not appear effective at curbing employee drug use, increasing productivity, or enhancing safety (Tunnell 2004). This led Tunnell to conclude that their utility is largely anthropological, a means to ritualistically evaluate and monitor outsiders and unfamiliars: "Since strangers, by definition, have no reputation or credentials, ordeals and surveillance are used to determine trustworthiness or reputability. . . . Drug testing, as an ordeal, is a highly ritualistic process for determining reputability"(Tunnell 2004, 105).

9. http://www.leadtds.com/law_enforcement/index.html.

10. http://www.leadtds.com/local_educators/index.html.

11. http://www.leadtds.com/law_enforcement/index.html and http://www.leadtds.com/local_educators/index.html.

12. http://www.dare.com/home/about_dare.asp.

13. http://www.dare.com/newdare.asp.

Bibliography

Acker, Caroline Jean
2002 Creating the American Junkie: Addiction Research in the Classic Era of Narcotic Control. Baltimore, MD: Johns Hopkins University Press.

Ackerman, Deborah L.
1991 A History of Drug Testing. *In* Drug Testing: Issues and Options. Robert H. Coombs and Louis Jolyon West, eds. Pp. 3–21. New York: Oxford University Press.

Agar, Michael, and Heather Schacht Reisinger
2002a A Heroin Epidemic at the Intersection of Histories: The 1960s Epidemic among African Americans in Baltimore. Medical Anthropology 21:189–230.
2002b A Tale of Two Policies: The French Connection, Methadone, and Heroin Epidemics. Culture, Medicine and Psychiatry 26:371–396.

Andreas, Peter
2009 Border Games: Policing the U.S.–Mexico Divide, 2nd ed. Ithaca, NY: Cornell University Press.

Arias, Enrique Desmond
2006 Drugs and Democracy in Rio de Janeiro: Trafficking, Social Networks and Public Security. Chapel Hill, NC: University of North Carolina Press.

Associated Press
2009 U.S. To Send More Drug Agents to Afghanistan. March 30.

Baker, James N. with Patricia King, Andrew Murr, and Nonny Abbott
1989 The Newest Drug War. Newsweek, April 3, 20–22.

Benjamin, Walter
2006 On Hashish. Cambridge, MA: Harvard University Press.
1978 Critique of Violence. *In* Reflections: Essays, Aphorisms, Autobiographical Writings. Peter Demetz, ed. Pp. 277–300. New York: Schocken Books.

Bertram, Eva, Morris Blachman, Kenneth Sharpe, and Peter Andreas
1996 Drug War Politics: The Price of Denial. Berkeley: University of California Press.

Biehl, João
2005 Vita: Life in a Zone of Social Abandonment. Berkeley: University of California Press.

Boon, James
1999 Verging on Extra-Vagance: Anthropology, History, Religion, Literature, Arts . . . Showbiz. Princeton, NJ: Princeton University Press.

Bourgois, Philippe
2000 Disciplining Addictions: The Biopolitics of Methadone and Heroin in the United States. Culture, Medicine and Psychiatry 24(2):165–195.
1993 In Search of Respect: Selling Crack in El Barrio. Cambridge: Cambridge University Press.

Bourgois, Philippe, and Jeff Schonberg
2009 Righteous Dopefiend. Berkeley: University of California Press.

Brady, Mary Pat
2002 Quotidian Warfare. Signs: Journal of Women in Culture and Society. 28(1): 446–47.

Butler, Judith
1995 Giving an Account of Oneself. New York: Fordham University Press.

Campbell, Howard
2009 Drug War Zone: Frontline Dispatches from the Streets of El Paso and Juárez. Austin: University of Texas Press.

Campbell, Nancy
2000 Using Women: Gender, Drug Policy and Social Justice. New York: Routledge.

Carr, Summerson
N.d. Scripting Addiction: The Politics of Therapeutic Talk and American Social Work. Unpublished MS.

CASA (National Center on Addiction and Substance Abuse)
2000 No Place to Hide: Substance Abuse in Mid-Size Cities and Rural America. New York: National Center on Addiction and Substance Abuse at Columbia University.

Chambliss, William J.
2001 Power, Politics and Crime. Boulder, CO: Westview Press.

Cole, Simon
2001 Suspect Identities: A History of Fingerprinting and Criminal Identification. Cambridge, MA: Harvard University Press.

Comaroff, Jean, and John Comaroff
2006 Law and Disorder in the Postcolony. Chicago: University of Chicago Press.

Courtwright, David
2001 Forces of Habit: Drugs and the Making of the Modern World. Cambridge, MA: Harvard University Press.

Das, Veena
2000 The Act of Witnessing: Violence, Poisonous Knowledge and Subjectivity. In Violence and Subjectivity. Veena Das, Arthur Kleinman, Mamphela Ramphele, and Pamela Reynolds, eds. Pp. 205–225. Berkeley: University of California Press.

DePhillips, Christopher, and Brian Sharkey
2006 How the Pharmaceutical Industry is Coming Under Attack, part 1. The Metropolitan Corporate Counsel (December), 34.

Derrida, Jacques
2003 The Rhetoric of Drugs. In High Culture: Reflections on Addiction and Modernity. Anna Alexander and Mark S. Roberts, eds. Pp. 19–44. Albany: State University of New York Press. (chap. 4, 3).

Devine, John
1996 Maximum Security: The Culture of Violence in Inner City Schools. Chicago: University of Chicago Press.

Drug Enforcement Administration (DEA)
N.d.a Clandestine Laboratory Indicators. Electronic document, http://www.dea.gov/concern/clandestine_indicators.html, accessed September 15, 2007.
N.d.b Methamphetamine. Electronic document, from http://www.usdoj.gov/dea/concern/meth.html, accessed September 15, 2007.
N.d.c Maps of Methamphetamine Lab Incidents, http://www.usdoj.gov/dea/concern/map_lab_seizures.html, accessed September 21, 2007.
N.d.d Methamphetamine. Electronic document, http://www.usdoj.gov/dea/concern/18862/meth.htm, accessed September 23, 2008.

Dubber, Markus Dirk
2001 Policing Possession: The War on Crime and the End of Criminal Law. *Journal of Criminal Law and Criminology* 91(4):829–996.
2005 The Police Power: Patriarchy and the Foundations of American Government. New York: Columbia University Press.

Dubber, Markus Dirk, and Mariana Valverde
2006 The New Police Science: The Police Power in Domestic and International Governance. Stanford: Stanford University Press.

Dumit, Joseph
2002 Picturing Personhood: Brain Scans and Biomedical Identity. Princeton: Princeton University Press.

Egan, Timothy
2009 Methland vs. Mythland. New York Times. Electronic Document,http://opinionator.blogs.nytimes.com/2009/07/20/methland-vs-mythland/,accessed September 15, 2009.

Ericson, Richard V., and Kevin D. Haggerty
1997 Policing the Risk Society. Toronto: University of Toronto Press.

Excerpts from President's Message on Drug Abuse Control
1971 New York Times. June 18: 22.

Feeley, Malcolm, and Jonathan Simon
1994 Actuarial Justice: The Emerging New Criminal Law. *In* The Futures of Criminology. David Nekin, ed. Pp. 173–201. London: Sage.
1992 The New Penology: Notes on the Emerging Strategy of Corrections and Its Implications *Criminology* 30(4) 449–474.

Foucault, Michel
1997 The Birth of Biopolitics. *In* Essential Works of MichelFoucault, 1954–84, vol. 1: Ethics: Subjectivity and Truth. Paul Rabinow, ed. Pp. 73–81. New York: The New Press.

1995 Discipline and Punish: The Birth of the Prison. New York: Vintage.

Freud, Sigmund
1936 A Disturbance of Memory on the Acropolis. *In* The Standard Edition of the Complete Psychological Works of Sigmund Freud, vol. 22. James Strachey, ed. Pp. 237–248. New York: Norton.

Friedman, Lawrence
1993 Crime and Punishment in American History. New York: Basic Books.
1994 Total Justice. New York: Russell Sage Foundation.

Garcia, Angela
2008 The Elegiac Addict: History, Chronicity and the Melancholic Subject. Cultural Anthropology 23(4):718-746.

Garland, David
2002 The Culture of Control: Crime and Social Order in Contemporary Society. Chicago: University of Chicago Press.

Goode, Erich
2006 Drugs in American Society, 7th ed. New York: McGraw Hill.

Goode, Erich, and Nachman Ben-Yehuda
1994 Moral Panics: The Social Construction of Deviance. London: Blackwell.

Greenhouse, Carol
2003 Solidarity and Objectivity: Re-Reading Durkheim. *In* Crimes Power: Anthropologists and the Ethnography of Crime. Philip Parnell and Stephanie Kane, eds. Pp: 269–291. New York: Palgrave.

Hagan, John, and Ron Levi
2005 Crimes of War and the Force of Law. Social Forces 83(4):1499–1534.

Hannah-Moffat, Kelly
2005 Criminogenic Needs and the Transformative Risk Subject: Hybridizations of Risk/Need in Penality. Punishment and Society 7(1):29–51.

Hargreaves, Guy
2000 Clandestine Drug Labs: Chemical Time Bombs. FBI Law Enforcement Bulletin 69(4):1–9.

Horn, David
2003 The Criminal Body: Lombroso and the Anatomy of Deviance. New York: Routledge.

Hull, Matthew S.
2003 The File: Agency, Authority, and Autography in an Islamabad Bureaucracy. Language and Communication 23:287–314
2008 Ruled by Records: The Expropriation of Land and the Misappropriation of Lists in Islamabad. American Ethnologist 35(4):501–518.

Hunt, Dana E.
2006 Methamphetamine Abuse: Challenges for Law Enforcement. National Institute of Justice Journal 254:24–27.

Jefferson, David J.
2005 America's Most Dangerous Drug. Newsweek. August 8: 41–48.

Kleinman, Arthur
1995. Writing at the Margin: Discourse Between Anthropology and Medicine. Berkeley: University of California Press.

Kraska, Peter
2003 The Military as Drug Police: Exercising the Ideology of War. In Drugs, Crime and Justice: Contemporary Perspectives,2nd ed. Larry K Gaines and Peter B. Kraska, eds. Pp. 288–308. Prospect Heights: Waveland Press.

Kulongoski, Ted
2004 In My Opinion: Why I'm Cracking Down on Pseudoephedrine Sales. Oregonian October 5.

Levi, Ron, and Mariana Valverde
2001 Knowledge on Tap: Police Science and Common Knowledge in the Legal Regulation of Drunkenness. Law and Social Inquiry 26(4):819–846.

Levine, Harry G.
1978 The Discovery of Addiction: Changing Conceptions of Habitual Drunkenness in America. Journal of Studies on Alcohol 39:143–174.

Levy, Robert, and Douglas Hollan
1998 Person-Centered Interviewing and Observation. In Handbook of Methods in Cultural Anthropology. H. Russell Bernard, ed. Pp. 333–364. Walnut Creek, CA: AltaMira Press.

Lineberry, Thomas, and Michael Bostwick
2006 Methamphetamine Abuse: A Perfect Storm of Complications. Mayo Clinic Proceedings 81(1):77–84.

Lovell, Anne M.
2006 Addiction Markets: The Case of High-Dose Buprenorphine in France. In Global Pharmaceuticals: Ethics, Markets, Practices. Adrianna Petryna, Andrew Lakoff and Arthur Kleinman, eds. Pp. 136–170. Princeton, NJ: Princeton University Press.

Lutz, Catherine
2002 Homefront: A Military City and the American Twentieth Century. Boston: Beacon Press.

Marks, Amber
2007 Drug Detection Dogs and the Growth of Olfactory Surveillance: Beyond the Rule of Law? Surveillance and Society 4(3):257–71.

Masco, Joseph
2006 The Nuclear Borderlands: The Manhattan Project in Post-Cold War New Mexico. Princeton, NJ: Princeton University Press.

Miller, Marissa A.
1997 History and Epidemiology of Amphetamine Abuse in the United States. *In* Amphetamine Misuse: International Perspectives on Current Trends. Hilary Klee, ed. Pp. 113–133. Amsterdam: Harwood Academic Publishers.

Mintz, Sidney
1986 Sweetness and Power: The Place of Sugar in Modern History. New York: Penguin.

Moore, Dawn
2007 Criminal Artefacts: Governing Drugs and Users. Vancouver: University of British Columbia Press.

Moore, Dawn, and Kevin Haggerty
2001 Bring It on Home: Home Drug Testing and the Relocation of the War on Drugs. *Social and Legal Studies* 10(3): 377–395.

Morgan, Patricia, and Jerome Beck
1997 The Legacy and the Paradox: Hidden Contexts of Methamphetamine Use in the United States. *In* Amphetamine Misuse: International Perspectives on Current Trends. Hilary Klee, ed. Pp. 113–133. Amsterdam: Harwood Academic Publishers.

Morgan John P., and Lynn Zimmer
1997 Social Pharmacology of Smokeable Cocaine. *In* Crack in America: Demon Drugs and Social Justice. Craig Reinarman and Harry Levine, eds. Pp. 131–74. Berkeley: University of California Press.

Musto, David
1999 The American Disease: Origins of Narcotic Control. Oxford: Oxford University Press.

Musto, David, and Pamela Korsmeyer
2002 The Quest for Drug Control: Politics and Federal Policy in a Period of Increasing Substance Abuse, 1963–81. New Haven, CT: Yale University Press.

National Association of Counties (NACo).
2006 The Meth Epidemic in America: The Criminal Effect of Meth on Communities. Washington, DC: National Association of Counties.

National Institute on Drug Abuse (NIDA)
2006 Methamphetamine Abuse and Addiction. Electronic document, http://www.nida.nih.gov/ResearchReports/Methamph/Methamph.html, accessed September 23, 2008.

Nolan, James L.
2004 Reinventing Justice: The American Drug Court Movement. Princeton, NJ: Princeton University Press.

Novak, William J.
1996 The People's Welfare: Law and Regulation in Nineteenth-Century America. Chapel Hill: University of North Carolina Press.

Office of National Drug Control Policy (ONDCP)
2007 National Drug Control Strategy, 2007: Fiscal Year Budget Summary 2008.

Ortiz, Fernando
1995 Cuban Counterpoint: Tobacco and Sugar. Durham, NC: Duke University Press.

Ove, Torsten
2006 Desperate Drug War Fought All Over West Virginia: Appalachia Home to Growing Crime Wave. Pittsburgh Post-Gazette, Sunday, May 21.

Owen, Frank
2007 No Speed Limit: The Highs and Lows of Meth. New York: St. Martin's Press.

Parnell, Philip, and Stephanie Kane
2003 Crime's Power: Anthropologists and the Ethnography of Crime. New York: Palgrave Macmillan.

Pasquino, Pasquale
1991 Theatrum Politicum: The Genealogy of Capital: Police and the State of Prosperity. *In* The Foucault Effect: Studies in Governmentality. Graham Burchell, Colin Gordon, and Peter Miller, eds. Pp. 105–118. Chicago: University of Chicago Press.

Penglase, Ben
2009 States of Insecurity: Everyday Emergencies, Public Secrets and Drug Trafficker Power in a Brazilian *Favela*. PoLAR: Political and Legal Anthropology Review 32(1):47-63.

Petryna, Adriana, Andrew Lakoff, and Arthur Kleinman
2006 Global Pharmaceuticals: Ethics, Markets, Practices. Durham, NC: Duke University Press.

Pew Research Center for the People and the Press
2001 74% Say Drug War Being Lost: Interdiction and Incarceration Still Top Remedies. Washington, DC: Pew Research Center for the People and the Press.

Pine, Jason
2007 Economy of Speed: The New Narco-Capitalism. Public Culture 19(2):357–366.

President signs USA PATRIOT Improvement and Reauthorization Act.
N.d. http://www.whitehouse.gov/news/releases/2006/03/print/20060309-4.html, accessed September 15, 2007.

Rafael, Vicente
1999 Figures of Criminality in Indonesia, the Philippines, and Colonial Vietnam. Ithaca, NY: Cornell South East Asia Program Publications.

Rawson, Richard
2007 Why Do We Need an Addiction Supplement Focused on Methamphetamine? Addiction 102(Suppl. 1):1–4

Reding, Nick
2009 Methland: The Death and Life of an American Small Town. New York: Bloomsbury.

Reinarman, Craig, and Harry G Levine
1997 Crack in America: Demon Drugs and Social Justice. Berkeley: University of California Press.

Rhodes, Lorna
2004 Total Confinement: Madness and Reason in the Maximum Security Prison. Berkeley: University of California Press.

Riles, Annelise
2006 Documents: Artifacts of Modern Knowledge. Ann Arbor: University of Michigan Press.

Rose, Nicholas
2007 The Politics of Life Itself: Biomedicine, Power, and Subjectivity in the Twenty-First Century. Princeton: Princeton University Press.

Sabol, William J., Heather Couture, and Paige M. Harrison, Bureau of Justice Statistics
2007 Prisoners in 2006. Washington, DC: U.S. Department of Justice.

Scheingold, Stuart
1991 The Politics of Street Crime: Criminal Process and Cultural Obsession. Philadelphia: Temple University Press.

Schneider, Eric C.
2008 Smack: Heroin and the American City. Philadelphia: University of Pennsylvania Press.

Shafer, Jack
2005 Crack Then, Meth Now: What the Press *Didn't* Learn from the Last Drug Panic. Slate, posted August 23.
2006 Methamphetamine Propaganda: The Government and the Press Are Addicted. Slate, March 3.

Siegel, James T.
1998 A New Criminal Type in Jakarta: Counter-Revolution Today. Durham, NC: Duke University Press.

Silverstein, Michael
2004 "Cultural" Concepts and the Language–Culture Nexus. Current Anthropology 45(5):621–652.

Simon, Jonathan
1993 Poor Discipline: Parole and the Social Control of the Underclass, 1890–1990. Chicago: University of Chicago Press.

Singer, Merrill
2005 The Face of Social Suffering: Life History of a Street Drug Addict. Long Grove, IL: Waveland Press.

Stalcup, Meg
2006 The "War on Drugs" and National Security. Unpublished MS.

Suo, Steve
2005b Bills Take Global Swipe at Meth. Oregonian. July 19.
2005a Mexico Cuts Imports of Meth Ingredient. Oregonian. November 20.
2004 Unnecessary Epidemic. Electronic document, http://www.oregonlive. com/special/oregonian/meth/, accessed September 15, 2007.

Taussig, Michael
1992 The Nervous System. New York: Routledge.
2004 My Cocaine Museum. Chicago: University of Chicago Press.

Tracy Sarah W., and Caroline Jean Acker
2004 Altering American Consciousness: The History of Alcohol and Drug Use in the United States, 1800–2000. Amherst: University of Massachusetts Press.

Tunnell, Kenneth D.
2004 Pissing On Demand: Workplace Drug Testing and the Rise of the Detox Industry. New York: New York University Press.

United Nations Office of Drugs and Crime (UNODC)
2005 World Drug Report. Vienna, Austria: UNODC.

United States Department of Justice, Bureau of Justice Statistics
2007 Drugs and Crime Facts. Washington, DC: U.S. Department of Justice.
1997 Prisoners in 1996. Washington, DC: U.S. Department of Justice.

U.S. Outlines New Drug War Strategy
2009 Electronic document, http://www.npr. org/templates/story/story.php?storyId= 105040484&ft=1&f=1070, accessed June 10, 2009.

Valdez, Angela
2006 Meth Madness: How The Oregonian Manufactured an Epidemic, Politicians Bought It and You're Paying. Electronic document, http://wweek.com/edito- rial/3220/7368/, accessed February 17, 2010.

Valverde, Mariana
1998 Diseases of the Will: Alcohol and the Dilemmas of Freedom. Cambridge: Cambridge University Press.
2006 Law and Order: Signs, Meanings, Myths. New Brunswick, NJ: Rutgers University Press.
2003 Law's Dream of a Common Knowledge. Princeton, NJ: Princeton University Press.

Wacquant, Loic
2009a Punishing the Poor: The Neolib- eral Government of Social Insecurity. Durham, NC: Duke University Press.
2009b Prisons of Poverty. Minneapolis: University of Minnesota Press.
2008 Urban Outcasts: A Comparative Sociology of Advanced Marginality. Cambridge: Polity Press.

Weisheit, Ralph, David N. Falcone, and L. Edward Wells
2006 Crime and Policing in Rural and Small-Town America. Long Grove, IL: Waveland Press.

Weisheit, Ralph, and Jason Fuller
2004 Methamphetamines in the Heart-
    land: A Review and Initial Explora-
    tion. Journal of Crime and Justice
    27(1):131–151.

Weisheit, Ralph, and William L White
2009 Methamphetamine: Its History,
    Pharmacology, and Treatment. Center
    City, MN: Hazelden.

World Health Organization (WHO)
2001 Systematic Review of Treatment
    for Amphetamine-Related Disorders.
    Geneva: World Health Organization.

Zhou Yongming
1999 Anti-Drug Crusades in Twentieth-
    Century China: Nationalism, History
    and State Building. Lanham, MD:
    Rowman & Littlefield.

Index

AA. *See* Alcoholics Anonymous

ABLE. *See* Adult Basic Learning Examination

Addiction: cognitive models of crime and, 66–70, *68*; counselors, 19, 67–68; crimes not excused by, 73–74; crimes seen as linked to, 70–72, 169n6; criminal behavior as symptom of, 61–63; as intervention medium, 61–62; knowledge of, 61–81; law enforcement focus and, 15; police presentations defining, 64; state lens of methamphetamine, 72–81; triggers, 142

Addictiveness, 133; defined, 65; thinking and, 67–69, *68*

Addicts: criminalization of, 62–63; drug offenders considered, 130; interviews with, 16–17, 135–40; treatment success rate, 19. *See also* Cases/case files; Drug offenders; Users

ADHD. *See* Attention deficit hyperactivity disorder

Administration, methamphetamine methods of, 22, 51

Adopt-A-Highway volunteers, 47–48, 56

Adult Basic Learning Examination (ABLE), 147

Albright, Wendell (guidance counselor), 91, 92, 93–94, 97

Alcoholics Anonymous (AA), 118–19, 133, 142, 161

Ammonia, anhydrous, 55

Amphetamines: 1960s/1970s, 23–24; quotas, 24; tablets, 23

Anhydrous ammonia, 55

Anthropologists, on "figures on criminality," 62

Anti-drug media campaigns, 80, 169n7, 170n8

Anti-meth ad campaigns, 80, 169n7, 170n8

Appalachian culture, 37–38

Arrests: Baker County first major, 111; income/class and, 105; Terry's, Christie, 143–44, 152

Attention deficit hyperactivity disorder (ADHD), 23

Auerbach, Mike/Wanda, 118–22

Awareness, methamphetamine problem, 37, 38–41

Baker County, 11–15; arrests per year in, 105; awareness of methamphetamine problem, 38–41; community events, 16; Community Readiness Assessment, 37; cost/availability of test kits in, 101; criminal justice system, 21–22; drug detection system, 88–91; ethnographic background on, 7, 11–15; Federal Drug Task Force in, 70, 104–5, 110–11; first major meth arrest in, 111; jail, 66–70, 71–72, 102; methamphetamine production in, 41–44; meth labs in, 40, 52–56; narcopolitics, 7–8; policing in, 44–49, 103–4; prosecuting attorney for, 20–21, 75–76; user image in, 84

Barker, Jimmy, 53, 56

Behavior, symptoms of addiction, 61–63

Benjamin, Walter, 167n5

Bennett, Joan, 87

Benzedrine, 25
Bible study meeting, 38–39
Blackstone, William, *Commentaries on the Laws of England*, 3
Board of Education, letter from, 112
Body, physical, 61, 77–81, *78*, 169n4, 169n7
"Body on drugs" poster, *78*, 78–80, 169n7
Bottoms, Lester (police officer), 100
Bourdieu, Pierre, 44
Breathalyzers, 89
Burdette, Ken, 135–40
Bush, Vice President George, 90
Bush, George W., 1

Califano, Jr., Joseph, 26
Carson, Shelly (addiction counselor), 67–68
CASA. *See* National Center on Addiction and Substance Abuse
Cases/case files, 17, 21, 54, 72–77; Auerbach, Mike/Wanda, 118–22; Culler/Swift, Burt/Mandy, 59–60; Curtis, Eddie, 75–77; Grate, Donnie, 43, 53–56; Hopper, Dwight, 72–74, 75; Johnson, David, 103, 104, 107–18; overview of Federal Drug Task Force, 110–11; pre-sentence evaluations in, 142–46; Stevens, Emily, 83–84, 87–88, 102; Stokes, Justin/Christie, 106, 122–27, 140, 155–56; Terry, Christie, 106, 122–27, 140–61. *See also* Interviews; Users
Casterman, Greg (staff attorney), 94–97
Chemicals, 56; precursor, 44, 46; use of widely available, 22–23
Children, 26, 92–93
Citizens: law enforcement concern of, 14, 20; mobilizing of, 46–47; policing by, 41; relations with law enforcement, 14, 20
Class: arrests and, 105; criminalization of drug users and, 98; drug-detection and, 85–86; middle, 83–102, 170n2
Cleanup, meth lab, 50, 168n3
Clinical information, 130–61; forensics and, 130; pre-sentence evaluations, 142–46; prison evaluations, 146–49; risk/needs profile for, 130; sentencing based on, 139–42; state intervention through, 150, 160; targeted punishment through, 152–56

Clinics, mental health, 138
Cocaine, 27, 50
Cochran, Janice, 20
Code Red, 92
Cognitive models, addiction-crime, 66–70, *68*
Combat Methamphetamine Epidemic Act, 28
Commentaries on the Laws of England (Blackstone), 3
Community: "imminent threat to," 107; lost vision of, 57; marginal members of, 127; policing by, 41, 44–49, 103–4; reentry into, 161; sentencing influenced by, 116–17, 121–22, 144; service, 160
Community events, ethnographic participation in, 16
Community Readiness Assessment, 37
Concerned Citizens United Against Crime, 14, 20
Confidential Informants, 103–4, 108–9, 111, 122–23, 124, 154
Controlled buys, 103–4, 108–9, 111, 122–23, 124
Conviction: rates, 32; Terry's, Christie, arrest and, 143–44, 152
Cooks, description by local, 43
Corbin, Joey, 38, 39
Cost, drug test kits, 101
Counselors: addiction, 19, 67–68; guidance, 91, 92, 93–94, 97
Country stores, 45–46
Cravens, Arthur (judge), 133–35
Crime: addiction in drug-related, 70–72, 169n6; addiction not excusing, 73–74; cognitive models of addiction and, 66–70, *68*; drug-related, 32, 70–72, 169n2, 169n6; drugs and, 30–35, 59–63; focus shift to criminal from focus on, 131, 149–50; penalties for meth-related, 12; property, 59–60, 76. *See also* Drug-crime connection
Criminality: behavioral symptoms of addiction, 61–63; "figures of," 62; physical features of, 61, 79–80, 169n7; thinking and, 67–69, *68*

Hinkle, Sandy, 38
History: erasure of political, 29; narco-politics legislative, 30–35; twenty-first century methamphetamine, 22–25
Hopper, Dwight, 72–74, 75
Hutchins, Glenda, 86–87, 102

Incarceration, class and, 102
Income, arrests and, 105
Informants: confidential, 103–4, 108–9, 111, 154; controlled buys, 103–4, 108–9, 122–23, 124; marijuana offenses used to obtain, 169n3
Informed observation, 87
Ingredients, meth production, 22, 24, 42
Inhalers, 23
Institutions: drug testing at various types of, 88, 170n4; risks of drug testing associated with various, 95
International Narcotics Control Board, 28
Interracial marriage, 153, 155
Intervention: addiction as medium for, 61–62; clinical information channel for state, 150, 160; middle-class drug testing form of, 98–102; military, 9–10; regulatory/legislative, 12; targeted, 8–9, 153–56, 165
Interviews: with addicts, 16–17, 135–40; DNR officer, 49–52; guidance counselor, 91, 92, 93–94, 97; with judge, 133–35; person-centered, 135–40; police officer, 70–72, 93; police officer/drug offender, 59–60; with probation officer, 129, 161; with sheriff's deputy, 20, 70–71, 77–79, 104
IQ, 149

Jail: Baker County, 66–70, 71–72, 102; class and, 102; treatment programs, 66, 67, 69–70, 71–72
Johnson, David (case of), 103, 104, 107–18; probation of, 113; trial of, 108–10
Judge: interview with, 133–35; sentencing role of, 150
Juridical field, 44

Keezle, Matt (DNR officer), 49–52
Kent, Charlie (state road worker), 48
Knowledge, 61; of addiction, 61–81; clinical, 130–61; drug search prior, 92–93; workers, 63
Korsmeyer, Pamela, 30–31

Latinos/Latinas, Baker County, 13
Law enforcement: addiction focus of, 15; citizens relations with, 14, 20; class basis of, 102; funding for, 1, 30, 167n2; methamphetamine response through angle of, 1, 21–22; military intervention in civilian, 9–10; narcotics focus on, 1–4; police power expansion within field of, 49–52. See also Policing
Law Enforcement Against Drugs (LEAD), 97–98
LEAD. See Law Enforcement Against Drugs; Local Educators Against Drugs
Legal habitus, 44
Legality: scientifico-legal complex, 131; student drug testing issues of, 93, 95, 171n6
Legislation: meth production chemicals, 41, 56; narcopolitics and, 30–35; over-the-counter medication 1970s, 27; PATRIOT Act, 1, 28, 30, 167n2, 168n2, 168n3; penalties for meth-related crimes, 12; policy changes, 163–64; political history erased by anti-methamphetamine, 29; search/seizure, 31
Liberalism, War on Drugs and, 31
Lively, Bobby (jail warden), 66, 69
Local channels, police power through, 43–44
Local Educators Against Drugs (LEAD), 97, 98–102
Lombroso, Cesare, 79
Lovell, Anne, 24
Lutz, Catherine, 31

Mackie, Dustin, 45
Mackie, Jerry, 45
Major structural contradiction, 43
Manchin, Joe, 12

Marginalization, 132; treatment fostering sense of, 132, 139–40

Marijuana, 27, 70, 169n3; informants obtained through offenses of, 169n3

Markets: expansion of medication, 27–28; interdependence of licit/illicit, 24, 27–28

Marriage, interracial, 153, 155

Mathews, Dana (board president), 94, 96

Mayo Clinic, 23

McDonald, Gil, 51–52

McKinney, Ronnie (sheriff's deputy), 100

Media: anti-meth campaigns, 80, 169n7, 170n8; "Body on drugs" poster, 78, 78–80, 169n7; class and, 83–85, 170n2; *Newsweek*, 25, 84–85, 170n2

Medications: market expansion, 27–28; over-the-counter, 27, 44

Medicinal use, 23

Mental health, 33, 145; clinic, 138

Messinger, Larry, 53, 54, 56

Methamphetamine: addictiveness, 65, 67–69, 68, 133; administration methods for taking, 22, 51; alleged proliferation of, 4–5; definition of, 22; distinguishing features of, 6–7; eastward spread of, 24–25; enhanced productivity from, 123; first synthesis of, 23; global trends, 27–29; increased domestic production of, 25; law enforcement emphasis/response to, 1, 21–22; medicinal uses of, 23; military use of, 23, 42; nicknames for, 87, 169n1; physical signs of use, 61, 77–81, 78, 169n4, 169n7; political role of, 1, 4; production process, 22–23; recipes, 24; research focus on, 6–7; rise in use of, 24; rural/white drug representation of, 25–26; statistics on proliferation of, 4; twenty-first century history of, 22–25; user experiences, 22, 83; "Vague Awareness" of, 37, 38–41; waste dumps, 48; as "white"drug, 170n2. *See also* Addiction; Production; Production process

Meth labs, 7, 22–23; Baker County, 40, 52–56; cleaning up after, 50, 168n3; DNR jurisdiction to deal with, 49–52; first, 24; funding for training on, 168n3; locating, 52–56; rural image of, 26, 40–41; statistics on incidents concerning, 40; superlabs, 28; West Virginia incidents of, 12

Methodology, research, 15–17. *See also* Administration, methamphetamine methods of

Middle-class, 83–102, 170n2; drug testing and, 96–97; parents, 92–93, 96–102; protection from scrutiny, 85–86, 96–97; shielding of, 85–86, 96–97; treatment facilities for, 102

Military: drug testing in, 90; intervention, 9–10; methamphetamine use by, 23, 42; Nazi, 42

Minnesota Multiphasic Personality Inventory-2 (MMPI-2), 147

MMPI-2. *See* Minnesota Multiphasic Personality Inventory-2

Montgomery, Daryl (deputy sheriff), 20, 77–79

Moore, Dawn, 97, 98

Morality, 11, 165

Morphine, 39

Musto, David, 30–31

NA. *See* Narcotics Anonymous

NACo. *See* National Association of Counties

Narco-enforcement bureaucracy, 164

Narcopolitics, 3, 5–11, 167n3; Baker County, 7–8; definition/background, 5, 167n5; drug testing in, 11; fissures in contemporary, 164–65; intervention focus on, 8–9; key features of contemporary, 8–11; legislative policy history and, 30–35; twentieth-century governance and, 6

Narcotics, 28; as global commodities, 5; law enforcement context for, 1–4; police power and, 22

Narcotics Anonymous (NA), 20, 67, 118–19, 133

National Association of Counties (NACo), 26

National Center on Addiction and Substance Abuse (CASA), 25–26

National Institute on Drug Abuse (NIDA), 25

Wechsler Adult Intelligence Scale-Revised (WAIS-R), 147
"Well-regulated society," 2
West Virginia, 7, 37, 47; characteristics of, 11–12, 168n10; DEA profile of, 11; drug trafficking and, 11–12, 104, 168n10; meth lab incidents, 12; population of, 167n7. *See also* Baker County

West Virginia Division of Environmental Protection, 47
West Virginia Prevention Resource Center (WVPRC), 37
World War II, 23
Worthen, Chris, 38
WVPRC. *See* West Virginia Prevention Resource Center

About the Author

WILLIAM GARRIOTT is an assistant professor in the Department of Justice Studies at James Madison University.